VIETNAM, VIETNAM

VIETNAM, VIETNAM

Minh Hiên
and
Luthfi Pirabeau

VANTAGE PRESS
New York / Los Angeles

FIRST EDITION

Published by Vantage Press, Inc.
516 West 34th Street, New York, New York 10001

Manufactured in the United States of America
ISBN: 0-533-08226-9

Library of Congress Catalog Card No.: 88-90333

I write
For the millions of my Vietnamese compatriots
Who died at the hands
Or because of the Communists,
But mostly
For the people around the world
Who are still free
And want to remain free.

—Minh Hiên

CONTENTS

INTRODUCTION

If one remains silent in front of an injustice, one becomes an accomplice of it.

—Albert Einstein

Why a book on Vietnam? Indeed, since 1975 people had better forget about it unless they wanted to be called reactionaries by those helping public opinion incubate its Vietnam syndrome: the confusion created by the loss of a battle thought to be for the right cause. They felt forsaken by God Almighty Himself, forgetting that the immediate is part but not the long view of history.

Later on, the subject was considered to be passé. Mind you, even thinking about it was not "in" anymore. However, Vietnam, having been buried rather quickly in political terms and despite Vietnamese refugees' efforts as well as those of some Westerners to clarify things—people who needed to understand the situation or at least to be informed about it kept asking, "How come we never heard anything about what really went on in Vietnam after the war? Of course we have seen pictures of Boat People, like anyone else, but that does not tell us why they fled their country and what is happening to those who stayed there." This book, or rather, this investigation should be for them and especially for the youngsters who said, "We've been had. We have had enough of novels; we want facts."

This investigation does not put aside the problems, mistakes, and flaws of former governments that have been held responsible for the current situation. The truth of the matter is that they were responsible for what they did or did not, exactly the way today's regime is reponsible for making promises its leaders knew they would not keep, and for using Marxist-Leninist terror to impose the dictatorship of a few upon a majority of people they claim to represent and serve. Since so much has been said, written, and commented about Vietnam, and there have been so many television programs, films, and reports on that country for the past forty years, we felt it was due time to focus on the thirteen years following the war, and to tell the reader what we know about how socialist Vietnam intends to conquer Southeast Asia, for how long it has planned to do so, how it is doing it, and how the West is dealing with the situation. In short, we tried to put a mirror in front of a system that says one thing, and does another. We have also tried to show the reader that information does indeed exist here in the West, but that a little effort is required of any one of us in order to get a clear idea of what is going on in our respective countries interacting in a world context. A clear picture on a silver screen today is no more granted than a message in Morse code was in 1840. Technology is by no means a guarantee of fairness and accuracy. As with a puzzle, we have to pick up the pieces across the political and media spectrum, then put them together in time and space, and finally hope that we will understand the situation before it is too late; at times, the picture is so shocking that some people try to tone it down. We have not; reality cannot afford it.

The tragedy today lies more with the fact that no matter what communist regimes have done in their respective countries and abroad, Marxism-Leninism is still being sold like an item in its box. It is described as the struggle against a filthy capitalism that exploits the masses. Yet we will see that it is not what some people want us to believe it is. Leninism made sure through violence that this perception would not be even questioned. Stalin confirmed it in blood, and since then the routine has been established to make the world used to the idea that Marxism is the way of the future, but we will have to put up with its violence first. The real victims are not the ones we believe, but ordinary people, free enterprise, and your neighbours. But mind you, it does not matter that some people have managed to get out of that box to tell us about their dreadful experience under a communist regime. No, we are still fed in the West with the idea that the grass is greener "out there" than "over here." Yet most people who have been able to go there, see for themselves, and come back, agree, that as imperfect as our society may be, it is still better than any communist regime pretending that socialism is the way of the future and that nations are longing for it.

We are also increasingly invited to "get together" with people who are more skilled at building prisons and filling graveyards than at feeding their populations. We are invited to work with the Soviets against an Ayatollah, a Quaddafi, or anyone else as stated on PBS, June 22, 1987, on the program "The Presidency and the Constitution." The presidency, we know it, is getting a lot of attention, but why the Constitution? Is it up to date? . . . Is it really what our forefathers really meant it to be? . . . Many people are turning around it, trying to find, or so it seems, ways to modify it.[1] Some even suggest that since times have changed, the president should not have the same control over the armed forces as he has previously held. Congress thought of that already in 1972 with the War Powers Act. On ABC's "Nightline" on November 17, 1987, Rep. Richard Cheney, a Republican from Wyoming, was even talking about a war between Congress and the presidency that has been continuing for at least a decade and a half. That is, a long time before Irangate. But as far as we Westerners are concerned, it is the invitation to join the Soviets to work against anyone else that should worry us: they are known to fight against their own people in the first place.

Now, by the way, the United States did fine with Quaddafi and had no need of the Soviets, too busy watching the U.S. navy and sending information to Libya. The subject of working with the Soviets to help the oil tankers sail freely through the Persian Gulf was brought up again on ABC's "Nightline" on June 3, 1987. When Leonid Brezhnev once did say that the Soviet Union's first target against the West, and the United States in particular, is the oil of the Persian Gulf? It was the same thing again on June 7, 1987, also on ABC, when someone said he did not mind having more Soviet ships in the gulf. Finally, in August 1987 on PBS, when the media were increasingly speaking of the Reagan-Gorbachev summit, Gwynne Dyer, the author of the series "War," said that the world will be politically united within a certain number of years. If all this is true, let us have a closer look at those we are supposed to associate with, why, and what it may do to us.

This book presents the victim's point of view rather than that of the *Raison d'Etat* that accepts massacres in the name of "higher goals"; "more important political achievements for the good of all"; it is constantly repeated, but usually ends up in "mistakes," always committed by "others." This is an account of a human tragedy that has devastated every part of the economic, social, political, cultural, and spiritual life of a country, with far reaching consequences for us all, right here in North America in particular, and in the West in general. The communists and their collaborators are affecting our way of life; we are democratically helping them build a system that is intended to destroy us in the end.

This is an investigation, not a novel. Communism has been so idealized and romanticized in the West, and people have so much projected their desires and fancies—or lack of them—on this "new cure-all" without analyzing what is in fact a ruthless recuperation of power, that a little bit of realism will not hurt. It shows how a regime has absolutely crushed a nation and its people through economic measures we are supposed to marvel about simply because they are socialist. But are these things happening only to others?

Minh Hiên, the coauthor who originated this book, knew Vietnam before and after the South fell to the North. He has been jailed by the French, and later on by the communists, for having fought in both cases for the freedom of his country and freedom in general. Because of his experience as a high-level economist, his work and responsibilities, and his travels throughout the country, he is well qualified to tell us what the situation is: "Before April 1975, one could hear rumors that, should the North invade South Vietnam, human rights and individual freedom would be suppressed. People were talking about the population being systematically impoverished, the suppression of real justice, and the monopolization and centralization of the economy, politics, education, and culture in the hands of a few who intended to eliminate capitalism and the bourgeoisie. Beginning in May 1975, things happened exactly as predicted, but we also discovered and experienced artificial famine decimating the ordinary people, men, women, and children, who had little to do with the so-called enemies of communism. How could that be? How could one starve in a South Vietnam that had always been considered a real cornucopia in that part of the world? And nobody was being told what was going on, not even a single word. . . . "

Lenin once said that Western capitalists and their governments would labor for the preparation of their own suicide. May this book and those in the bibliography present a clear picture of how nations with a great past have fallen, victims of ruthless people who know how to manipulate individual and collective hope for a better life into disaster and how this is beginning to happen here in the West.

NOTE

1. On Vermont ETV, on September 17, 1987, Vermonters were asked to answer the call to amend the Constitution. A vast majority of them said that it would change it beyond recognition, and that it would give too much power to those advocating the changes.

THE HISTORY OF VIETNAM IN A NUTSHELL

Since they never made peace in good faith, and that in their design to invade all their treaties were only suspensions of war, they were including conditions in them which would always ruin the State accepting them.

—Montesquieu

If one wants to sum up thc history of Vietnam, one might say that the search for food and power by the hungry bellies of the North is the dominant and most sustained geopolitical constant of that country. It led to Saigon on April 30, 1975.

Some believe the Viets, inhabitants of the northern part of the land, came from Mongolia, others believe they came from Tibet, but all agree they came mostly from South and Southwest China. As for the Vietnamese themselves, they prefer to keep their origins shrouded in mystery. It is also recorded that some two thousand years ago and probably earlier, what is today's Vietnam was also inhabited by Negritos, Australoids, and Melanesians who came from the Pacific after they migrated from the mainland itself.

During the reign of Hong Bang (289–258 B.C.) the first federal state of Van-Lang was established in the North during the first millennium. It was to be replaced by that of Âu-Lac (Thuc Andüong-Vuong dynasty: 250–207 B.C.). In 208 B.C., this state under the influences from farther north was integrated in the Chinese empire as what was for China the Nam-Viet or "Land of the South." That was an improvment over Giao-chi, an earlier name the Chinese gave to the Vietnamese, meaning literally "the people whose toes are looking at each other." Later on still, the emperor Vù-Dê (Wou-Ti) annexed the land in 111 B.C. and Vietnam became a Chinese province.

There were already deep differences dividing the North and the South, where Hindu kingdoms had been established during the first centuries of our era. The most important of them was that of Champa, stretching from Quang-Binh to Binh-Thuan. The Chinese stayed in *Vietnam* for more than a thousand years—some say 1,147 years—during four periods of domination and left behind them political, religious, economic, social institutions and a form of centralized government they invented, in which the emperor is all-powerful and the subjects owe him absolute obedience.

During the thirteenth century A.D. the Mongols of the emperor of China Kublai Khan (1214/15–94) tried to occupy the country in order to get access to warm waters, but were repelled by the Viets, independent since A.D. 939. The Chinese again imposed their domination on Vietnam from 1407 to 1427. They were expelled, once more, by Lê-Loi, founder of the Lê dynasty (1428–1527), interrupted by the usurpation of the Mac-Dang-Dung in 1527. However, it was said that the Chinese would collect the tribute until the arrival of the French colonialist administration, in the nineteenth century.

When the Lê dynasty was restored (1528–1788), *Vietnam* or the *Vietnams* were governed by two families of the same northern stem, very closely related, but which became enemies: the Trinh up north, and the Nguyên Phuc down south. And here you have the old story of North and South: they fought seven wars between 1627 and 1672. To find their geopolitical depth, the Nguyên had to go farther down south, where they met the resistance of the Khmers (Cambodians), already established there for five centuries, and fought six other wars among themselves, from 1658 to 1748, and four against the incursions of the Siamese (Thais) in 1715, 1738, 1771–72, and 1788. During these wars one of the main strategies was to get hold of the rice, to cause famines. From 1790 to 1801 and for the first time in the history of the country, Nguyên-Phuc-Anh, king of the south, brought Vietnam together in 1801. The country will remain united until the arrival of the French administration some decades later, which will divide it again into three colonies based on the former kingdoms: Tonkin up north, Annam in the center, and Cochin China down south.

The people of Southeast Asia, who killed each other, and occupied and colonized their neighbors over the centuries the way others did and would later do elsewhere in the world, saw the Arab settlements established in the region as early as the year 700 become European colonies. To know what colonialism means, just turn the table on those who have practiced it at one time or another for, say, the past four thousand years: almost everybody. Third World countries of today were the kingdoms and empires of before yesterday. Europe was the power of yesterday, and the empires of today will have disappeared by tomorrow. Everyone wants to be the dominant power, and for as long as possible.

At this point in history it is interesting to note that Marx, in his own time, favored colonialism—followed in that by many European leftists—because it was opening countries to his ideological market, and would, by reaction, accelerate their fall into the communist basket. Later on, after World War II, the Soviets would not think differently in terms of decolonization. The West being the symbol of the latest form of colonialism, newly independent countries would automatically turn to the USSR for support.

World War I was the beginning of the end for the European empires. In *Vietnam* in 1930, a Nguyên-Ai Quôc,[1] posing as a nationalist, was fighting the French, and later he would struggle against the Japanese. In fact, he had been trained in the Soviet Union between 1923 and 1925; he was an agent of the Komintern (the Communist International), and he had just established the first cells of the Indochinese Communist party. On May 28 of this same year, 1925, Stalin delivered a speech at the University of the Oriental Communist Workers (where revolutionaries such as Nguyên-Ai-Quôc are trained) on the expansion of communism in Southeast Asia, especially China and Indochina.

In 1932 the Communist party of Indochina—created by Nguyên-Ai-Quôc—was accepted as member of the Komintern and announced its aim as stated by Stalin: the establishment of communism in all of Indochina. In 1941, the same Nguyên-Ai Quôc became *Ho Chi Minh.*[2] Instead of turning Vietnam from colonialism to freedom, he engulfed it in communism.

Toward the end of World War II at Yalta, *Vietnam* was divided into North and South, on both sides of the seventeenth parallel. This was confirmed at the Geneva Conference of 1954, after the departure of the French from Indochina. The neutrality

Map Showing History of Vietnam

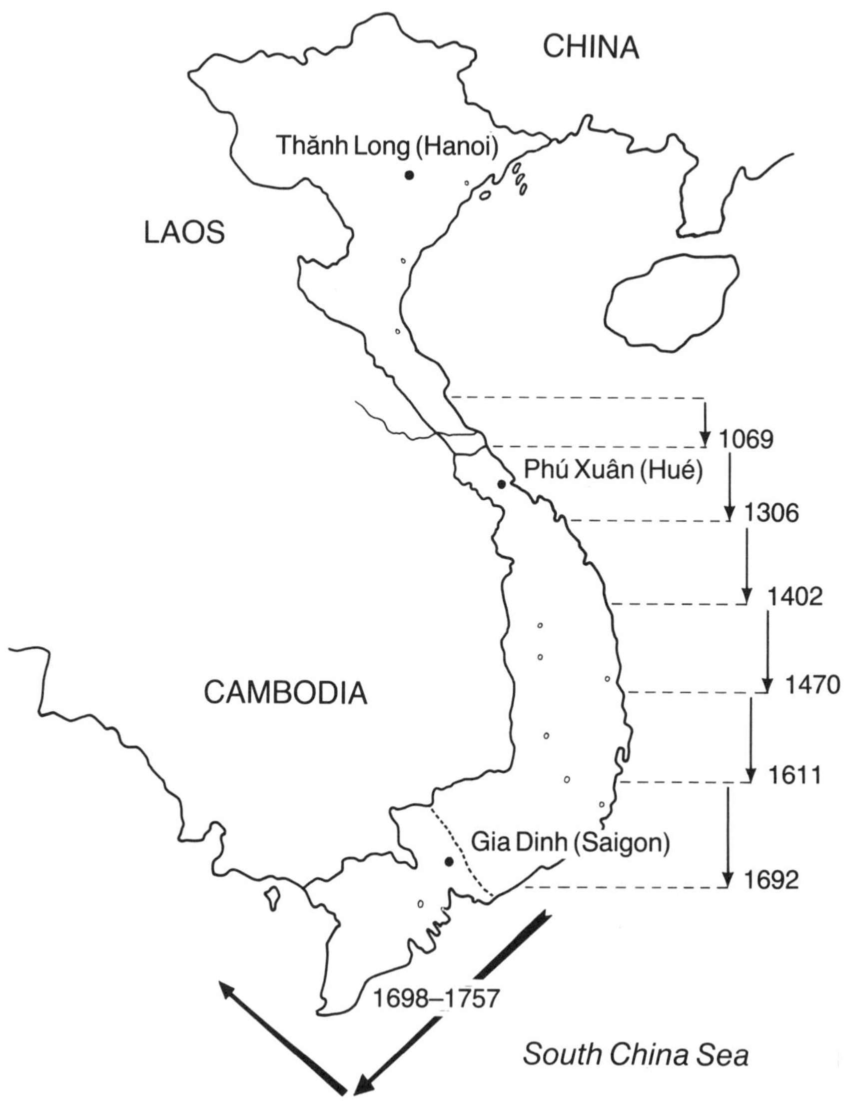

of Laos and Cambodia was also established during this very same conference, to maintain the new peace in the region and avoid an invasion of *Vietnam* through these two countries. The neutrality of Laos was reaffirmed at the Vienna Conference of 1962. In 1973, after the war between North Vietnam—backed up by the USSR and China—and South Vietnam and the United States, the Paris Accords signed by North Vietnam, the Vietcong (the revolutionary provisional government created by Hanoi, which would be eliminated soon after the invasion of South Vietnam by the North), South Vietnam, the United States, the USSR, China, Great Britain, France, Canada, Poland, Indonesia, and Hungary were supposed to ensure the neutrality of South Vietnam.

None of these treaties or accords has been respected by the communists, and in April 1975 the North Vietnamese invaded South Vietnam, the result of a forty-five to fifty year strategy aimed at transforming all of Southeast Asia into a communist bastion.

Under the disguise of self-determination, Third World countries were promised recognition, power to the people, freedom, self-respect, and a decent life. They soon discovered that if getting rid of colonialism was a good thing, it did not necessarily lead to freedom—on the contrary.

NOTES

1. Nguyên-Ai-Quôc (Nguyên the Patriot) was the pen name that Phan-Van-Trüong gave him in Paris; Nguyên-Tât-Thanh was his real name.
2. Ho Chi Minh means "the one who reaches light"; in this context, I was told, with *Chi* (to reach) *Hô* may also mean "fox." It is also said that Ho Chi Minh may have had at least a dozen different names during his life.

THE INVASION

The way to feel about things is to suffer from them.
—Gustave Flaubert

And the South Vietnamese will suffer.

Centuries ago, Sun Tzu had already warned that when the enemy is making speeches full of humility but continues his preparation for war, he is going to advance. The Paris Accords had given time for preparation, and on April 30, 1975, columns of *bô-dôis*, the North Vietnamese soldiers, entered Saigon, the capital of South Vietnam. Soviet-made tanks broke through the iron gate of what was already called the "former presidential palace." In Hanoi this was called a "liberation." In South Vietnam it was already borne as an invasion, an occupation.

First, the foreigners were expelled; they were embarrassing witnesses. The Vietnamese of Chinese origin—the Hoa—opposing the new regime were stripped of everything. The farmers—the class on which the Communist party bases its legitimacy—were liquidated, and the religious groups were eliminated simply because their members refused to worship Marx and his associates. They were replaced by Party members, soldiers and farmers from North Vietnam.

Vietnamese being expelled, liquidated, replaced? In the name of what, by the way, since the North was talking "brotherhood" before the invasion? Did not Pham-van-Dong himself say that it would be stupid and criminal to invade South Vietnam? Two weeks after the fall of Saigon, hadn't the president of the United States, Gerald Ford, declared that no repression had been reported from *Vietnam*?[1] And Hanoi's delegate to the United Nations, Hà-van-Lâu, also ambassador to Cuba, had he not declared that there had never been any bloodbath in Vietnam?

Yet Sir Robert Thompson in his 1972 report to the U.S. government was already warning—before the signing of the Paris Agreements in January 1973—that should South Vietnam be invaded by the troops of the North, 3 to 5 million South Vietnamese would be massacred.[2] French general Raoul Salan evaluated the number of potential victims at 3 million.[3]

Saigon fallen, South Vietnam is dressed with red flags on which Hanoi's slogans are written in golden letters: "Nothing is more precious than freedom and independence," and "To go forward fast and to firmly establish socialism," the whole thing steeped in a sauce of "reconciliation," "clemency," "tolerance," "magnanimity," et cetera. Knowing who has written these recipes of a doubtful "cuisine," one also knows who will have to swallow them.

Meanwhile, since the Great Spring Victory,[4] people in the free world—who have never lived under any communist regime—are praising Marxist ideology, the equality and justice in countries under its rule versus the exploitation and injustice within the capitalist nations. Strangely enough, though, no one has ever seen any of these procommunist collaborators splurge on a one-way ticket to experience the life of their dreams in one of the totalitarian countries of their choice where the regime, it is claimed, is so humane.

At the same moment, but in North Vietnam this time, the bureaucrats, the militants of the Party, and the soldiers who are going on a mission to the South receive strict orders: they will have to show that they are superior to the vanquished, whatever the circumstances may be, in order to cultivate the myth of the invincibility of the North Vietnamese troops and of the communist militants.[5] This is not only due to the fact that since the Americans—who had never lost a war in the history of their country—have been defeated by the Vietnamese (and the USSR and China and at home), they wanted to wrap themselves in turn in this legendary cloak, but simply because it is part of the communist ideology and propaganda that the world should believe they are indeed "ten feet tall" and make people look up to them in a sort of worship.

Needless to say that from now on the invaders who have been taught that the population of the South is hostile and mean—one wonders why, by the way—and thus fear assassination attempts and the South Vietnamese who, facing the occupation, will have humor as the only weapon against stupidity, ignorance, arrogance, and cruelty will look at each other as enemies, not as brothers.

There are two fundamental reasons for this kind of attitude on the part of the North Vietnamese cadres and settlers: first the annihilation of the Indonesian Communist party, second the setback they suffered during the Phoenix campaign.

In the first case, the communist leaders applied in Indonesia the same strategy they used everywhere else: they sowed the seeds of disorder and exploited the situation in order to take over power at the opportune time. With a slight difference, however, this time: the Indonesian authorities were able to cut them short in their attempt to seize power and wreck the country.[6]

In short, they made them swallow their very own recipe and experience their own strategy. They did not like it. In 1965 the Indonesian government outlawed the Communist party (PKI); out of nearly 2 million members, 1,700,000 were arrested. The Party was decimated.

In the second case, and the communists did remember it, too, the Phoenix campaign put the undercover cells out of action. According to William Colby, it was conducted by the CIA, the Counterespionage Service, the security, and the police of the former government, from 1968 until 1971.[7] It eliminated 20,587 communist militants and won back some 17,000 of them. A hard blow for the North, especially when one knows what the North Vietnamese had accomplished during three decades (1945–75) to "free" a South Vietnam not really in a hurry to be "liberated."

What is important, however, beyond the figures of agents eliminated on both sides of the fence, is that the military, the judiciary, the intelligence and counterintelligence services, in short the entire South Vietnamese defense system, was infiltrated to the core by communist agents. Despite all of this, it seems that most of them had been spotted, and were executed, and in some instances others were turned against the North, whose leaders thought they had the situation under control. This shows that nothing was clear and simple for either side.

There is maybe another reason why the North Vietnamese were very careful with the South: that was the experience of the Chinese communists against the nationalists in Mao's time. During the fifth campaign against the communists, the nationalists, who had been well trained by their German advisers and duly equipped, were well coordinated and advancing slowly and carefully. The communists realized then that for the first time they did not have the initiative. Unexpected result: they lost ground and disbanded. Had South Vietnam a similar ace in its sleeve?

Therefore, one can understand the significance, and the implications on the international scene of events such as these: they show to the world that communism can be defeated when there is a will. However, some decision makers in the West want to integrate it into their economy system—the way sedentary people have been integrating nomads throughout history—rather than to fight it, while others still, favor the concept of containment. Often, though, both are influenced by people who are dealing with the communists. Public opinion being more and more aware of this fact tends to disengage itself, in distrust, from the political aspect, which is maybe what was intended in the first place.

There was probably another reason for the attitude of the North Vietnamese toward the South Vietnamese population: they never referred to the events that took place during the Têt Offensive[8] in 1968—starting at 3:00 A.M. on Tuesday, January 30—but they remain very vivid in the memory of the people of the South even today. Regular units of the NFL and the North Vietnamese army, backed up by the guerrillas, attacked on all fronts. They stormed some thirty cities and forty towns and thirty-five American and South Vietnamese positions. These places fell to the North, who broke the truce established at that time and were occupied for three weeks during which—particularly in the city of Huê[9]—fifty-eight hundred people disappeared.[10] Later, when they were taken back by the South Vietnamese and the American forces, mass graves were discovered by chance, with chained corpses of children and adults buried in them.

Three weeks: 5,800 dead. The North Vietnamese had lost no time, and maybe they were worried now that they had to face the South Vietnamese population they were pretending to "liberate" as "brothers." For the world watching, propaganda was still talking "brotherhood," "clemency" (for whom, by the way?) and the construction of a "new country" (at what cost?), but everyone knows that when there is a murderer in a family, hatred from the other members is twice as strong than in any other circumstance—first, because of the crime itself and second for the betrayal of the family's trust. So it was and still is with

Vietnam. However, for those who died during these three weeks it was still a milder treatment than the one reported by Géneral Henri Jacquin in his book *La Guerre Secrète en Indochine (The Secret War in Indochina)*[11]: " . . . children cut in slices, nailed alive on doors, raped women ripped open with a knife like at the slaughter house; breast and cheeks cut; heart, liver and lungs found boiling in pots . . . "

The communist leaders were also silent when it came to the "feat" of the North Vietnamese battalions in the cities of An-Lôc and Quang-Tri during the spring of 1972 and Banmethuot during the spring of 1975. They pounded entire columns of civilian refugees, leaving dislocated corpses scattered all over the roads.[12] In the provinces of Binh-Dinh and Quang-Ngai (Central Vietnam) the *bô-doîs* shot people simply because they were suspected of having worked with the government.[13]

There is nothing surprising in this. The communists, in a hurry to establish socialism as quickly and as firmly as possible, do not hamper themselves with agreements or international conventions of the Red Cross to warrant protection to the wounded, the prisoners of war, and the civilian population.

NOTES

1. Voice of America, mid-May 1975.
2. Sir Robert Thompson, British assistant of Gen. Gerald Temple and expert in counterguerrilla warfare in Malaysia, inventor of the "strategic hamlets" (not to be confused with those in "ink blot" used in Africa by Field Marshal Lyautey), former secretary of defense of the Malaysian Federation, former adviser to President Nixon, went many times to South Vietnam.
3. General Raoul Salan, *L'Indochine Rouge (Red Indochina)* (Paris: Presses de la Cité, 1975), p. 13.
4. Title of a work praising the deeds, during the Ho Chi Minh campaign, of North Vietnamese general Van-Tiên-Dung, who entered Saigon in 1975. The Great Victory was won over South Vietnamese troops short of fuel and ammunition. Published first in the People's Army Daily in April–May 1976, it has become a book.
5. From the revelations made during the Fourth Congress of the Party, held in December 1976. At the First Congress, in Macao, China, in March 1935 there were six hundred Vietnamese members; 766,349 at the Second Congress in Tuyên Quang, North Vietnam, in February 1951; there were 500,000 in Hanoi for the Third Congress in September 1960, 1,550,000 in Hanoi for the Fourth in December 1976, 1,700,000 in Hanoi for the Fifth Congress in March 1982, and 1,800,000 in Hanoi for the Sixth Congress in December 1986.

6. Not only Indonesia, but also Thailand, Singapore, Malaysia, the Philippines, and Brunei, which are forming the ASEAN, do not accept communist parties or parties obedient to communist ideology.

7. William Colby, *Honorable Men: My Life in the CIA* (New York: Simon and Schuster, 1978), 219–236.

8. The New Year in Vietnam.

9. Huê is a city of Central Vietnam, formerly center of the ancient kingdom of Champa. Since then, the former imperial capital, renowned for its palace, the citadel, the river of perfumes, and the numerous tombs of emperors of the Nguyên dynasty.

10. Figure by Jean Lartéguy in *Voyage au bout de la Guerre* (*Journey to the End of War*) (Paris: Presses de la Cite, 1971), p. 171.

11. Olivier Orban, *La Guerre Secrète en Indochine*, p. 176; on p. 168, another massacre is also mentioned, so horrible that no one dared to claim responsibility for it.

12. Lê-huy-Linh-Vu, *Les derniers trois jours au quartier général du général Giai* (*The Last Three Days at the Headquarters of General Giai*) (Saigon). and "L'été sanglant" ("The Bloody Summer") by Phan-nhât-Nam, Saigon.

13. *The Memoirs of Richard Nixon*, Warner Books Corp.; p. 434.

THE PILLAGING OF SOUTH VIETNAM

One pillages the enemy because one covets his riches.

—Sun-Tzu

With the arrival of the North Vietnamese troops, the South Vietnamese administration began to disintegrate, and part of the people took this opportunity to help themselves in abandoned houses and stores. Waves of *bô-dôis* invaded the country, swarming cities and hamlets and streets and houses on their way. Agents of the fifth column, sympathizers, and profiteers were there as well to offer their services as informers and spies for the invading troops. Soon afterward, however, these people were replaced by the cadre's colonizers, or indoctrinated settlers from the North who called them "the revolutionaries of the Division 304."[1]

The Bamboo Curtain had fallen, in every sense of the term. First, small units of *bô-dôis* occupied all the buildings of the armed forces of the South, took possession of all the military vehicles, the stockpiles of weapons, ammunition, food, and *matériel*, and all the public buildings, embassies, and consulates except that of France. Then, with the help of the communist police, they occupied strategically located buildings, drew up the inventory of personal estates, collected public funds and private fortunes, and seized factories, universities, et cetera; in a word everything, in compliance with Marxist-Leninist ideology, which forbids private property and gives the state control over everything in socialist countries.

According to Voice of America, the military booty, worth $5 to 8 billion,[2] was gathered and quickly sent to the North, of course, and before it could be turned against the invaders. Of this booty Vietnam was to supply F-5 fighters, helicopters, M-48 tanks, M-113 APC, and air-to-air missiles to Iran, according to press reports from the gulf. The captured U.S. equipment, worth $400 million, would be paid for in cash and oil in equal parts.[3]

As for public funds, they simply have changed hands. It is as easy as that; keys and locks do not even know who are the new owners. As far as civilian booty is concerned, matériel, equipment, machines, merchandise, private estates, antiques, private collections, medical equipment, medicine, as well as the supplies of the Red Cross, et cetera, everything that constitutes the life of a country one can think of, was taken down, collected, indexed, stored, then finally shipped to the North, preferably at night, by cargos and convoys—a real work of ants. South Vietnamese sent by cargo ships to the North to be re-educated noticed that in the Haiphong harbor two huge warehouses were filled up to the roof with mattresses and beds taken away from hospitals in South Vietnam. On thc national highway linking the North and the South, Minh-Hiên himself saw endless convoys of trucks loaded with booty from South Vietnam moving day and night.

Drama, however, became horror when the communists took hold of rice, Vietnam's staple food. We will deal with this in the next chapters. To the general booty were added the very secret documents that could not be destroyed before the arrival of the communists and which got the security service busy for quite some time. People were executed on the spot, others, innocent, but being namesakes—which is frequent in Vietnam—and those who had worked for the former government were shot as investigations proceeded.

This being said, the pillaging did not go without some troubles, since some ammunition warehouses occupied by the People's Army exploded underneath the feet of the soldiers, in Cân-Tho, Sadec, and other places. For example, the Long-Binh ammunition warehouse (a former large U.S. base) was literally blown up in the sky in May 1975. The explosion was heard more than one hundred kilometers around. It killed many people and caused heavy material damage, never reported by the communist press of course.

Colonialism is no more a European invention of the sixteenth century than is pillaging a creation of the nineteenth-century West. Even a hasty glance at history reveals that war, colonization, torture, and famine are indeed creations of peoples whose empires thrived a long time ago. The colonialist West did not escape this tradition, which began several thousand years ago, when the nomads found out that it was easier to plunder the sedentary populations than to work themselves.

If it were indeed enough to conquer and plunder others to become developed nations, countries would have been wealthy throughout history. In fact, barbarians who destroyed civilizations spread their underdevelopment and brought Europe back to the Stone Age.

The pillaging of a country at war with another is not exactly pretty, but when it comes to plundering compatriots it is like stealing from your own brothers.

NOTES

1. The very one that took part in the battle of Diên-Biên-Phu in 1954, but here the figure 304 is a date: thirty of fourth, or thirtieth of April, the day Saigon fell. In the present context it means "the revolutionaries of the last hour."

2. Olivier Todd in *Cruel Avril 1975/La chute de Saigon* (*Cruel April 1975/The Fall of Saigon*) (Paris: Robert Laffont, 1987), evaluated the war booty as follows:

312 planes
502 helicopters
550 tanks
1.330 guns
90.000 hand guns
791.000 rifles
15.000 machine-guns
47.000 grenade-launchers
63.000 anti-tank weapons
12.000 mortars
42.000 trucks.

3. Weekly magazine *Jane's Defense*, London, November, 1986. This does not mean that the entire war booty was worth $400 million, only the part sent to Iran.

THE POLICE NETWORK

> *The Universe has as many different centers as there are living beings in it. Each of us is a center of the Universe, and that Universe is shattered when they hiss at you: "you are under arrest."*
>
> —Alexander Solzhenitsyn

The communist security service arrived on the heels of the soldiers rushing into the South. They occupied, with the police and the People's Committees (administration branches of the blocks, districts, cities, provinces, and regions created in haste), all the public buildings still vacant and confiscated private houses for their personnel.

Once in place, they began to deploy a huge network of information, like a web whose tightening became strangulation as investigations of the more and more controlled population proceeded. At the lower level, one finds the local cell, called street cell, of about ten houses put under the constant surveillance of a security agent who observed absolutely everything happening in his or her cell.

These cadres erupt into houses at any time of the day or of the night to search or bark orders:

- "Group meeting!" (Block or district.) Every family must send a representative to listen to the "news" or official statements. These night meetings take place two or three times a week, and those attending them sit on their heels, dominated by the standing cadres and overwhelmed by their logorrhea.
- "Shopping!" In theory this means to get rice, flour, sweet potatoes, vegetables, fish, meat, wood, coal, salt, mercurochrome, et cetera. In fact, one obtains one item at a time only. That is when there is something to get, period.
- "Fatigue parties!" They are simply forced labor.
- "Gathering declarations!" At this point one has to be a mailman, handing prospectuses and collecting detailed declarations that would send entire families to their death.

Every cadre knows his cell inside out. Anything unusual is immediately recorded: strangers (that is, Vietnamese who do not belong to the cells), doors closed during the day, noise, or silence, in short, anything out of the ordinary or slightly disturbing.

The mesh became tighter and tighter every day: intrusion in the personal life of individuals and infiltration of all social and religious organizations, setting up of new ones such as the Young Communist Brigades, the Young "Avante-Garde" (has anyone ever seen backward youths, by the way?), women, seniors, intellectuals, patriots, and "hair splitters," or what-have-you, to replace the ancestral structure. Not to forget the so-called Homeland Front Committees, supposedly designed to defend the country in case of danger, but whose real purpose is in fact to provide recruits for the invasion of Cambodia or Laos or to fight against China.

Then the security and the police undertook vast simultaneous actions to change the country in depth:

•Strict surveillance of anything hostile or even signs of dissatisfaction.

•Repression of any opposition, even the slightest one; people were arrested and disappeared.

•Organization of mass movements for "spontaneous" demonstrations.

•Imprisonment of capitalists and "bourgeois" and extortion of valuables.

•Seizure of personal and real estate and fortunes.

•Exchange and invalidation of banknotes in order to prevent any direct economic trade with the outside world and to bring all the money in the hands of those in power.

Meanwhile, the declarations gathered among the population are carefully examined: name, first name, nicknames, assumed names, sex, age, profession, activities, paternal and maternal ancestry and lineage of the family's head, the spouse, living members of the family, the deceased, place of abode, children and parents abroad, level of education, degrees obtained, foreign languages known, religion, activities under the French administration and under the "new American imperialists," personal and real estate, surface of the house, of the farmland, number of cattle, horses, fruit trees, everything, absolutely everything. Can one imagine what it would have been like if these people had computers? Big Brother would look like a choirboy by comparison.

The workers of the confiscated enterprises and the prisoners of the reeducation camps must give the name of two people they know and love most, the name of two people that they hate most and the name of collaborators that they know to have worked with the Americans. This source of information is added to the secret documents left by the Americans and the secret services and which have not been destroyed; they are scrutinized in every detail.

Thanks to this huge mass of information, the communist security proceeds meticulously and tirelessly, twenty-four hours a day, to run the deadliest manhunt ever. Usually, to capture the victims on their day's lists the security agents of one locality go to another one, or in the capital they go to another part of the town where they have little chance of being recognized by the people.

In his book, *A Viet-Cong Memoir,*[1] former RPG's justice minister Trûóng-Nhu-Táng writes that about three hundred thousand people were arbitrarily arrested, anywhere, any time, for any reason, no rights granted; they just disappeared. Other people were also arrested by military and police organizations dealing severely in Saigon and in the provinces, but the figures are unknown, even today.

Those who were arrested will never know if they have been victimized because of a shady denunciation, vengeance, or simply homonymy.

While pursuing socialization and the establishing of state control as set by the Party, the prime task of the communist security remained the following:

- To look for, track down, and eliminate the nonevacuated agents of the CIA. (By the way, one wonders why their names were left behind.)

•To find, capture, and punish the defeatist traitors.

•To arrest and imprison the "rebels."

•To liquidate the enemies of the proletariat and of Marxism-Leninism.

•To suppress the intelligentsia and the opponents of the regime.

•To control the discontented.

•To expel the foreigners and the Chinese.

•To get hold of the population.

In order to do that, the North Vietnamese searched for and eliminated anyone suggesting that this was far from a brotherly revolution. They also wiped out even the mere memory of the American presence.

NOTE

1. Truong-Nhu-Tang, *A Viet-Cong Memoir* (New York: Harcourt Brace Jovanovich, 1985).

THE ANTI-AMERICAN CAMPAIGN

May God send lice to tyrants, dogs to lonely people, butterflies to children, minks to women, boars to men, and to us all an eagle to take us to Him.

—Ukrainian proverb

This time the eagle was gone. And the communists would make sure it would not land again in Vietnam.

This anti-American campaign was conducted as soon as the communists arrived in Saigon in April 1975: search and arrest of Americans who had not been able to flee and of the people who had worked with them (suspected agents of the CIA, priests, businessmen, et cetera). Then the embassies, except that of France, and the residences of the diplomats, in which the *bô-dôis* established their quarters, were seized.

The warehouses, merchandise, and vehicles of American or other foreign companies were confiscated. The building of the USIS (U.S. Information Service) and the Abraham Lincoln Library on Le-quy-Dôn street were ransacked and the books burnt in the street. Before rewriting history in Marxist terms, one needs to eradicate everything else in order to avoid any possible comparison.

Places and hotels rented to American organizations and agencies to shelter GIs between 1965 and 1973 were requisitioned. Apartments rented to foreigners, and particularly to Americans, were confiscated. Houses in residential areas rented—or not—to American civilians or belonging to professors of Thu-Duc University were also confiscated. Families living in these houses were thrown out in the street on the spot, forbidden to take anything with them, not even clothing.

Progressively and as the communists were taking the census of the people the security confiscated their homes. Reason: collaboration with the Americans. Families or close relatives of absentee owners were thrown out in the street without further inquiry. Some who had never rented a room to any American were expelled in the same fashion: they simply owned the luxurious hotel Bach Kim at the corner of the Hông-Thâp-Tu and Cao-Thang streets.

In the provinces it was even worse. The provincial security confiscated the houses of former South Vietnamese officers and civil servants; they were accused of having built them with the "blood of the people." Strangely enough, however, the same people in the name of whom these expulsions were committed did not benefit from them at all. Like the big owners who in the cities could be accused of having been in contact with the Americans, the big merchants in the countryside were accused of illicit trading, speculation, and dealing on the black market. Their houses and warehouses were therefore confiscated. Houses whose owners were related or allied to important people in the former government were also taken by the communists. As for those whose names were linked, in one way or another, with the American presence, they were subjected to constant attacks during the meetings and were branded "American-Thieu-Ky," "American-Diêm," or "American rebels."[1]

These confiscations in the name of a people who would not even see the colour of the loot were followed by an anti-American propaganda campaign.

During the month of May 1975, the entire Vietnamese population was invited to regular meetings to listen to the cadres praising the "heroic People's Army, who won a decisive victory over the Americans." One detail, however, was never mentioned during these meetings: this victory took place against an American army gone for two years already, the last GIs having been evacuated between January and April 1973, the first *bô-dôis* entering Saigon April 30, 1975.

The authorities were also making a lot of noise about the myth of the soldiers' invincibility, claiming that for "100 battles engaged by the Marxist-Leninists, 100 victories have been won." Sun-Ťzu himself would have retorted that winning one hundred victories in one hundred battles is not exactly the acme of warfare "savoir-faire." The Têt Offensive of 1968 was never mentioned however, since it was a defeat for the communists; of course, and thanks to a certain Western press it appeared to be a victory for the North Vietnamese simply because some *bô-doîs* came under the windows of the U.S. embassy in Saigon.

At that time, though, in Saigon, the North Vietnamese were preparing an exhibition titled "Crimes Perpetrated by the Americans," right in the pharmacy's faculty yard (was this place chosen to get emergency care for their ideology, should they need it?) standing at the corner of the Trân-quy-Cap and Lê-quy-Dôn streets.

Flabbergasted visitors could find a Soviet bomb, a Soviet-made T:72, and Kalachnikovs. Sorry, the propaganda committee forgot to change the slides left by the Soviet and the Chinese arms dealers. So, to start again: flabbergasted visitors could see a CBU bomb,[2] an amphibious M-113, a Howitzer, M-16 rifles, the table showing 7,700,000 tons of bombs, rockets, missiles, shells, and ammunition used in Vietnam, Laos, and Cambodia and 64 million liters of defoliants[3] used by the U.S. Army during the war in Vietnam, and pictures of the 169 dead in My Lai killed by American soldiers in March 1968.

Were the visitors really flabbergasted? Yes indeed. First, because everyone knows that My Lai was used as a base by the communist guerrillas and that the inevitable was bound to happen there, especially right after the Têt Offensive during which the communists themselves had killed five thousand, eight hundred civilians in Huê alone. Second, because they could not see the difference between the deadly Soviet weapons and the deadly American weapons. What they knew, however, was that those who were carrying the American weapons had respected their freedom, whereas the other had reduced them to slavery.

Meanwhile, not even a hundred yards away, Soviet SAM 3 were being erected on the ground of the former Gia-Long palace, at the corner of Gia-Long and Công-Ly streets, renamed Nguyên-thi-Minh-Khai and Nam-Ky-Khoi-Nghia.

Flabbergasted are the Vietnamese when it comes to My Lai, because if most of the Western media have focused persistently on the 169 dead of this hamlet, they have been extremely discreet about the five thousand, eight hundred people massacred in three weeks by the communists during the Têt Offensive in 1968. Decaying corpses of the victims were found, by chance, hands and feet tied, lying in mass graveyards, exactly like in Katyn, where 4,143 Polish officers were murdered by the Soviets and found in February 1943.[4]

Now, in a more profound manner, the North Vietnamese inculcate hatred of the Americans in their children. They teach them how to count the number of GIs killed daily by their guerrillas. In the streets, groups of policemen pick up all the publications and tapes in English. Young people sporting American-style clothes or haircuts are arrested and punished in public.

In 1975 a music professor, TVK, back from Paris to Ho Chi Minh City, where he was to visit his family, had to lecture on the perverse, immoral, and repugnant life of Americans in the United States. Up to a point, one could understand this professor being asked to talk about the French, since he was coming from France, but about the Americans when he had been as many times in Washington as in Moscow?

During this anti-American campaign, the South Vietnamese were called on to give away all the U.S. dollars they had in their possession and to "deposit" them at the bank. Not to obey such a "request" would have meant, of course, severe punishment; we need not insist on that. Besides, and in order to strengthen the citizens' hearts, security agents searched every inch of each house: walls, floors, ceilings, furniture, toilets, flowerpots, piles of household linen, everywhere, in order to extirpate the symbols of that spurned capitalism.

One must not draw too hastily the conclusion that these symbols were, say, burnt in the street, like the books of the Abraham Lincoln Library, for instance, and that life was about to continue as before, without banknotes. No. Discredited indeed were the green dollars, gold bullion, and precious stones, but all of them were entrusted to the one and only bank, state-owned of course, replacing all of the forty-five Vietnamese and foreign banks closed since the invasion.

Within the framework of this anti-American campaign, the cadres and the *bô-dôis* bought French and Japanese products at the flea markets, rather than those "Made in the USA," of course. The French and the Japanese, who are thus separated in a symbolic manner, will have to accept the fact that from then on they are not capitalists in the eyes of the North Vietnamese.

In the same spirit, Hanoi for months, had been asking the U.S. government to pay $3.25 billion[5] said to have been promised by former president Richard Nixon in order to rekindle the North Vietnamese economy ruined by the war, that is, if North Vietnam had respected the Paris Agreement and had not invaded the South. This not being the case, the U.S. government refused what could have amounted to financing socialism, whose goal is to destroy democratic countries.

On the other hand, since the signing of the Paris Agreement in 1973 establishing the neutrality of South Vietnam, the United States has demanded the return of some two thousand, five hundred MIA (Missing In Action). Once in a while, the North Vietnamese send back a few skeletons.

Now what about the American prisoners? Former soldiers, NCOs, and officers have declared in front of U.S. television cameras that they had the proof that some of their compatriots and comrades in arms are still alive in Vietnam. The March 23, 1985, *Gazette* of Montreal, Canada, revealed, based on an AP wire datelined Washington, that former U.S. Marine Robert Garwood stated that up to seventy Americans were still in captivity when he left Vietnam in 1979.

In his book *Dead End,* former communist cadre Xûan-Vū[6] describes the story of one of these war prisoners. On the bank of a brook where he had come to quench his thirst when crossing the province of Kontum, nearby the Ho Chi Minh Trail, Xuân-Vū tells how he discovered, by chance, a cage about three foot high built with trunks as big as a leg. Inside, an American prisoner, covered with haematomas,[7] lived—if one might say that—crouching, in rags, his hair long and shaggy, one foot chained to a tree that served as a corner pillar for the cage.

The warden with whom Xuân-Vū had begun to talk explained to him how a *bô-dôi* hidden in high grass had managed to call a chopper's attention with distress signals from the ground. While one soldier jumped off the helicopter to check the situation, another *bô-dôi* shot at the aircraft, which had to leave the soldier, now prisoner in the cage.

At lunchtime, *bô-dôis* sat down in front of him so that he could see and smell the food, so with cigarettes at the time of tea break. Afterward, one of them would throw a handful of rice at him and a pail of water. What he could get was what he had to survive with. Sometimes he got a cigarette, but the *bô-dôi* "for-got" to light it.

In another instance, relatives of one of the coauthor's neighbors, living in Saigon at the time, said that, while crossing the province of Quang-Ngai in Central Vietnam during the exodus of 1975, they saw two Americans, instead of the usual water buffalo, harnessed to a plow. It was along the Transnational Road Number 1 connecting Hanoi with Saigon. When the two men slowed down, they were beaten with a rattan or bamboo stick. And these witnesses added: "The communists will never let the Americans go free and alive, because they would have too many things to tell."

In his book, *The Red Carcan*[8], Pham-quôc-Bao tells in what circumstances he also had the opportunity to meet other prisoners. As an intellectual and a former officer,[9] the author, captured by the communist police, spent more than five years—from 1975 to 1980—in various jails of Ho Chi Minh City and in reeducation camps in North Vietnam. Toward the end of 1977, he was transferred with thousands of other prisoners[10] on board the ship *Credit Commercial 1*, renamed *Song Hüong* (*River of Perfumes*), to the Quang-Ninh camp, near the coal mines of Dông-Trieu; later still to Camp Number 5, sadly known as the Ly-Ba-Só camp, located in the province of Thanh-Hoa in the northern part of Central Vietnam. No one has ever got near the camp, built at the foot of a mountain.

During the fall of 1978, the directorate of the camp received an urgent order for several thousand woven bamboo baskets, which, the author learned later, were to be used for packing oranges for the Soviet Union. Needless to say, the prisoners had to work without interruption to fulfill the order in the prescribed time. In October, a team, of which the author was part, was sent by carts to deliver the baskets to an orange grove some three kilometers away.

Waiting for the workers in charge of the delivery, the prisoners who brought the baskets remained outside the camp, but took the opportunity to have a look inside. Three tall men dressed in black cotton were picking oranges. When they finally got within close range, the workers asked them not to point them out with their fingers, nor to stare at them too long, because they were strictly watched. When they turned their heads the newcomers saw "their blue eyes and pointed noses." They were able to exchange a few sentences. The men dressed in black cotton were former commandos, and they were not alone. Indeed, Pham-quôc-Bao and the prisoners with him could see other tall men among the trees, but were not able to know about their number, nor about their fate. For all we know, no one has ever heard that any of these "giants with pointed noses and blue eyes" has been able to leave Vietnam alive since 1975.

In June–July 1985, Hanoi announced that twenty-eight skeletons had been found. As of August 2, 1987, one thousand, eight hundred Americans are still missing. Does this mean that out of the two thousand, five hundred MIA, seven hundred of them could have been set free and we never heard anything about it?

NOTES

1. Referring to the Americans Gen. Nguyên-Van-Thiêu, Gen. Nguyên-Cao-Ky, and former president Ngo-dinh-Diêm.

2. A CBU bomb had been used fifty kilometers north of Saigon on April 17, 1975. World public opinion prevented the further use of the Cluster Bomb Unit.

3. Gérard Le Quang, *La Guerre Américaine d'indochine* (*The American War of Indochina*) (Paris: 1973 Editions Universitaires), p. 117.

4. Alexandra Kwiatkowska Viatteau, *Katyn, 1940–1943, La Mémoire du Siècle* (*The Memory of the Century*) (Brussels: Editions Complexe, 1982), p. 50. In fact, fifteen thousand officers disappeared, but only some five thousand have been found in the mass graves.

5. A letter of former president Richard Nixon to Prime Minister Pham-van-Dong, February 1, 1973.

6. Book published in Vietnamese in 1973 (six months after the signing of the Paris Agreement). Most books such as this or even the publishers are difficult to trace back. We do not know either what Xuân-Vū became after he left the Party. The former secretary of education who prefaced Xuân-Vu's book is still in jail.

7. Because the poor guy had been badly beaten before he was thrown into the cage.

8. In Vietnamese, published by The Vietnamese, Westminster, California, p. 149, not yet translated into English.

9. Professor of English, later on Lt. Pham-quôc-Bao was jailed in 1975 and released from the camps in North Vietnam in 1980. He arrived in Ho Chi Minh City in October the same year and found refuge in Indonesia in January 1981 with other Boat People. He now lives in the United States.

10. Vietnamese and Cambodians.

THE RE-EDUCATION CAMPS

The next day came and went.

—Mark Twain

In Vietnam weeks and months were to come and go and people were to be forgotten.

Once the South had been invaded, and the weapons and ammunition were under control, the most important preoccupation of the Party was to seal the fate of the South's armies and authorities who for thirty years had fought in order to keep their country out of reach of the North Vietnamese. For failing to recognize the "blessings" of communism, these men, women, and children would be executed as "rebels."

Those who refused to surrender killed themselves, like Trân-Chanh-Thành, former minister of information under Ngô-dinh-Diêm, and the generals Nguyên-Khoa-Nam, Lê-van-Hung, and Pham-Van-Phu. Others ran away. During the last few days of April 1975, 135,000 people managed to escape the North Vietnamese invaders. Then, there were those, like Dr. Phan-huy-Quat, ex–prime minister, Trân-Van-Tuyên, lawyer, and the ex–vice prime minister and scholar Hô-Huu-Tuong, who died in the camps.

During the very first week of May 1975—that is, right after the fall of Saigon—loudspeakers[1] called the NCOs and the hamlet's chiefs, in other words all the lower ranks in the hierarchy, to register for the "lenient policy courses of the Center."[2] They had to take with them a blanket, a mosquito net, and food for a week. Seven days later, those people who are not of interest to the communists, at least for the time being, came back with a piece of paper certifying that they had followed the courses given by Hanoi. Then, one week later, when the population was a little bit reassured about the fate of some of its members—now listed with the communist police—Hanoi starts a new "political training" campaign. Large posters on the walls of the city, inflammatory speeches broadcast by loudspeakers more and more present in the daily life of the people, articles in the one and only newspaper of the Party—the *Liberated Saigon*—everything was done to make known the official statement of Trân-van-Trà, commander-in-chief and president of the city's military committee: "All civilians or soldiers, retired or not, and even veterans who have assumed any responsibility are required to register for the political courses."

This time, however, registrations were conducted in schools, not in the street anymore, like the last time, and, the statement insisted, everyone must bring clothes, a blanket, a mosquito net, and food for ten or thirty days, depending upon the categories determined by those in charge of the registration.

Despite their fear, all concerned high-ranking officers, ministers, deputies and political leaders, writers and journalists, et cetera, came to the registration "offices" with their bundles. The last day, during the curfew, the city was totally plunged into darkness and the convoys of "volunteers" went to the courses of "lenient policy."

Ten days went by, then thirty days, then two, three months. Nothing. The new policy instructors were probably having a hard time penetrating the brains of these people.

Without news of their relatives since their departure, distressed by rumors finally getting through ("accidents" had occured along the way), and totally unaware of the places where the members of their families were being detained, mothers and wives decided to confront the police in order to get some information. They went to the former Ministry of the Interior (Home Office) facing the cathedral of Saigon.

The police officers bludgeoned and dispersed the poor women, like, for instance, in Tân-sa-Châu, a town where three weeks after the fall of the capital about one hundred Catholics led by a few priests took to the streets to demonstrate against the suppression of liberties and were savagely beaten, arrested, and imprisoned.

Not knowing where to turn, the women decided to discretely approach the officials of the National Front of Liberation who had access to Commander-in-chief Trà, the signatory of the official statement on re-education. One of these officials reported:

•September 2nd, 1975, official holiday of the Democratic Republic of Vietnam, we talked to the commander-in-chief during the reception given at the Palace of Independence:

•"General, in your statement, the length of reeducation for the rebels was set at 10 and 30 days depending upon the person. Three months have elapsed and now the families are anxious to get news of their relatives."

•"Oh, yes . . . We have managed to put all of them in jail," answered the commander-in-chief.[3]

Besides, one of the Party leaders would tell later the ex–vice prime minister Nguyên-vàn-Hao that the communists have been successful in two very important instances:

•To lure the Americans into leaving Vietnam, and

•To deceive the "rebels" and jail them in the reeducation camps.

Other statements warned the latecomers and recalcitrants. For them, there was only one way: exile by whatever means, in order to evade the police net closing in more and more every day.

In the camps and for those who had not died "accidentally" begins a long wait. They have to fill out an extremely complete and complicated questionnaire, and their declarations will be checked several times. Those who have a "debt of blood," that is, the men and women who fought the communists, are separated from the others and disappear.

During a visit of the Amnesty International delegation in Vietnam from December 10 to the twenty-first, 1979,[4] the Hanoi government declared that there were four categories of prisoners:

•The military "rebels," that is, those who fought against the communists.

•The "rebel" authorities, that is, the civil servants who worked for the former government.

•The agents of security, police, and counterespionage forces.

•The militants of the political parties and "reactionary" organizations such as those opposed to communist ideology.

Other categories should be added to these four, but the communists did not mention them:

•The clergy: Buddhist, Catholic, and Protestant, and the faithful of various sects.

•The "enemies of the proletariat": capitalists, bourgeois, intellectuals, et cetera.

•The politicians.

•Those opposed to Marxist-Leninist ideology, in particular the writers, journalists, and publishers.

•The men and women who fled the regime.

•Delinquents and common criminals.

•The 220,000 communist militants who joined the nationalist cause.

•The seventeen thousand agents recruited by the CIA who could not be evacuated in April 1975.

It is difficult to know the exact number of re-education camps dotting the country. According to the magazine *Van-nghê-tien-phong*[5] (*Vanguard Letters and Arts*), no. 177 (June 1983), estimating by counting the post office boxes whose numbers are published in the people's daily, there could be 1,200 camps with between 500 to 1,000 prisoners in each, which means a total of 600,000 to 1,200,000 prisoners. According to the document "The Penitentiary Regime in Vietnam–78 Charter," published by the Movement for the Defense of Human Rights in Vietnam, no re-education camp has fewer than one thousand prisoners of both sexes and of all ages and there would be a total of about eight hundred thousand prisoners.

When one speaks of prisoners of both sexes and of all ages, there is a reason for that: for instance, according to Nguyên-Thanh-Dân, now a refugee in Montreal, Canada, a young boy of twelve was jailed for having reported to the police of the former government a hideout where he found two Kalachnikovs just after the Têt Offensive; that was seven years earlier. The communists did not forget and jailed him when they took over South Vietnam.

Interviewed by journalists in April 1977 in Paris, then prime minister Pham-van-Dong[6] declared that 95 percent of the prisoners in the re-education camps had been released, a delicate euphemism, since these prisoners have no rights, not even that of possessing a ration book. Only 5 percent had to stay in jail for various reasons, numbering fifty thousand. The most elementary arithmetic reveals that if fifty thousand prisoners represent 5 percent, 100 percent means there is a grand total of 1 million. When queried about the fate of Trân-van-Tuyên, already mentioned,[7] the then prime minister declared that he was "in good health"; in fact, Mr. Tuyên had been transferred from the South to the North, where he died in the prison of Lao-Kay, in April 1976—one year earlier.

To Amnesty International, visiting Hanoi in December 1979, the communist authorities stated that from 1975 to 1979 only forty thousand people were detained in the camps:

- Twenty-nine thousand military "rebels," that is, servicemen of the former government.
- Seven thousand "rebel" officials.
- Three thousand agents of the former government's security.
- Nine hundred militants of the political parties and "reactionary" organizations.

All of which was in direct contradiction with the figures given by Pham-van-Dong himself (fifty thousand still in jail, representing only 5 percent of the prisoners). Now, one also knows that beyond the estimates and figures forwarded by the Movement for the Defense of Human Rights in Vietnam and what seems to be the plausible figure of 1 million prisoners, there were at the time of the fall of Saigon 1,100,000 soldiers in the South Vietnamese army, retired officers not included. There were also more than 280,000 civil servants in all fields. It is unlikely that the 220,000 communist militants who joined the nationalist South or the 17,000 agents recruited by the CIA were allowed to run loose.

Several books and articles have been published about the reeducation camps, describing the horrible, inhumane, and atrocious conditions in which victims died:

•*Trai Dâm Dùn (The Camp of the Dun Lagoon,* known as the Lý-bá-Só camp)[8] by Trân-vān-Thai. Editor: Song Moi (New Life), Saigon, 1970. Reedited by Song Moi, in 1979, Forth Smith, AR, 73913, U.S.A. U.S.A.

•*Le Gulag Vietnamien* (*The Vietnamese Gulag*), by Doàn-vān-Toai, Robert Laffont, Paris, 1979.

•*Nhúng Năm Cai Tao Ó băc Viêt* (*The Reeducation Years in North Vietnam*), by Trân-huỳnh-Châu, published by TTNS (monthly news), Culver City, California, 1981.

•*Nhân Loai Da Thäy Gì Tü Hoa Nguc Vietnam* (*What Does Mankind Know about Hell in Vietnam?*), by Lê-tân-Trang, published by Liên Minh Dân Chu, 1982, Santa Ana, California.

•*Cùm Do* (*The Red Carcan*), by Pham-quôc-Bao, published by The Vietnamese, 1985, Westminster, California.

•*Dai Hoc Máu* (*Bloody University; or 1685 Days in the Reeducation Camps*), by Ha-thuc-Sinh, published by Nhâm Vān, 1985, San Jose, California.

•*Trai Cai Tao (Reeducation Camps),* by Pham-quang-Giai, published by Liviko Printing, 1986, Houston, Texas.

•*Day Dia Nguc (Down to Hell),* by Ta-Ty, published by Thang-Mo, 1986, San Jose, California.

•"Les prisons du Vietnam" ("Vietnam's Prisons"), an article by Marie-Thérèse de Brosses, *Paris-Match* no. 1541 (December 8, 1978). A collection of accounts from three refugees of the Hai-Hong cargo ship.

•"Mes prisons au Vietnam" ("My Prisons in Vietnam"), an article by Jean Lartéguy, *Paris-Match* no. 2533 (November 22, 1981). From the account of Lê-van-Duc, a lawyer.

Never has the saying "Vae Victis" ("Woe betides the vanquished")[9] been so real than in Vietnam for those opposed to the regime or Marxist-Leninist ideology. The penitentiary system is a disgrace at all levels and seems to have eliminated, we are told, 30 percent of the prisoners in most of the camps. Beside the fact that they are starving, the prisoners are without news from their families, who themselves have no support whatsoever. In most cases the prisoners do not know what they are being accused of, they are not judged and therefore they do not know how long they are going to remain prisoners, and yet they have to undergo self-criticism sessions. They are also mentally and physically tortured—although the degree and intensity may vary from one camp to another—and, of course, there are executions.

For the prisoners who have been transferred to the North the treatment is even more painful and ends up at times with lapidation. At the bottom of this abyss of despair, some prisoners become insane, like the former director of the Public Property Service, Lê-van-Truong, who died in the psychiatric hospital of Biên-Hoa in April 1977. Others killed themselves, like former M.D. colonel Vo-Khac-Tuy, who worked at the military hospital of Saigon and was transferred to Haiphong.

Some prisoners who had become crippled or too old were released, like General LVK, for example; some others were freed simply because they had fallen in such a state of total hebetude and lethargy, like ex–minister of finance Luu-vân-Tinh, incarcerated despite distinguished services rendered to the communists as an underground agent. Then there were those who were freed because they were on the threshold of death, like the scholar Hô-huu-Tuong.

The prisoners were condemned to hard labor in unhealthy areas. They were compelled to cut down trees, bamboo, and rattan; they were compelled to toil carrying heavy blocks of stone and tree trunks, with a food ration limited to a handful of wheat flour or a piece of manioc. Gnawed by a hunger never appeased, deficiency diseases and malnutrition weakened their bodies and exposed them to tuberculosis and, ultimately, death. The absence of medicine, hoarded in the North, meant their condemnation, as in the case of Bành-ngoc-Quy, ex–vice director, of Vice President Trân-van-Huong's Cabinet, and Nguyên-dinh-Luong, specialist *and* adviser to the Minister of the Economy, husband of Vu-thi-Thoa, M.D. Dysentry *and* malaria alone exacted a very impressive toll.

The prisoners who transgressed the camp's rules, in order to secure a bit of food, for instance, were locked in underground cells, too narrow to allow them to lie down or stand up, or in steel containers (recuperated U.S. conex, about 1.5 meters by 1.5 meters by 1.5 meters) overheated by the sun, without water, without food, until death claimed them. The case of one police officer and judo trainer is well known: tortured by hunger, he tried to unearth some forgotten tubercles of manioc. Caught red-handed, he was condemned on the spot, had his hands tied behind his back, was placed between four executioners, and was beaten to death with wooden rods. Those who escaped and were brought back were immediately shot on the spot. The bodies of the executed were buried hastily, and the families were never notified of the deaths.

NOTES

1. Used for brainwashing. American prisoners in Korea, for instance, remember what this was like.
2. *Centre* here means the North, Hanoi.
3. Conversation reported by an official still living in Ho Chi Minh City who prefers to remain anonymous.
4. Pages 294 to 300 of the Amnesty International report on Vietnam, 1980.
5. Published in the United States.
6. Replaced in July 1987 by Pham-Hung, which is a militant's name, of his real name, Pham-Van-Thiên. He passed away on March 10, 1988, and was replaced by Vo-Van-Kiêt.
7. Lawyer, leader of the South Vietnamese Nationalist party, vice prime minister in 1965–66, at one time member of the delegation led by Nguyên-Tuong-Tam, who participated in the French-Vietnamese preliminary conference of Dalat in 1946.

8. This was a real concentration camp, baptized "re-education camp" to fool public opinion. The author escaped from this hell located in North Vietnam, on the twentieth parallel, before the fall of Saigon.

9. (Livy) V, 48.

SUPPRESSION OF FREEDOM OF EXPRESSION

Considering the virtues demanded from a valet, does your excellency know many masters who would be worthy of being servants?

—Pierre de Beaumarchais

Journalists and politicians criticizing our "imperfect" world could be asked this question. After the taking over of the South by the North and in order to avoid a similar treatment, the communists made sure that the media of the opposition were silenced. True enough, the media, in the communist concept, are one of the major tools in shaping the new socialist man in the struggle against capitalism.[1] What kind of man and woman is our media shaping?

The journalists and reporters, writers and publishers who for some reason had managed to avoid the early massacres were jailed, like Nguyên-kiên-Giang, Huynh-thanh-Vi, Thanh-thuong-Hoang, Hô-huu-Tuong, Son-Diên-Nguyên-viêt-Khanh, Doan-quoc-Sy, Cao-Giao-Nguyên-trân-Huyên, Doan-kê-Tuong, Dang-Giao, Chu-vy-Thuy, Phan-nhât-Nam, Thai-làng-Nghiêm, and many more.

Those who were spared by this repression had no more newspapers, no paper, no pencils, no ink, and no printing shops to practice their profession. From the little newspaper boys to the directors, the printers, the journalists, and the editors, everybody was destitute, without any work compensation, no unemployment insurance, or whatever. Thus the South Vietnamese press and its twenty dailies or so and its reviews and periodical publications began to disappear. Fast. The country was silenced. One newspaper only, the *Liberated Saigon*, the Party's own, of course, replaced all the publications: No more international, national, regional news; no more crimes, murders or suicides; no more thefts and no more rapes, no more accidents nor incidents, all bad for the Party's image. Everything is finally "perfect."

Radio and television are, of course, strictly used for official statements and the Party's propaganda.

Besides, people were "invited" to see only what the Party wanted them to see, like the popular tribunals, for instance, conditioning the public, and the Party made sure that they listened to what the Party wanted them to hear. No one knew exactly what was going on outside a circle of a few hundred meters. The ferocious vigilance of the security force was such that the individuals listening to even the most insignificant noncommunist murmur were having a hard time trying to spread news from VOA, the BBC, or even the Australian radio. Only by word of mouth did people manage to learn that one night, for instance, the security had conducted a manhunt in such and such part of the city, that convoys of prisoners had left for the camps where the re-educated become zombies, and that rice and booty were sent up north by dark in order to prevent the population from knowing what was going on and how.

In May 1975 a demonstration at Tân-Sa-Châu against the exactions of the cadres towards the Catholics from the North who had found refuge in the South in 1954 was not published in the Party's newspaper. Despite that, the people knew it had been harshly repressed, the priest imprisoned, and that the North Vietnamese had opened fire on the crowd. No one knows the exact figure, but it is said that there were about ten killed and more wounded.

There is news heard in Vietnam that will never be published anywhere else in the world. Early one morning in May 1975, for instance, the people found, to their very great surprise, a proclamation signed by Huynh-Tan-Phat, prime minister of the provisional government created by Hanoi, posted on walls in Saigon. Three days later, these posters with the ten articles referring to the neutrality of South Vietnam had disappeared. The red and green flag with a yellow star in the middle and the national anthem of this pseudo-government were proscribed.

There is other news that is known around the world, but not in Vietnam, or when Vietnamese learn about it, it is later, much later, after the events have taken place and are even forgotten. In October 1975, for example, an H-12 helicopter flown by former lieutenant Hô-xuan-Ngai landed on the coast of Thailand. The same month, the refrigerator ship *Chiên-Thang* (of the Denis Brothers Company) found refuge in Singapore. In November the S/S *Vaico 2* took refuge in Thailand. The following year, the S/S *Vaico 16* anchored in the Philippines with 150 "illegal" passengers and a load of one thousand, five hundred tons of first-quality rice expected in Haiphong, North Vietnam. In April 1977, the S/S *Song-Be 2* found refuge in Darwin, Australia, with 182 refugees on board. The following month, the towing ship no. 1 of the State Ship Construction Company arrived in Singapore with ninety-three refugees. In October of the same year, a civilian DC-3 was "hijacked" by four "pirates" and landed in Singapore. On March 22, 1978, a military DC-3 flown by two communist pilots also landed in Singapore. One month later, the S/S *Vaico 24* also arrived in Singapore.

Finally, there is news that is partly known in Vietnam and partly known in the rest of the world, like, for instance, the story of the S/S Vietnam *Thuong-Tin 1*, with a cargo of about ten thousand tons, the pride of the merchant marine of the former regime. After four months at sea,[2] this ship arrived in sight of her home port, Saigon, in the afternoon of April 29, 1975, and anchored in the middle of the river that gave its name to the capital city, in front of the place known as the Pointe des Blagueurs. Commanding Officer VVT, going home, passed through a city in effervescence. The next day, April 30, 1975, a few hours before the arrival of the North Vietnamese troops, VVT met Commander NNT, his replacement. After consultation, the two men decide to leave the country aboard the cargo ship. NNT's family being ready to embark, VVT went aboard and brought the ship alongside the quay. As soon as the ship reached the wharf, NNT and his family climbed up on board, while VVT ran home—about one kilometer away—to pick up his wife and children. But thousands of people who had closely followed the movements of the ship, packed on the quay, used this opportunity to embark immediately in a confusion beyond description. Fearing the worst, NNT cast off with three thousand refugees on board, leaving thousands of others ashore, among whom VVT, who had just arrived with his family to see the ship sail away. By invading the ship, the refugees had completely upset two men's plan to escape together.[3]

When the cargo ship arrived at the junction with the Donai River at the height of Nà-Bè, she was hit by an antitank grenade, fired from the shore by arriving North Vietnamese troops. The first salvo killed five passengers among whom was Chu-Tu, the journalist and director of the daily *Song* (*Life*). What follows is part of the information known and reported throughout the world. The ship headed for Guam, where more than one hundred thousand refugees had managed to escape with the U.S. 7th fleet, coastal vessels, with cargos of all tonnage, in other words with anything that could float or fly. Then, after the tribulations of the flight, the refugees of the S/S Vietnam *Thuong-Tin 1* found themselves standing in line to fill in forms, keys to a new life in another country.

As strange as it may seem, something unbelievable happened: among the 100,000-plus refugees on Guam Island, 1,547 people prompted by agents who had boarded with them in Saigon[4] discovered all of a sudden that they had made a "mistake"; they had been carried away by the flow of refugees, and they had left their families behind. They were nostalgic and wanted to go back to Vietnam, absolutely, and now. People with experience were telling them that doing so would not exactly be safe and that it might be disapproved of by the communists, whereas for the moment, at least, they had a unique opportunity to leave hell behind. Nothing worked. They protested, destroyed their camp, set their shanties afire, initiated a hunger strike, and demanded to be sent back to Vietnam, in order, they said, to "serve their homeland." Funny, especially because that was precisely the very moment Hanoi chose to claim the cargo ship, which it contended belonged to North Vietnam. Finally, after a crash course attended by a new pilot and a new crew selected among the discontented, who were then given plenty of food and clothing, the American authorities shipped back all these people eager to join the gulag. The boat left the island on October 19, 1975. Here ends the part of the story known outside Vietnam. The conclusion was a Vietnamese one.

Instead of going to her home port of Saigon, the Vietnam *Thuong-Tin 1* headed for Nhatrang, where she stopped at the deserted quay of Câu-Da. All we know about the 1,547 "refugees" is that they have been searched four times:

•First, to take their gold and jewelry.

•Second, to deprive them of their dollars.

•Third, to strip them of their valuable clothing.

•And finally, to take any food they had.

Instead of being awarded a medal for services rendered to the nation, these refugees were sent to jail for having been in contact with the Americans.

You will remember that the North Vietnamese and their collaborators complained about the censorship of the press before April 30, 1975. With about ten dailies in Saigon alone, five in Chinese in Cholon, and a dozen wide-circulation periodicals, magazines in French and English, weeklies, and bimonthly reviews, one wonders how that was possible. It is true that at times certain news pertaining to national security was suppressed, and that may be why the communists complained about a so-called censorship.

By the way, what happened to all the media there before April 30, 1975? They do not exist anymore. The only paper, four pages "thin," is the only authorized publication since May 2, 1975, that is, two days after the invasion. It is called the *Liberated Saigon*—why not the *Liberated Ho Chi Minh City*?—and is the official medium of the Vietnamese Communist party, translated into Chinese for the Hoa of Cholon.

However, this very same May 2, 1975, another newspaper, the *Tia-Sang*[5] was circulated, as usual, in the streets of Saigon. But when the newspaper boys took off like a flight of sparrows with their papers under the arm, the security policemen ran after them and confiscated the newspapers. The owner and the chief editor of the journal were thrown in jail.

Before the fall of Saigon, people used to go to work with one or two papers under their arms. Today, with a minimum of 1 million cadres and a population starving for news, the Party is unable to peddle its only paper, the *Liberated Saigon*. Orders have been given to the cadres to force those who can afford it to subscribe to it. It is also read and commented on during group meetings in the evening, and at lunchtime in the factories.

In order to enhance the content of the paper and try to make it more attractive to the public, the picture of "X," for instance, is published showing her husking rice paddy[6] to pay the farm tax[7] to such and such a service; when everybody knows too well that there is no such thing as a cooperative farm for the moment. The figures of such and such a factory are published showing a production well above the average of what used to come out of the same plant under the best conditions, before the arrival of the North Vietnamese, when the product cannot be found anywhere.

Later on, it would be published that the population of the North had been fasting for two consecutive days in order to help their "compatriots" from the South and send them 240,000 tons of rice when everyone knew too well that all convoys were going one way: north. Therefore, as far as news is concerned, the South Vietnamese are doing without. Aware of the boycotting of the daily, the Party than decided to publish another one by the end of 1975, to make people believe that there was freedom of expression. This time, the morning newspaper *Tin-Sang* was headed by former deputy and communist sympathizer Ngô-Công-Duc, fiercely opposed to the former government. With such references there is no doubt that the "menu" would be "à la carte;" that of the Party, of course. More "businesslike," with classified adds, slightly critical articles, and very impersonal dull-witted jokes, and the same "news" as in the first paper, but presented differently. This daily disappeared in 1980, when the Party estimated that it could do without public opinion and even the appearance of it.

However, the more the communists try to strangle freedom and erase even the memory of democracy, the more South Vietnamese try to beat the system. They sell, rent, and lend every possible book by Vietnamese authors salvaged from the Marxist-Leninist flames. Among the most read foreign books are George Orwell's *Animal Farm* and *1984*, and Solzhenitsyn's stories, a real "How to Do in Hell." As for those who are dreaming about getting out of the country, they read Henri Charrière's *Papillon*.

The communists themselves recognize that there cannot be any freedom of speech, press, and so on and so forth for the foes of socialism. Since no one is allowed to speak and/or to write freely in South Vietnam, does this mean that all South Vietnamese people are considered enemies of socialism? As seems to be the case, how come revolutions are done in the name of the people?

NOTES

1. *Kratkiy slovar-spavochnik politinformatora i agitatora* (*Short Dictionary–Reference Book for the Political Informer and the Agitator*) (Moscow, 1973), in *A Lexicon of Marxist-Leninist Semantics*, ed. Raymond S. Sleeper, p. 169.
2. In this case, from January to April 1975. After each rotation of four months, the commanding officer and his crew were replaced by the team who had been on leave during that period of time.
3. Minh-Hiên, who knows the two commanders well, says that VVT believed for a long time that NNT had betrayed him. However, he managed to escape Vietnam in 1979, with his family and other Boat People. They were picked up by a British vessel. VVT and NNT, reunited in Canada, have been able to tell each other their adventures and have therefore clarified the situation.
4. To infiltrate the groups of refugees and try to go through the immigration screening of the host countries and set up cells among these Vietnamese groups.
5. *The Rays of Light* (approximate translation), not to be mistaken with the *Tin-Sang* (*Morning News*) of the ex-deputy and communist sympathizer Ngô-Công-Duc, published from 1975 to 1980.
6. Rice with its envelope.
7. Tax created by the communists which did not exist under the former government.

THE MANIPULATION OF THE MASSES

The aim of totalitarian education has never been to instill convictions but to destroy the capacity to form any.

—Hannah Arendt

Once freedom's suppressed or about to be, the North Vietnamese replace it with something else, the way mosquitoes while sucking their victim's blood inject a liquid—often carrying disease—to prevent coagulation. Here the communist system prevents the population from collecting itself in its effort to resist annihilation. Indoctrination comes in very early, along with propaganda, and tries to take a targeted society, people, or nation away from its political, cultural, religious, social, and economic foundations and principles—here, in South Vietnam, four thousand years of civilization—and replace everything with the Marxist-Leninist system.

In Vietnam, blackmail with food is the main tool to indoctrinate the population, a kind of Pavlovian technique: "you go our way, you get enough food to survive; you don't, you starve." If people are afraid of the security force, police, and informers, they fear even more the withdrawal of the rationing card. To keep it, one has to regularly attend the meetings organized by the cadres and submit oneself to propaganda, indoctrination, and brainwashing. When the rice ration decreased from twelve to eight kilograms per month, the heads of families showed their discontent and only a few delegates went to the meetings. In 1980, when the rice ration was suppressed, the people refused to obey, at the exact time the Party decided it could do without public opinion anyway.

As in all communist countries where education is monopolized by the state, teachers are one of the most important transmission belts between the regime and the population. In order to eliminate the directors, rectors, and teachers, the North Vietnamese resorted to "titularization"—investigations over three generations enabled them to "prove" that most of these people had ties with the former government—and then they fired them. Through this process they were also able to detect former sympathizers who could be used again; after a period of indoctrination they were put in charge of children who at a very early age learned to betray and denounce their family and friends in the name of ideology.

Students at the primary-school level carry the hopes of the regime. Soft, "unpolluted," malleable, and innocent, they will be, once initiated, the supporters of a regime that needs them to perpetuate itself in its privileges. During the five-month transition period following the invasion, that is, from May to September 1975, the communists sent students from the secondary level to the usual summer "vacation," where they learned the fine art of delation and denunciation, and with the promise that a good collaboration with the revolution would entitle them to go back to school come fall. In September these students had to undergo an "exam" that most of them failed to pass. Unaware of the test results, they were told, however, that because of their answers they didn't meet the standards established by the new system. Their personal past, and the antirevolutionary antecedents of their parents had classified them as "unfit for socialism," and they were banned from schools. Those who "passed the exam"—there are always some of them—were deemed fit to participate in anti-Americanism courses, to learn delation, and that the class struggle consists, before anything else, in getting hold of all the goods and the means of production in the name of the people, but for the benefit of a few. Good students become examples for others and have the privilege of carrying a red scarf around the neck; another way of getting strangled by communism.

During their holidays, students are required to do collective work: gathering old papers, cleaning up the streets, farming, or gathering scrap iron. It was during one of these fatigue duties in January 1976 that children were killed by a hand grenade forgotten in the bushes of Ly-Thai-Tô Street.

Students that the ruling class deem fit for the service of the regime are grouped by teams of eight or ten and placed under the surveillance of a pseudo-student responsible for noting every single move they make. Once they are well under control, the courses of indoctrination and self-criticism represent most of their schedule; collective gardening—"culture"—represents the practical aspect of their training.

The submission test of these new recruits consists in fighting among themselves in order to have the right to use their excrement as fertilizer in the garden. The student who manages to make it is awarded a good mark.

I was discussing this point with Minh-Hiên, asking him how could it be that people proclaiming the nobility of their intentions could use such means in total contradiction with what they call the restoration of human dignity, when I came across an article of *Paris-Match* dated December 13, 1985. In an interview, the French writer Lucien Bodard said, "They tortured Yu Ping-Po and his likes. They were sent to the most desolate places of the country. They were obliged to spread human shit [sic] with their own hands, and then required to glorify its good smell."

This was twenty years earlier, during another revolutionary storm, in Mao's China.

DISINFORMATION

In politics, what is believed becomes more important than what is true.

—Talleyrand

Today, what we know about politics is what we see on, but mostly through television. Disinformation—not exactly your everyday household word, not even to be found in many dictionaries—begins with the intent to deceive and takes all forms of lies, just like the insects that have learned the language, sound, the light signals of the glowworms, approach the familiar lantern insects, and under the pretext of "getting together" and telling them love stories, kill them and eat them, leaving only a parched envelope blown by the wind of history.

Transposed, this means that words, pictures, cultural clichés, and promises are being expressed in the same manner in the East as in the West. But the definition of terms and their finality are totally different right from the intention. We have all heard the words "I love you." It may be for ourselves, our body, our mind, et cetera, but some would love us dead. The word *peace* has probably two dozen different meanings in the Marxist-Leninist vocabulary, but it means something closer to war and revolution than an inner state allowing progress to develop.

In Vietnam before the invasion of the South by the North, the communists were talking about "peace," "reconciliation," and "national harmony," words that to people of goodwill ring like "clemency" and "tolerance," and the possibility of good relations at a real human level may mean exactly the contrary in the minds of those who are planning to conquer the world. That is why under the cover of words like *justice* and *equality* we have seen factual horrors happening.

In Vietnam, the relation between the words and the facts takes the following form. For instance, the Politburo of Hanoi says, and the cadres repeat: "The *bô-dôis* of the People's Army have taken advantage of their victory over the South, and this has caused the Centre [government of Hanoi] many political, economic and social problems," meaning that those in charge are not responsible for what happened in the South, but that the soldiers are.

During the Nuremberg trials, the Nazi underlings declared that they had received their orders from their superiors, who themselves received them from Hitler . . . already dead. Therefore, had one followed their way of thinking, none of them would have been guilty of anything. Here it is the same, but the other way around. Should there be a communist Nuremberg, for instance, the communist officers and cadres would say that they only respected the "will of the people." Therefore, no one will be held accountable for the atrocities committed since 1917, or it will be—in their own words—entire nations who supposedly asked them to act in such a way.

Such is the situation that one would almost pity the government of Hanoi whose soldiers were making life so difficult for it; they—the soldiers—are the ones who invaded the South! More subtly, since the soldiers sprang from the population, public opinion cannot be judge anymore and part of a situation where its government is acting in its name.

However, the South Vietnamese people now know very well that the invasion of their country was not a fortuitous event, but the consequence of a plan prepared a long time ago by the Politburo of Hanoi. In his book titled *The Great Spring Victory* of April 1975 Gen. Van-Tien-Dung tells how he was reporting every evening to the Politburo about the evolution of the operations and how the members of this supreme office, not ignorant at all of a situation that supposedly slipped through their fingers—one would wonder how—took all the necessary decisions to invade the South. It was not the actions of the *bô-dôis* that embarrassed the Politburo of Hanoi, but plans A, B, C, and D, to conquer Laos, South Vietnam, Cambodia, and later on Thailand, which were at the root of the political, economic, and social evils the Party is complaining about. Now if the soldiers did not behave exactly like gentlemen, whose fault is it?

Another example: "If president Ho Chi Minh were still alive, the situation of the South would not be so dramatic. The actual state of affairs is due to the bad conduct of the leaders. Alive, Ho

Chi Minh would have shown an example of integrity and austerity to the militants of the Party."

As we can see here, Ho Chi Minh, like Hitler and Stalin before him, was molded into a legend, being idealized. The use of the conditional tense suggests that the model would have made things different. This is also an admission that things are not going so well, this time not because of the footsoldiers, but because of the leaders who are commanding them. This also suggests that with the first statement, the footsoldiers were not under the control of their officers and cadres anymore, since they have made so many mistakes. Yet the fact that these same officers and cadres seem to have taken control again does not improve the situation either, or so it seems with this second statement.

Now to suggest that the South would be better off if Ho Chi Minh were still around is to forget that he has been there before and the North is the proof of his failure for the same reasons. On top of that—and assuming that he had not betrayed anyone, which history itself refutes—it does not dismiss the fact that every human being is responsible for his or her own actions.

"The cadres are corrupted by the hollow wealth of the South. As soon as it will be impoverished, completely despoiled, the conduct of the cadres will be good."

It is very peculiar that people talking about false wealth are laying their hands on it and sending it to North Vietnam. Yet they are correct on one account: when Vietnam will be starving to death everybody will indeed have good conduct, that very quiet manner of the mass graves. The only ones who are going to be corrupted at that point and to the core, under the circumstances and by the real abundance of cadavers, will be the maggots and possibly the Nomenklatura itself, which will have managed to keep itself comfortable. But you can bet a lot that at this kind of feast the maggots will have the last word.

Now what about what appears outside Vietnam, although transmitted by some of the Western media, looks and/or sounds like a communique from Hanoi or Moscow?

Bashed daily by the most powerful medium of clichés that ever was—TV—and finished, knocked out by the written media, the public is soon in the ropes. In this very case, the war between Vietnam and the United States—or the struggle between two principles—appears to be more like a conflict between the presidency and part of the U.S media, a political group not accountable to the public through elections.

A typical example of this is the military victory of the American-Vietnamese forces during the Communist Offensive in 1968, known as the Têt Offensive. It was transformed into a psychological defeat on the screen and on paper, which was exactly what Moscow and Hanoi had intended in the first place, with the help of some of the media, some politicians, and the resounding effect of a small fraction of American public opinion. True enough: if we are victorious, how can we later on get together with an enemy? Therefore, we "have to" be induced into believing that we "lost."

Yet it is the communists who lost beween forty-thousand and seventy thousand men during the Têt Offensive.[1] In 1972, another attempt by the North Vietnamese was also defeated. If the U.S. Congress had allowed continued support for the South Vietnamese, instead of cutting down by 60 percent,[2] North Vietnam (and the USSR and China) would have been *militarily defeated.*

Again, when the communists took the city of Huê they killed five thousand, eight hundred people, but we never heard of it and never saw it on T.V. What we were given to see was that some North Vietnamese soldiers were under the U.S. embassy's windows and the killing at My-Lai.

This being said, one wonders why the Americans and the South Vietnamese did not pursue their advantage at the time of the Têt Offensive. Propaganda or not, the victory of the American–South Vietnamese troops would have been a *fait accompli*, a fact.

After the invasion of the South by the North, even impartial journalists—maybe this explains that—had all the difficulties in the world in obtaining credible information. When they managed to go to Vietnam, they were literally walked around, fed well, and entertained when a few blocks away the people were starving. And most of all, they were very carefully watched.

No journalist has been able to detect the subtle drifting, artificial but real, the replacement of the Southern population by that of the well-indoctrinated North. This means that if, for instance, the policy of "transparence" were to reach Vietnam, these well-trained and brainwashed people would, to our amazement, vote very "democratically" for the communist candidates, filmed by Western cameras. That may one day be the state of the art in terms of disinformation and manipulation on an unprecedented scale.

World public opinion has sent aid to a country that normally is producing and exporting rice; it fed the communists, believing it was helping the South Vietnamese, the Laotians, or the Cambodians, who are being replaced exactly the same way. Drawn into the situation by real, genuine charity, it was engaged unwittingly in a dreadful process, which we are going to talk about a little later.

In 1985, for the anniversary of the fall of Saigon, an American TV network offered to its public pictures of a "serene" Vietnam and, without saying "prosperous," at least "well fed." A young woman looking at the camera pours some rice on a heap, not too big, but not too small either. The picture seems harmless, almost pastoral. When one analyzes these pictures, one realizes that the young woman is too photogenic and too well fed, podgy, to be a country woman bent all year long over paddy fields. Her way of looking at the lens while checking with the crew when and how to pour her rice is not natural; it is not a spontaneous shot taken in the middle of a day-to-day routine of life in that country. Her action is not part of a continuation of events either, such as harvesting, bagging, or distributing rice. It is an isolated act. Anyone who has worked on a farm knows these things. The point is that these pictures have been taken in April, 1985, with a background of green paddy fields. This cannot be the time for harvesting, since it usually takes place in February and in August (that is, when there is a second harvest). The size of the paddy heap has nothing to do with real farm work, such as bagging for instance, even less for distributing rice. No, it tends to show that Vietnam still produces rice indeed, but not enough, which justifies the request for food aid from the West.

When one also knows, for instance, that in his book *The War of Desperation: Lebanon 82–85,*[3] John Laffin writes about Americans filming Roman ruins on the outskirt of Beirut as an example of Israeli bomb damage, and when we know that some TV crews have "worked" their interviewees to make them say what the journalists wanted them to say, a very first question arises: why are we fed lies? A possible answer could be: to make the journalist's point of view look good, in the hope—and the knowledge—that practically nobody will be able to check out the facts. Indeed, how many of you readers knew anything about harvesting rice in Vietnam? How many of you know that it was not the Romans who put an end to Jewish resistance in A.D. 66–73—if one is to believe the filming of the American crew—but that it was the Jews who bombarded the Romans with Howitzer artillery shells from the heights of Massada, so that these people could film it some nineteen centuries later? All this looks too much like Soviet TV work showing to Western visitors "happy farmers" harvesting in the fields, that is, until everybody discovered that the actors hired for the show arrived too late on the scene that day, jeopardizing the entire propaganda program.

Now, do you remember the picture seen all over the world showing General NNL, former director of the South Vietnamese police, pulling the trigger on a civilian? Yes, you do; it has been shown so much and so often. That is what the communists wanted Western public opinion to see, and that is exactly what was shown to us by our media. Sometimes, it is just plain sensationalism.

But the real story is something else. For a moment think about the picture of a group of demonstrators waving flags and the voice of a reporter commenting that this event shows the massive support for such and such a cause. Indeed, that is all you see on your screen. Now pull the TV camera away, and you'll see that the only massive thing is the girl sitting on the shoulders of a bearded guy surrounded by a dozen demonstrators gathering as closely as possible in front of the camera. That is the difference between reality and what the public is made to see, and therefore to believe.

In this case, the picture was taken "unexpectedly" by a photographer of an American agency who believed that General NNL would only threaten the communist commando, for he was one, in civilian clothing. When he dropped dead on the pavement, the photographer knew that he had just shot the picture of his life; someone's shot became instant fame for another. Such has been the case, for he thus received the Pulitzer Prize.

So far, so good, everything is all right, if we may say that: a photographer doing what he is paid for is at the right place at the right time, shoots the picture of his life, and is rewarded for it; no qualm with that. But what propaganda has done with the picture, out of context, has been extremely disinforming.

As a matter of fact, what the public did not know—and neither did the photographer, it seems, at the time—was that half an hour before the taking of the picture, one of the general's officers (a colonel, a friend in fact), his wife, and their children had been literally butchered by that very communist commando and his comrades, dressed in civilian clothing to make people believe they were peaceful citizens going about their daily lives. The general had just been informed of this when he got hold of the commando. The critics of such an action never took the care to explain what their reaction would have been, or that of the communists for that matter, if they had been confronted with the same situation and circumstances. Another thing has been said of this: the execution was brutal. Again, those who expressed this view never explained what their reaction would have been, noting, by the way, that the murder of his colleague and friend, his wife, and their children was certainly more abominable than an execution.

This being said, the general soon afterward had a leg snatched away by a hand grenade. Had he lost his life, no one would have shot any picture. Interviewed later, but before he was wounded, he said that he could have seized the picture or have had the film destroyed had he wanted; but he did not do so in order to respect the freedom of the press. We are still waiting for something similar on the part of the North Vietnamese.

Minh-Hiên, the co-author and initiator of this book, ought to know: two of the general's sisters have been friends of his family.

NOTES

1. Forty thousand according to ABC's "Our World: 1968"; 50,000 according to Gérard Le Quańg in *La Guerre Américaine d'Indochine* (*The American War*

of Indochina) (Paris, Editions Universitaires), 85,000 destroyed houses, of which 18,000 in Saigon alone, 14,300 civilians killed, 24,000 wounded, 30,000 Vietcong and North Vietnamese killed, 20,000 out of action. Still according to this author, ten thousand South Vietnamese were killed, five hundred MIA, two thousand Americans killed, seven thousand, five hundred wounded. From 1961, to January 1973 1,153,175 soldiers died during the war in Vietnam, 45, 928 Americans, 180,676 South Vietnamese, 921,350 North Vietnamese and Vietcong, 5,521 allies (Korean, Thais, Australians, and others); 70,000 according to Nguyên Van Canh in his book *Vietnam Under Communism, 1975–1982* (Stanford: Hoover Institution, Stanford University).

2. *National Review*, May 3, 1985. Interestingly enough, more than two thousand years ago Sun Tzu wrote that as far as government expenses are concerned, 60 percent represent the deterioration of the war material, meaning that what has been used will not be replaced.

3. John Laffin, *The War of Desperation: Lebanon 82–85* (London: Osprey), quoted in the *Newsletter of the Canadian Institute of Strategic Studies*, December, 1986, p. 8.

COMMUNIST XENOPHOBIA

According to the *Concise Oxford Dictionary*, xenophobia is a morbid dislike of foreigners.

The ostensible goal of communist xenophobia is to reinforce the imperviousness of the Iron and/or the Bamboo Curtain in order to ward off the influence of democracy on the people controlled by the communists and avoid what could possibly be the largest migration ever toward freedom. Freedom, as understood in the West, means everyone has to make decisions for himself or herself several times a day, while in the East freedom seems to be the ability to follow the Party's line, for which, in return, you are said to obtain food and shelter.

However, how will people feel and what is going to be the population's reaction when they realize that so many million of their fellow citizens and family members have died just to "get together"?

To achieve total control over the entire Vietnamese population, the Communist party sends away all foreigners not sharing its ideology. They could be witnesses, and they could denounce the actions of the regime and force it to do what it most dislikes: to face itself and recognize that the will of a few is not that of a nation. In fact, some foreigners will be detained under the accusation of having worked with the CIA, but this will be mostly to wring money from them and see their reaction.

This maneuver of expulsion is aimed directly and primarily at:

- All those who have admitted having sojourned even briefly in Vietnam—journalists, and representatives of international organizations, such as the Red Cross, for instance. The Vicar Apostolic (Rome) was expelled in May 1975. At this point, by the way, those who leave do it without major problems. The ambassador of France will stay.

- All European and Asian nationals—whether they are French, Hindus, Japanese, Pakistanis, South Koreans, Taiwanese, Filipinos, and so on—who have had ties or relations in South Vietnam: family, business, tourism, et cetera.

•Those of mixed origin: Indo-Vietnamese, Eurasians, Vietnamese in fact for several generations, speaking Vietnamese only, but of foreign origin.

Paradoxically, even if they have been summoned to leave the country immediately, the departure of these "foreigners" is postponed—except for the first category—because of the investigations the communist security force runs to stop those who might have worked with the CIA. On top of that, all the financial files are examined with the utmost care, in order to make one pay off his or her remaining taxes, debts, or loans.

Gathered in Saigon/Ho Chi Minh City and lodged with relatives, friends, or relations for a period that will last as long as it takes to receive an authorization to emigrate toward freedom, these "foreigners" must sell their jewelry, clothes, and family belongings in order to survive in the capital. When they leave the country, they must abandon everything else: houses, properties, farms and herds, plantations, stores, and warehouses. Everything that can be discreetly slipped into the linings will be "removed," most of the time, by the custom officers, the cadres, and eventually the pirates.

The "foreigners" are therefore completely stripped of everything, and even that is not a guarantee of departure. The case of the Amerasians, that is, of a good number of children born of American and Vietnamese parents, is still not solved. This elimination of anything foreign to communism, which can "pollute" the ideology and hinder the fast and strong progression of socialism, can be traced back to Stalin and his killing—or imprisoning—of those who had been in contact with the West. Ukrainians in the thirties are examples of that. Solzhenitsyn in the forties is another among many. The same thing applies to Cambodians. This is an indication of what was going to take place in Vietnam.

In 1679, three thousand Chinese soldiers and four generals of the deceased Minh (Ming) dynasty looked to Vietnam for a place of refuge against the new Manchurian dynasty of the emperor K'ang-hi or Thanh Khang-hi (1661–1722). King Hiên of Vietnam gave them asylum in the South he was then conquering in Dông-Pho (Gia-Dinh), Lôc-Dà (Biên-Hoa), and Dinh-Thuong (My-Tho). In 1680, the Cantonese Mac-Cuu arrived in Hàtien, where he laid down the foundations of a prosperous colony placed under the protection of the Nguyên Vietnamese kings. Their descendants—Vietnamese of Chinese origin or Hoa—were persecuted by the Tay-Son of Central Vietnam, in 1777, for defending their king of the South. Twelve thousand of them were also massacred for trading iron, copper, and sulphur, all essential materials for the war industry.

This little flashback is to show that the antagonism between the Hoa—Vietnamese of Chinese origin who came later—and the Vietnamese (whose origins are also Chinese but more distant) is nothing particularly new. In fact, it is the eternal conflict between Vietnam and China. With the coming of the communists, this confrontation will take on a new meaning.

For four centuries, from the seventeenth to the twentieth, the Chinese who came mainly from South China, like their ancestors who populated Nam-Viet at its beginning, have been the absolute masters of the economy in Vietnam (national and foreign trade, small and medium-sized enterprises, big business and finance, and communications), with only one interruption, in 1782, during the intervention of the Tay-Son troops—from Central Vietnam—under the command of Nguyên-Nhac, the older brother of the emperor Quang-Trung-Nguyên-Huê.

To maintain their economic supremacy, the Hoa—or, once again, the Vietnamese of Chinese origin—made sure they were not interfering with the political peripeteia of the country. They preferred instead to weave their economic, cultural, and judicial web and establish a code of conduct among themselves to collaborate with or corrupt the various powers in office while remaining neutral in every respect, a state within the state, with its laws and way of conduct.

Their control over foreign trade was facilitated by the settlement of colonies in all the Southeast Asian countries and around the world. In Vietnam in particular, the Chinese colony took off rapidly, thanks to the constant influx during these four centuries of new Chinese immigrants and their demographic progression. In 1975 there were in the South between 1.5 and 2 million Hoa in Cholon, to which one must add another million of them who left the countryside for refuge in the city in order to close up ranks against the communist invaders.

During the French presence, from 1863 to 1954, the Chinese Compradors[1] collaborated with the Cholons in every sphere, sharing the fruits of colonization. At the beginning of the sixties, American financial aid and the presence of half a million GIs brought a certain prosperity to South Vietnam, even abundance. But the Chinese were those who, presenting themselves as Vietnamese, benefited most from this growth. They invested their fortunes in urban and rural estates.

In July 1955 President Ngô-dinh-Diêm granted them Vietnamese nationality, which would allow them to concentrate all their attention on Taiwan. Among them, the young manipulated by Peking and Hanoi would become pro-communist activists. After the fall of South Vietnam in 1975, the Chinese community found itself under the control of the communists, with all that entails: cessation of normal activities, arrests, systematic pillage, et cetera. The Chinese community then turned to China in the hope that it would use its influence with Hanoi to salvage the goods and riches of these "compatriots."

But Peking could do nothing for those Chinese who had legally become Vietnamese. Therefore, in Cholon as early as May 1975, a forest of red flags of the People's Republic of China bedeck the buildings and the houses of the Hoa as a sign of sympathy for the victory of the People's Army from Hanoi, then supported by the PRC. Everywhere posters in Vietnamese are praising Ho Chi Minh. However, instead of welcoming the Hoa, the North Vietnamese ordered them to take away the flags and dismissed or degraded the Chinese militants within their ranks. The night of September 19, 1975, will be remembered as the Saint Bartholemew moment of reckoning for the big businessmen, the rich industrialists, the shareholders, and the presidents of large companies who were arrested and tortured by the communists. Some, struck with panic, killed themselves before they could be dragged into the jails.

During the terribly painful "investigations," those who had been arrested had to reveal and abandon all their properties to their torturers: personal real estate, valuable articles, and fortune entrusted to relatives or friends. In short, all that capital had to put up with the Marxist-Leninist guillotine. Counts of endictment: speculation, trading on the black market, illicit trading, inflation, and what have you. Arrests were going on at a good rate and extended to relatives and friends. The Chinese community went through a tragedy of its own while desperately waiting for the intervention of Peking.

By the end of September 1975, the Hoa community knew what to expect: the BBC announced that Lê-Duân, the secretary of the Vietnamese Communist party, and Pham-van-Dong, the then prime minister of Hanoi who came especially to Peking to attend the anniversary of the People's Republic of China, celebrated on October 1, were not welcomed and had to return to Hanoi. Maybe they came to strike some kind of a deal with China in exchange for the Hoa, but it seems that Peking did not exactly appreciate the invasion of South Vietnam, nor the massacre of the Chinese community. However, to Peking, having tried on April 20, 1975, to prevent the invasion of South Vietnam by the North—to no avail[2] —the visit of Lê-Duan and Pham-van-Dong, agents of Moscow, may have been perceived as a provocation.

Harassed by communist security forces, stripped of all their possessions and means of subsistence, the Hoa underwent a very tough test. The adults were assigned to "public labor," while their children were impressed into the Vietnamese army. All the Chinese were accused of being part of the fifth column.[3] Peking remained silent; it was a Vietnamese problem, and the Chinese who lived in that country had freely accepted the Vietnamese nationality for twenty years by then. This tense situation would climax in 1978 when North Vietnam invaded Cambodia. Peking would bring its aid programs to an end and call back its technicians. Meanwhile, in order to escape the communist exactions and to survive the famine caused by a food blockade the Hoa of South Vietnam resorted to various stratagems:

- Plotting against and blackmailing the communists who are commiting the exactions.
- Dispersion and dissimulation of merchandise.
- Sabotage and camouflage of essential mechanical parts of machinery.

Refugees

CHINA
SOUTH KOREA
Taipei
TAIWAN
Macao
HONG KONG
BURMA
Hanoi
Haiphong
LAOS
Gulf of Tonkin
Hainan
Vientiane
Pak Sane
Nong Khai
THAILAND
5,458 Vietnamese
38,353 Kampucheans
86,377 Laotians
Da Nang
Ubon
Paksé
VIETNAM
1,873
PHILIPPINES
Manila
Bataan
13,391
Bangkok
Aranyaprathet
Phnom Penh
South China Sea
Ho Chi Minh City
Songkhla
Pattani
Kota Bharu
Pulau Bidong
Trengganú
MALAYSIA
8,309
Klang
Kuala Lumpur
Singapore
159
Kuching
Brunei
EQUATOR
Galang
2,356
SUMATRA
BORNEO
(KALIMANTAN)
CELEBES
6,626
INDONESIA
USA 824,000
CHINA 272,132
FRANCE 101,432
CANADA 122,964
AUSTRIA 1,675
WEST GERMANY 23,2
UNITED KINGDOM 17,3
SWITZERLAND 9,428
NEW ZEALAND 7,369
NETHERLANDS 5,835
NORWAY 5,135
BELGIUM 4,255
JAPAN 5,211
DENMARK 3,275
ITALY 3,016
SWEDEN 2,862
AUSTRALIA 108,481
ARGENTINA 1,282

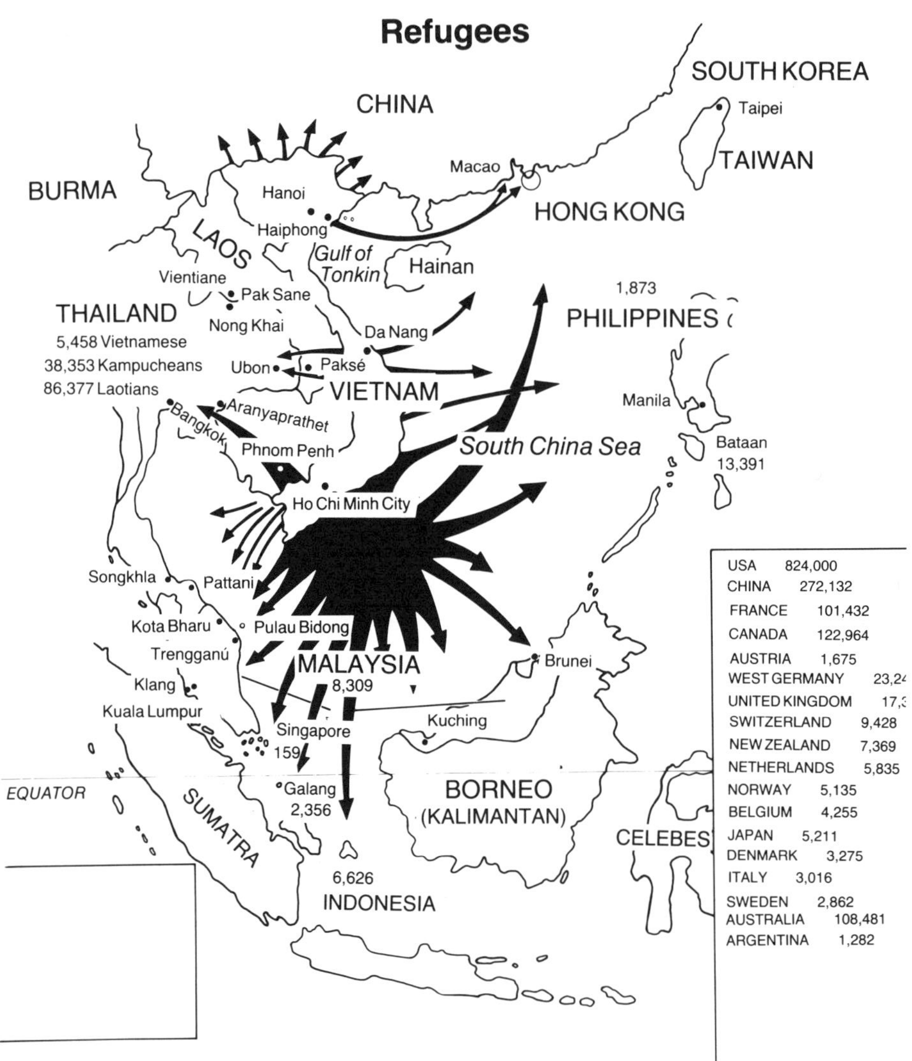

•Corruption of the cadres craving after gold, money, good food, and beautiful girls.

•Telling anyone who wants to listen to them that they are not stateless people, that they have always been Chinese, and that it was Ngô-dinh-Diêm who imposed the Vietnamese nationality upon them.

It is a struggle for survival. Many of them will flee the country.

However, in taking the Vietnamese nationality, these Chinese hoped to take advantage of it, especially to leave Vietnam, and establish themselves in neighboring countries. But no one, it appears, seems to want these immigrants known by all to be Chinese before anything else. Taiwan, for example, refuses them categorically, including the refugees found later at sea. Who are they really? Friends or agents? Peking would accept these "compatriots," but in turn, they did not seem too eager to go back to the "motherland." It also depends whom we are talking about: during the Sino-Vietnamese conflict of 1979, more than 250,000 poor Chinese[4] established for several generations in North Vietnam (Hanoi, Haiphong, Moncay, Hongay, Campha, et cetera) and who had lived for more than three decades under the Vietnamese communist regime (1945—79), picked up their few belongings and crossed the Chinese border. They were parked in camps, waiting integration into "agro-cities." South Vietnamese fled toward the West.

NOTES

1. Intermediaries. Every French company had to deal with them in their import-export transactions.
2. Philippe Richer, *L'Asie du Sud-Est* (*Southeast Asia*) (Paris: Imprimerie Nationale).
3. Hidden enemies living in any country like other citizens, but who will in due time reveal themselves for what they are. Some call them krypto Nazis, krypto communists, et cetera, from the Greek *krypton*, "hidden," neutral adjective *krypto*: "hide."
4. Up to 263,000, according to the United Nations High Commissioner for Refugees, have crossed the Chinese border during the first seven months of 1979, 279,000 up until 1985–86. They had to flee Vietnam, but could not afford to go elsewhere.

THE TRADING OF HUMAN LIVES

There are the living, there are the dead, and there are those who are at sea.

—French proverb from Brittany

This became true of the Boat People.

The North Vietnamese authorities were facing a Chinese community collecting itself, pulling together, organizing itself, and, beyond words, beginning to fight back. They decided to eliminate them and the threat they represented for the system.

To escape communist ascendancy, but mostly to escape a certain death, the Hoa would have no other choice but to pay 10 taels of gold, that is, 270 grams per person, to the security forces and the go-betweens who organize their departure for freedom. What is left of the gold and jewelry is entrusted to family and friends, but all the personal and real estate automatically became the property of the state.

After the exodus of April 1975, which saw 135,000 Vietnamese escaping the country, the trading of human lives became more and more sordid during the following years. The world discovered, with horror and disgust, boats crammed with corpses, raped women, children traumatized for life, and old people dazed to death. After seventy years of publicity selling socialism to the world, the Boat People are the extra proof, if need be, of what it really is and does.

At that time, everyone tried his or her luck a little bit any way he or she could. Some refugees managed to escape, some were shipwrecked, and others never got the opportunity to leave the country, the boats being sold were nonexistent or the hulls were completely rotten. Besides, if the first escape had been possible, it was thanks to the courage and determination of those who chose freedom, but also due to the fact that, at least at the beginning, the authorities had difficulties establishing total control over the one thousand, seven hundred kilometers (one thousand, one hundred miles) of the South Vietnamese shores. That would change.

The statistics of the United Nations High Commissioner for Refugees published in *Réfugiés* (*Refugees*), no. 17, of May 1985 reveal when and how many human lives were traded by Hanoi.

	LAND PEOPLE (Laos, Cambodia, VN 3%)	**BOAT PEOPLE**		**ODP (Orderly Departure Program)**
Exodus before April 1975		67,443[1]		
1975–76:	112,045	5,619	Did not pay	
1977:	29,780	15,657		
1978:	62,839	88,712	Paying from	
1979:	188,114	205,448	now on	1,919
1980:	92,318	75,833		4,706
1981:	24,882	74,754		9,815
1982:	5,185	43,825		10,057
1983:	9,280	28,055		18,987
1984:	18,334	29,154		(October) 25,130
1985(February):	5,941	2,453		
Total:	548,718	569,510		70,614
Plus:	272,100[2]	400,000[3]		
Total:	820,818	969,510		70,614

This means that a total of 1,928,385 refugees have left Southeast Asia, including those who escaped before April, 1975, the Land and the Boat People, and the ODP.

The Cambodians and Laotian Land People who saw the thrust of the communists in Cambodia (they entered Phnom Penh April 17, 1975) and Laos (they established the People's Democratic Republic of Laos on December 2, 1975), and most of all Cambodia (December 24, 1978) and in setting up of the Heng Samrin government on January 7, 1979—particularly the Hmongs who had worked with the CIA—took refuge in Thailand.

It was only in 1979 that Vietnamese, using the back and forth movement of the Vietnamese *bô-dôis*, managed to cross Cambodia to reach Thailand. Of the remaining 155,940 Southeast Asian Land People (3 percent were Vietnamese), an estimated 100,500 made it through to Thailand, while an estimated 33 percent died in this attempt to reach freedom. Furthermore, when China went to war with Vietnam on February 17, 1979, the Hoa of the North (272,100) crossed the Sino-Vietnamese border; 9 percent were North Vietnamese, and 1 percent were South Vietnamese who could afford only to pay one tael of gold instead of the ten required in the South. Among them, Minh Hiên estimates that about 100,000 did not pay anything because they lived close to the border and had just to cross it.

As for the Boat People—the 5,619 who escaped in 1975–76, and the 15, 657 who fled in 1977—we are certain that they are the "real Boat People" in that they left the country on their own. Most of these people fled by groups of about ten per boat, for an average of one thousand, three hundred to one thousand, five hundred a month.[4] It was at the beginning of 1978, with the tension between China and Vietnam, that the Hoa were expelled from the country. Of the 969,510 Boat People, at least 400,000 of them (40.3 percent) died at sea for lack of food or water or because of sharks, pirates, sabotage, et cetera; a third of them were children.

In Vietnam the Hoa and the Vietnamese authorities called this operation of expulsion the "semi-official emigration." It was headed by Gen. Nguyên M. of the secret service and organized by the communist security and the police. Outside the country, the operation was coordinated by Tay Kheng Hong, a rich Chinese merchant of Cholon who was especially released from jail in April 1978, to run this operation.

Among all the Hoa expelled, a minority of Vietnamese (2 to 3 percent) managed to leave with them by paying twice as much in gold, thanks to the Hoa intermediaries and the police agents in charge of controlling the departures. We must bear in mind that the Hoa are the ones who were expelled, not the Vietnamese. However, some of them managed to leave with the Hoa, while a clandestine network helped Vietnamese escape the country, but that represents a small percentage of all the refugees who fled Vietnam.

As far as the ODP (Orderly Departure Program, July 1979) is concerned and once they are established in some thirty host countries, the Hoa help their compatriots to get out of the Southeast Asian camps and, most of all, to legally get out of Vietnam. The signing of an accord between that country and the UNHCR in Geneva (July 20, 1979) will create a great deal of pain for those who had already paid for their escape. In all instances it postponed their departure, and in some cases it cancelled it. When they finally took off, the planes were loaded with 80 to 90 percent Hoa and 10 to 20 percent Vietnamese.

In Saigon, all the operations were taking place in the former Kim-Long gold trading house on Le-Thanh-Ton Street. When passengers were finally given the green light to leave the country, they were searched from head to toe and were stripped of every particle of gold and jewels slipped into the linings. As they say there, "the waters are not safe around here." Indeed, some boats never left, others sank just outside the harbor, and still others were ransacked by the pirates.

In these boats of fortune—if one might say that—crammed with people who eat, drink, try to sleep to rebuild a worn-out nervous system, and have to relieve themselves, the time when there is not enough food and water and too much of other things came very quickly. It then became extremely urgent to navigate along the shores in order to reach a neighboring country as fast as possible, but it is in these waters that pirates were still prowling. The larger boats, stronger and better equipped, tried to reach Hong Kong, Malaysia, Indonesia, Singapore, Brunei, or the Philippines directly, even Australia. Some figures and some facts give us a striking picture, like slides, of the tragedy these people had to go through:

BOAT NUMBER		LEFT FROM	ON	NUMBER OF REFUGEES	ARRIVED AT
CAT	159	Dai-Nagi	May 19, 1978	175	Trengganu, Malaysia
VT	668	Vung-Tau	June 1978	273	Pulau Besar, Malaysia
VT	262	Vung-Tau	June 1978	179	Trengganu, Malaysia
VT	669	Vung-Tau	June 1978	315	Pulau Tengah, Malaysia
VT	017	Vung-Tau	July 22, 1978	394	Kuantang (Pahang), Malaysia
VT	404	Vung-Tau	October 18, 1978	247	Mersing, Malaysia

CAT represents the initials of Can-Tho Province. VT represents the initials of Vung-Taù Province, formerly Cap Saint-Jacques. According to this list, it must have been a good loading dock, many boats having left from there. A baby died at sea and a refugee went over board and was devoured by a shark during the journey of *VT 668*. If we find many Vietnamese pharmacists in the West today, it is because there were already six aboard *VT 262* alone. On board *VT 017* there were two engineers, two ex-officers, and two doctors.

VT 669 weighed anchor at the same time as *VT 668*. After four hours at sea, the engine broke down and the boat had to go back. She could leave again only three days later, quite lucky to be able to do so. In July 1978 a boat arrived in Hong Kong with 135 people on board, announced the BBC. A Taiwanese fishing boat rescued 238 people near the Vietnamese shores; a good thing it was fishing that far away, is it not? The S/S *Chevalier Paul* en route to Singapore rescued 181 people. In August of the same year, another Taiwanese fishing boat rescued 450 people, also near the Vietnamese coast; it must have been the brother of the one before. A boat arrived at Kuching (Sarawak, Malaysia) with 310 people on board. An American battle cruiser en route to Hong Kong saved 310 and then 106 refugees. Figures and names well aligned on a page suggest tragedies, heroism, and sordid stories we will never hear about. It is a page of individual destinies in the middle of a book mankind is having a hard time finishing, because it is too big. Thirteen years after the fall of Saigon, refugees still play their lives heads or tails with death.

On April 30, 1985, when the North Vietnamese celebrated the anniversary of the invasion of the South, Premier Pham-van-Dong was given plenty of time on the air by an American TV network. Around this time, a group of 119 Vietnamese (lawyers, seminarians, a musician, Catholics, and deserters—of these last no one knows whether they were running away from the country or infiltrating the band) wended their way along the shore and managed to escape. They were rescued by the team of Médecins du Monde (Doctors of the World) aboard the oceanographic ship *Jean Charcot*, and the frigate *Victor Schoelcher*. Aboard one of the ships an avowed communist had a hard time believing what he was seeing. The crews would rescue 520 people in all during this campaign.[5] A refugee will tell[6] that her group left without water nor food. Some died of hunger, others of thirst, and there were those who killed themselves. Eighty-six children died during this journey. All six members of her family had died around her, and she was lying down to wait for death to pick her up as well. This journey had an average of seven dead a day on that boat alone.

The most important phase of this "semi-official emigration" by cargo ships flying foreign flags began in May 1978. No more fooling around; this time it was going to be big. Tay-Kheng-Hong, a Chinese merchant and director of the import-export company VITIMEX of Cholon, was authorized to leave Ho Chi Minh City in April 1978, and was given the task of setting up this massive emigration operation from abroad. Hong took the necessary steps among the Chinese communities of Ho Chi Minh City, Hong Kong, and Singapore. Inside the country, the Party appointed Brig. Gen. Nguyên M. from the counterespionage service[7] to direct the operation. The communist security force established the list of passengers who were to embark on every cargo ship anchoring near the southern tip of the Vietnamese shore, and cashed in the fare in gold (bullions, taels, and others) and in jewelry. As for the organization of Tay Kheng Hong, it collected, among the Chinese communities, the funds to charter the cargos. These boats, many of which were to be cut up by the oxyacetylene torch of demolition contractors, were declared fit for the service again. Taiwanese crews and captains received precise instructions to act as discreetly as possible. But all that stir finally attracted the attention of the authorities of Hong Kong, Singapore, Taiwan, Malaysia, and Peking.

From Hong Kong, reconnaissance aircrafts patrolled the South China Sea looking for ships crammed with refugees en route for the city known as the door between the East and the West. As early as June 6, 1978, the People's Republic of China offered to send two ships to Vietnam: the S/S *Minh Hoa*, a liner of fourteen thousand tons, was to sail to Haiphong in order to repatriate one thousand Chinese from North Vietnam, and the S/S *Truong-Ly*, a cargo ship, which was to sail to Ho Chi Minh

City, where she was supposed to embark one thousand, four hundred Hoa. On June 20, 1978, the two ships arrived in sight of Vietnam, but Hanoi is said to have refused categorically to let the ships enter territorial waters. It would have been to recognize that the activities of the "semi-official emigration" were taking place. Or was it an act of revenge on the part of Pham-van-Dong and Lê-Duan for not having been received in Peking in 1975, on the occasion of the anniversary of the People's Republic of China? Maybe, but it was frustrating for China that this rejected attempt to help the Hoa came right after a statement by some of them at a press conference, in Hong Kong, where they complained about the lack of help the Vietnamese of Chinese origin were receiving from Peking.

This massive emigration operation by cargo ships flying foreign flags officially started sometime around mid-August 1978. It began with the tragedy of the S/S *Southern Cross* under Honduran flag. The cargo ship anchored at Cat-Lai, on the river Donai, six kilometers away from Ho Chi Minh City. The transfer of passengers from the shore to the ship was done at night with small boats. The lack of discipline, confusion, and irritation prevailing in such a situation, became a general rush and excitement. The boats, heavily loaded, capsized. Many refugees immediately disappeared into the water, and were swept along by the currents, extremely strong in that part of the river. Scared by the disaster, the Hoa community beat a retreat and waited anxiously for the outcome of the *Southern Cross*'s journey, which took place in spite of this. She arrived in sight of the Malaysian shores on September 2, 1978, but was denied anchoring. The High Commissioner for Refugees, Mr. Poul Hartling, himself had to intervene so that the ship could touch land. This success gave hope again to those who had remained on the waiting list and who had already paid for their fare. Despite the initial catastrophe, this was the kickoff signal of the "semi-official emigration" campaign.

Cargo ships followed one another and anchored near the Vietnamese shore:

SHIP	**ARRIVED AT (in)**	**ON (in)**	**NUMBER OF REGUGEES**
S/S *Southern Cross*	Malaysia	September 2, 1978	1,200
S/S *Hai-Hong*	Port Klang (Malaysia)	November 1978	2,518
S/S *Tung-An*	Hong Kong	December 1978	2,364
S/S *Ha-Lung*	Hong Kong	December 1978	600
S/S *Huey-Fong*	Hong Kong	December 23, 1978	3,546
S/S *Sky Luck*[8]	Boyan Island (Philippines)	January 31, 1979	573[9]
THEN IN	Hong Kong	February 7, 1979	2,642[10]
S/S *Sibonga*[11]	Hong Kong	May 24, 1979	982
S/S *Sen On*[12]	Hong Kong	May 26, 1979	1,400

In 1978, with the discovery of the Boat People, the first accounts and the first pictures of their tragedy appeared. Médecins du Monde in Paris launched a campaign, Un Navire Pour les Réfugiés (A Boat for the Refugees), joined by a West German charitable organization, the Cap Anamur Society, and SOS Boat People of the Vietnamese themselves in several countries. Here are the results of their charitable work:

1979: The hospital ship *Ile de Lumière* (*Island of Light*) rescued five hundred people and anchored at Pulau Bidong, where the personnel cared for forty thousand refugees.

1981: The *Akuna II* (in cooperation with an international organization of twelve nations against pirates) rescued one hundred people.

1982: The *Goelo* (a coaster) escorted by the *aviso Le Balmy* (French navy) rescued 1,208 people, from June 1982 to January 1983. During July, August, and September 1982, they rescued 119 people in one boat and 240 in five others.[13]

1985: The *Jean Charcot* (oceanographic ship) escorted by the frigate *Victor Schoelcher*, rescued 520 people.

1986: The *Cap Anamur II* rescued 888 people. In the first boat on March 19, 1986, were fifty people (thirty-nine women, 8 men, and three children); in the last, on July 24, 1986, were twenty people.

1987: The *Ile de Lumière* from April 9, 1987, and still at sea at the time of this writing rescued ninety people in two boats in the first thirty-six hours of her journey. By November 9, 1987, 228 Boat People have been rescued by *Médecins du Monde.*[14]

Total: 3,534 people.

In July 1985 the Soviet cargo ship *Poisk* en route from Vietnam to Sakhalin rescued thirty-seven refugees aboard a boat in distress somewhere in the South China Sea. Getting wind of this, the Filipino government offered shelter to these people. The commanding officer of the cargo ship answered that he was awaiting orders from Moscow. Then, there was total silence. On July 11, 1985, Mr. Leon Davico, spokesman for the UNHCR in Geneva, announced that the thirty-seven refugees had been returned to the Vietnamese authorities. No one knows what happened to them since.

In February 1986 the Indonesian government denounced Vietnam for still trading human lives for gold. The Vietnamese authorities are using new, stronger, better equipped boats. Once they have disembarked their human loads on some Indonesian island, they return to Vietnam for another trip. That same month, the Indonesian navy intercepted a flotilla of five boats near its shores. The refugees have been accepted by the Indonesian authorities, but the Vietnamese crews were put on one boat and sent back home, while the four other boats remained in Indonesia.

NOTES

1. Barry Wain, *The Refused: The Agony of the Indo Chine Refugees* (Simon & Schuster, New York, 1981).
2. 90 percent Hoa, 10 percent Vietnamese.
3. Minh Hiên took the lowest figure, five hundred thousand according to the Asian Relations Center of Sophia University, Tokyo, January 1980. There were six hundred thousand according to Richard Nixon in *No More Vietnams* (Arbor House). Four hundred thousand of them died at sea, a third being children.
4. Figure forwarded by the chief of the refugee camp of Cherating, Malaysia.
5. From the reports of Georges Ménager for *Paris-Match* of May 5, 1985, and "Thalassa," TVFQ 99, August 5, 1985.
6. Ibid.
7. The one in charge of finding the former agents of the CIA. A native of the South, he also knows the Chinese very well.
8. The *Sky Luck* was in fact the *Ky-Lu*. Once at sea the letters "S" and "ck" were added to make it the *Sky Luck*.
9. The captain who had embarked 3,215 passengers on board his ship was refused the authorization to disembark them in the Philippines. However, he managed to leave 573 of them on a small island.
10. In Hong Kong, this same captain managed to disembark the remaining 2,642 passengers; he was arrested and jailed for one or two months, then released, after having paid a fine. It is said that since then many captains have left their ship just before touching land.
11. The S/S *Sibonga*, under British flag, did not embark refugees in Vietnam, but rescued two boats overloaded with Vietnamese and at the point of disaster.
12. The S/S *Sen On* was flying a Panama flag, but her home port was Singapore, where her services had been required.
13. When the boats are old, small, crammed with some dozens of people, and equipped with five-to-ten horsepower engines, you can be sure that these are escapees. When the boats are new, loaded with one hundred people and over, and equipped with forty to fifty horsepower engines, you know that their convoy has been organized by the Vietnamese authorities.
14. "Thalassa," TVFQ 99.

PROFITS MADE FROM THE TRADING OF HUMAN LIVES

The price of a man drops when he has no more the use of his freedom.
—Ho-Chi-Minh

To recover their freedom the South Vietnamese will have to pay in gold.

According to the statistics of the UNHCR, 88, 712 "semi-official" refugees left Vietnam in 1978; by 1979 they were 294,160, and 200,000 had their departure postponed or even cancelled because of the Geneva Conference of July 20, 1979. During this same year, marked by the conflict with China, 272,100 Vietnamese crossed the border and are said to have been the only Land People to have bought their freedom. Minh Hiên estimates that the first one hundred thousand did not pay, since, living so close to the border, they just had to cross it, whereas other refugees had to pay one or two taels of gold. Therefore, it seems that out of a total of 820,818 Land People from Southeast Asia (Cambodians and Laotians) only 172,000 Vietnamese have paid one or two taels of gold.[1] The richer South Vietnamese had to pay ten, twenty, and even thirty taels of gold per person, without distinction of age, plus expenses for false identity papers, their authorization to leave the country, et cetera.

Prices have doubled, and we hear that they have gone up again. However, since we do not know exactly when the prices began to rise and since the number of the refugees began to drop sharply in 1982–83, we are going to calculate the profits made from the trading of human lives at the rates of 1978–79.

Back then, the tael of gold (twenty-seven grams[2]) was worth about two hundred U.S. dollars. Using these figures:

- 172,000 North Vietnamese who paid a minimum of one tael of gold (U.S. $200): U.S. $34,400,000.

•For the Boat People totaling 969,510 and the 70,614 ODP People it cost them at the very least ten taels, or U.S. $2,000 per person. which means a total of $2,080,248,000.00.

All told it gives a grand total (Land People, Boat People, and ODP) of U.S. $2,114,248,000.00, over $2 billion. The French wire agency AFP mentioned on May 25, 1979, a figure of U.S. $241 million just for the month of April of that year.[3] This information was given by a Vietnamese source in Hanoi who wishes to remain anonymous.

In these figures are included the four hundred thousand Boat People who died at sea. They too paid their way out, but disappeared in the waters of the South China Sea. What is not included are the South Vietnamese who paid twenty and even thirty taels of gold to get out, plus more gold to get false papers as "Chinese" citizens for every member of their family, plus still more gold for the authorization to leave the country and the fact that every operation needed some hand greasing to help these papers to be released.

Now if we add these $2 billion dollars or so to the war booty evaluated at U.S. $5 to 8 billion, we reach the figure of U.S. $7 to 10 billion. That is not all; in fact it is only the beginning. There was the gold found in banks reserves and private safes; foreign currencies, precious stones, jewels, art collections, factories, plantations and farms, hospitals and offices with the equipment of the aforesaid, herds and reserves of grain, and warehouses of any kind of business you can think of as part of the daily life.

According to "L'Etat du Monde 1983"[4] the total exports of Vietnam in 1975 was one hundred eighty-eight million dollars. The trading of human lives alone represents more than eleven times that figure. For 1982 and according to the same source, Vietnam's total export was $428 million; the trading of human lives would still represent some five times that figure. The trading of human lives and the war booty alone represented thirty-seven times up to fifty-three times the total exports of Vietnam in 1975, 16.3 to 23.6 times the total exports of Vietnam in 1982, plus everything else seized in the country.

There are other advantages to be added to that list:

•The rapid reduction of number of mouths to feed.

- The confiscation of all the goods these people left behind, which are not likely to be reclaimed.

- The expulsion of the malcontents, those opposing the regime and representing a threat in the heart of the country.

- The opportunity to have communist agents infiltrate the West, therefore to create unrest and social problems and to install organizations that will exploit the Vietnamese communities to finance socialism.

Despite all this, Hanoi never ceases to ask for Western aid.

Thanks to their expertise and contacts, the Hoa have helped a great number of their relatives and compatriots to go back to freedom and to escape death. But good charity begins with oneself. Vietnamese in general had to embark on boats that were not too reliable, while the Hoa left on cargo ships secured from pirates and communists—or at least much more—since this "semi-official" emigration was organized by their compatriots and the Vietnamese authorities.

International public opinion and the Geneva Conference in July 1979 have momentarily brought this traffic to a halt or at least slowed it down, but as we shall see, it is still going on today. At that time, the North Vietnamese were furious to see their source of income drying up, but even more so the refugees who wanted to leave the country.

Among the most desperate, four thousand, five hundred people were waiting in July 1979 for the authorization to leave with a ship flying a Panamanian flag, anchored at Ba-Lai, in one of the nine mouths of the Mekong. After two weeks under a hot sun and still without authorization, the human cargo had practically exhausted their reserves of food and water. They rationed what was left. Then they rationed the rations. Corpses began to line up in the alleyways. The survivors gave all they still possessed to buy the few supplies that managed to reach the ship. Finally, ten days after the Geneva Conference, that is, thirty-five days after they boarded, the bony ghosts of the survivors were disembarked and sent to temporary camps on the deserted beach of Thanh-Phu in the Bên-Trê province. Then in small groups these refugees with broken dreams were brought back to square one: Ho Chi Minh City.

To bring some order into the "semi-official" emigration, the Geneva Conference called by the High Commissioner set up the Orderly Departure Program (ODP). It began, in fact, several months later, in December 1979. Two thousand refugees per month would be allowed, in theory, to leave Ho Chi Minh City by plane for Bangkok in Thailand. From there they would be dispatched to the Western countries.

To sum it up, the Vietnamese who could, left in April 1975, then clandestinely and in small groups in 1975, 1976, and 1977. In 1978–79 those who left did it with the "semi-official emigration." Later on still, they would try to bring their family with them, thanks to the family reunion plan. But except for the few who managed to flee in the first hours, they all had to pay a price for their freedom.[5]

One could believe that since the Geneva Conference, things would be orderly indeed. In fact, the "semi-official" emigration still continues. A boat arrived in June 1985 in the Philippines with three hundred people on board. When it comes to a few refugees, one can be sure they are clandestine. But when they number several dozens with a new boat, we know the journey has been organized. This time, however, it is not the refugees who pay for their fare in Vietnam anymore—they have not enough left to do that—but their relatives who are now in the West. It is a form of terrorism: a communist state holds a nation hostage, and the ransom is paid by the members of that community in the world.

NOTES

1. The others who lived in MongCay, LaoKay, Hongay and Campha, for instance, near the border, just had to cross it.
2. Some say that today it is worth thirty-six grams, but Minh Hiên maintains the figure of twenty-seven grams.
3. *Le Devoir* (Montreal), May 25, 1979.
4. *The State of the World*, La Découverte/Maspéro.
5. According to W. R. Smyser, U.S. diplomat serving with the UNHCR in Geneva, in "Refugees: A Never Ending Story" (*Foreign Affairs*, Fall 1985), 1,500,000 refugees would have been relocated, while 150,000 would still be waiting in transit camps.

INTERNAL PASSPORT AND TRANSPORTATION

1974 (Dec.): Internal passport for peasants.

—G. P. Armstrong

The Western media dwelling on the internal passport in South Africa were telling the truth at that time. Since then and at the time of this writing, laws have been passed in South Africa to abolish it, among other things. In South Vietnam, on the other hand, it was imposed—along with curfew to facilitate arrests—in 1975 and is still in force today. What these two countries have in common is that the media never talked about the laws abolishing it in South Africa, nor about its implementation in South Vietnam.

The North Vietnamese compel the South's population to stay in the same place, on the same spot, in the same house, one could almost say from the cradle to the grave. Moving is forbidden. This allows the cadres, the police, and the security forces to thoroughly know the people under their surveillance, to prevent them from knowing what is going on elsewhere, and to help the police in the arrests and the repression of individuals and of groups.

The South Vietnamese society was in complete shambles in April 1975. Saigon was overcrowded with refugees from all over the country: from Central Vietnam (Huê, Danang, Qui-Nhon, Nhatrang, Phanrang, Phantiêt), from the Plateaux (Pleiku, Kontum, Banmethuot, Dalat, Lamdông), and even from Cambodia. Saigon had fallen into the hands of the North Vietnamese, who sent the refugees back home, where they found only ruins, ashes, or simply cadres from the North living in their houses.

Profiteers posing as war amputees settled on the city's sidewalks and then began to build shacks on empty sites. They were soon thrown out by the security forces because they had no family booklet. Members of families who were in charge of keeping the house were also thrown out in the street, and the buildings were confiscated. Those who had large houses were compelled to host *bô-dôis* under their roof, as in any occupation by an enemy army. All the homeless and jobless people were sent to the NZE, the New Economic Zones, of which more later.

It is forbidden to have a second residence, be it a cottage, cabin, or even a shack; those that are discovered are confiscated. All real estate transactions are forbidden. Apartments and houses from which the tenants are gone for more than two days and without any authorization are ransacked and finally confiscated. Since August 1975 every family must have an identity card delivered by the local People's Committee on which the number, the name, and all information concerning every member of the family appear. It is forbidden to host any person foreign to the family. If, perchance, a relative happens to come to visit, he or she is to be reported to the security agent of the cell whose job is to watch every move of the people under his, or her surveillance. One must be aware that surveillance is extremely tight; it is not only an agent of the cell in charge of it. First, you have several people's committees: for food, surveillance, politics, youth, women, housing, and what-have-you. Therefore, people are always under surveillance at any one time of the day or the night. The presence of any person foreign to a neighborhood must be reported.

The confiscated houses are allocated to the cadres and their families, who have come from the North. Moving being strictly forbidden, extorted bribes for that kind of operation are exorbitant, if not prohibitive, needless to say. Most of the Hoa have paid astronomical sums of money to leave the provinces and settle in Cholon in order to reinforce the Chinese community.

To go from one city to another, one has to have an authorization delivered by the local police where the person lives, established from the ration card of the applicant. Once this person has reached her destination, she must go to the local police to get her authorization countersigned, then back home, to go again to the local police to give back the authorization.

The security and the police systematically search the people at all the major crossroads and the rivers' most strategic choke points. They check the travel documents, the bills and title deeds of the bicycles (motorbikes are rare and private cars forbidden). Forgotten or lost papers mean that the bicycle is confiscated and that the traveler has to return home on foot.

The police themselves, of course, reserve the right to refuse any authorization without explanation. There is no problem, though, for the sympathizers who are selected, then transported by plane, and invited to visit the tomb of Ho Chi Minh in Hanoi. Of course, some people can travel indeed, like those poor women who in 1980 made a round trip of two thousand kilometers on foot, by car and by train to visit for few hours a jailed husband, father, or brother, transferred to the North—but they paid a stiff price for it and sacrificed all they had. They were lucky even to be able to visit their relatives.

It was forbidden for the North Vietnamese who settled in the South when whey fled the North in 1954–55 to go back and visit their hometown or birthplace; they are lucky if they can stay alive, period. On the other hand, 1.5 million cadres and their families (which means an estimated 3 to 5 million people) have been sent to the South, and several million farmers of the Red River Delta, in the North, have been transferred to the Mekong Delta in the South, to the Plateaux region, and to Central Vietnam where the populations have been literally decimated, and to Cambodia. Well-indoctrinated, they are there to consolidate the regime and maybe one day vote, give the impression to Westerners that everything happening politically there is democratic.

If someone wants to have a good idea of what the levelling of a society is and to what kind of equality the class struggle leads, just look at transportation. Any vehicle is considered property of the state, which monopolizes gas, oil, tires, and spare parts, as a matter of fact, everything related to transportation, whether on the ground, at sea, or in the air.

The upper class of the North travels freely. Air transportation is exclusively reserved for the leaders of the Party. It was during one of these occasions that a civilian DC-3 going to the island of Phu-Quoc was hijacked on October 27, 1977, by four "pirates." The line from Ho Chi Minh City to Hanoi, the only one with a regular weekly flight, is restricted to the communist leaders. It was like that as well with the Hanoi-Bangkok line, at least until 1980, when it was also used for the ODP. The superb limousines, considered to be war booty, are reserved for the high-ranking cadres and the minibuses for the middle cadres on duty.

Traffic is limited to the subaltern cadres and the proletarian class dwelling in the cities. Barely one fifth of the one hundred thousand workers of Ho Chi Minh City own a motorbike. That is because they are coddled by the regime, which needs them in the state's factories. These twenty thousand or so "privileged" are allowed a monthly ration of five liters of gas; they sell them on the black market to make ends meet and feed their family.

The subaltern cadres are a little better off, since they can buy Japanese motorbikes from the South Vietnamese, who have no gas to run them and have to sell them for a piece of bread before they are requisitioned.

The population can hardly move. Private cars are out of the question. Requisitioned trucks are being used for the transportation of the war booty towards the North. Other means of transportation are requisitioned for the soldiers, the cadres, and their families. The motorbikes are for the workers—that is, those who can afford it—and the subaltern cadres. There are the bicycles, of course, when one can find one in good working order. Therefore, considering the situation, one goes the old-fashioned way: on foot.

Needless to say, the profession of bicycle thief is flourishing. Of course there are buses sometimes. Overcrowded right from the start, they will be able to stop only at the terminal, unless they run out of gas or break down, which happens quite often. This has helped the old tradition of the cyclo-rickshaw to be in again. Economical, they have quite taken off and are of course criticized by the Party, who sees there a form of private enterprise, "inhumane and degrading."

When one needs to go on a longer journey, one takes the three-wheeled Italian Lambros on which fifteen people are packed on three benches. When they collapse under the weight they are not replaced, of course. Then there are the taxis; yes, there are some. State-owned, controlled by the security forces, with gas rationed, they are here for the tourists and the journalists who will later report that "nothing has changed in Vietnam," and for the cadres and the security service. Then when someone really needs to travel far . . . well, forget about it. There is still the trans-Indochinese train built during the French regime, but parts of the railway having been sabotaged during the war by the communists themselves, there is a good chance that the travelers will be obliged to repair them, an opportunity to stretch their limbs a little bit along the way. The cars, like buses, are so overcrowded right from the start that usually, the train cannot accept other travelers before the terminal at the other end of the line.

As for the buses, which ensure the liaison between the cities and the provinces, one has to queue a day in advance to be able, maybe, to purchase a ticket. Then the battle for it is fierce and the black market hikes prices very high. It is not uncommon to see the happy winner with a black eye. He has been lucky, a person in the queue has fainted and has been trampled down, while others waiting farther down the line have had their pockets visited by pickpockets who abound in the neighborhood. It is better not to have someone in the family dying in another part of the country. In the province, since the terminals are quite far away from any center, those who have to buy a ticket have to bring along their sleeping mats and camp on the spot until the wicket opens; the only thing sure about it is that it is going to be after curfew hours. Finally, when someone has managed to get hold of a ticket, he must expect to travel two or three times more slowly than before, because of the frequent police controls and systematic searches.

The passport to travel inside the country or, as it is euphemistically called, the authorization to move, the exorbitant price, the administrative hassles, and the real dangers discourage the Vietnamese from undertaking a journey they cannot manage on foot. With time and distance, family ties are stretching, then breaking; so do most relations.

The Gas and Lubricant Company of the state has been transferred from Hanoi to Ho Chi Minh City and replaces Shell, Esso, and Texaco, which even during the war managed to supply and distribute gas and oil in South Vietnam. All their equipment has been destroyed, of course, or confiscated. Of the numerous service stations, only a few are kept in working order, and the system makes sure that quantities to be distributed are just enough to wet the rationing tickets. In such conditions, what usually has to happen does. The workers who are having a hard time making ends meet go on foot and sell their monthly five-liter ration on the black market. All those who, like their colleagues who happen to handle rice, find themselves manipulating gas are up to their neck in the black market.

Then there is the Army; it is stupendous. Between the jeeps and the trucks for the daily service, it is said that all the "spare" gas not only improves the menu on the table and in the beds of the officers and those of the *bô-dôis* as well, but that it helps make a lot of money indeed.

Since May 1975, with all the war booty that had to be evacuated to the North, the convoys have not ceased to make the eighteen-hundred-kilometer journey separating Hanoi and Ho Chi Minh City. Since the invasion of Cambodia, other convoys have been doing the same thing on the two thousand kilometers separating Phnom Penh from Hanoi. As any one of us has probably done at one time or another with cargo trains, Minh Hiên has counted the number of trucks in convoys using the national Highway 1, linking the North to the South. He found an average of three hundred trucks per convoy, believe it or not. From Ho Chi Minh City to Hanoi or from Phnom Penh to Hanoi, trucks are using their own fuel. But on their way back they are empty and pull one another. In an average convoy of three hundred, one hundred are pulling the two hundred others. At twenty liters minimum per truck and for one hundred kilometers, this does represent a saving of eighty thousand liters for one convoy traveling from Hanoi to Ho Chi Minh City. And these convoys have been driving for a long time, day and night.[1]

All that fuel is then sold at a high price on the outskirts of the main cities or on the black market, right downtown. It will then reach a very, very high price for those who can still afford it and even more for those who are planning to escape by boat. In his book *Le Défi Mondial*[2] Jean-Jacques Servan-Schreiber quotes the formula of Georges Clemenceau, who when evaluating World War I said that a drop of oil would have the value of a drop of blood. The Gas and Lubricant Company seems to have made its own the words of the "Tiger"—Georges Clemenceau's nickname—and is prompting everyone and all to save the precious fuel. Commendable. But everyone has a personal, different

THE COMMUNIST ECONOMY: TO GOVERN BY THE STOMACH AND TO PROLETARIANIZE THE PEOPLE

There are three ways to keep conquered countries accustomed to live according to their laws, and free: one, destroy them; two, live there in person; three, let them live according to their laws, exact tribute, and create an oligarchical government which will keep you their friendship.

—Machiavelli

In South Vietnam the North Vietnamese came to live in person, exact tribute, and create a communist oligarchy to keep the South Vietnamese population under control. But instead of letting people live according to their laws, they make sure they are obeying their own set of rules. We are going to see how—point number one—this system is destroying South Vietnam.

Until the invasion in 1975, the economy of South Vietnam was able, despite war and sabotage, to provide for the needs of the population, to resist the invasion from the North, and to achieve development and reconstruction. Not a small deed. One was even talking about prosperity, due in fact, it is true, to the presence of GIs and the support of free nations.

Since the North Vietnamese takeover, the economy and the human situation are in a disastrous state. But why should we be surprised? The North Vietnamese who took refuge in the South in 1954–55 had already warned the people: "Hanoi has hoaxed the population for a long time, repeating endlessly that the South is poor, that it suffers under the American yoke, and that the North must make a sacrifice to help the unfortunate compatriots of the South," who had no desire whatsoever to be "liberated."

Once the South conquered, the propaganda of the North changed: "the opulence of the South is fake and is the hypocritical work of American imperialism." The problem with that is that the North Vietnamese did not exactly understand why the

American hypocrisy was giving chubby cheeks to their southern neighbors, while the nice words of the North were leaving them with empty stomachs. They were absolutely amazed to see the people down south comfortable with what they had.

After having set up a police network, eliminated the "troublesome elements," and taken the booty and the food away, the police and the security forces started within four months a census that would give Hanoi a pretty good idea of how many useful mouths would need to be fed:

- The cadres and their families, the agents and the police, and the soldiers who ensure the setting up and the expansion of the system. They receive a comfortable quantity of varied foodstuffs with their units.
- A small number of workers who ensure the operation of the state-owned factories. They receive their barely sufficient rations through their department.

As for the nonuseful mouths, the population hostile to the regime will receive starvation rations through the cells of every block.

From May to September 1975, the authorities took every measure to make rice—the staple food in Southeast Asia—scarce as well as food in general and anything essential. Everything is monopolized. The most gigantic scheme in the country is a food blockade that triggers an artificial famine. Beginning as of October, the "rice card" is issued to every family. Those who have no home or permanent address and those who have moved without authorization do not receive the precious card. People who have been "re-educated" and are "set free" and have lost their citizenship do not receive the card. Families that are allowed to have it can go to the cell that handles rice for their district and buy at the official price of 0.40 dông a kilo of poor-quality rice[1]:

- Twelve kilograms per month or four hundred grams per day and per adult.
- Six kilograms per month or two hundred grams per day and per child under twelve years old.

This is in a world where twenty countries alone produce 1,676 billion tons of grain for a population of about 4.6 billion people.[2] This means about one kilo of grain per day and per person anywhere in the world, without any consideration of age. Only grains, think about it. To that, potatoes, soya, beef, pork, fish, poultry, vegetables, et cetera are to be added.

This kind of attack against the population is always "telephoned." It means that, one way or another, the information concerning restrictions is announced, tested beforehand with the public, in order to know its reaction. For example, before the invasion the North Vietnamese rumors of "reconciliation," "reunification," "clemency," "brotherhood," et cetera, were circulated to lull the southern population. This time, to impose the rationing of rice, unknown up until that day in the history of South Vietnam and to make sure that there will not be any riot, the communists pass along messages such as "times are hard," "the weather is bad" (it always works, even if the South Vietnamese have not seen any climatic change), "rice is in short supply" (which is true since it has been shipped to the North) and "it will have to be shared on a more egalitarian basis," the usual trick.

At the beginning, the naive population smiled about it. It is well known that the most cruel and inhumane way to go or to come back to liberalism is communism, or, the communists have never seen so much rice in their life, that once they get used to it, things will be normal again. In short, most people thought things would improve with time.

South Vietnam having always lived in opulence, its people could not understand the meaning of these measures, their implication, or the threat carried by sentences such as "the opulence of the South is artificial," or "rice will have to be distributed on a more egalitarian basis." What the people discovered, however, was that during the curfew hours entire convoys and cargo ships were leaving the South to deliver the rice to the North.

The only way out for the young who had to accept 12 kilograms of poor-quality rice per month at that time was to join the army and go to Cambodia to get 21 kilograms of first-quality rice and adequate rations of meat, fish, and vegetables. Meanwhile, his family would remain on starvation rations and would be condemned if the rationing card were to be lost. It is not replaced.

In the financial sphere, the only Japanese bank and the

American, the British, the South Korean, and the Taiwanese banks had time to leave Vietnam before the arrival of the North Vietnamese. But the communists took hold of the French Bank of Commerce (Banque Française du Commerce), the National Bank of Paris (BNP), and the fifteen or so South Vietnamese and Hoa banks. It is said however, that the sixteen-ton gold reserve of the National Bank of Vietnam was evacuated to Taiwan during the night of April 24, 1975, with the family of the former president Nguyên-van-Thieû. We do not know much about the fate of other banks.

As in Kampuchea (Cambodia)[3] the very first monetary measure taken by Trân-Duong, governor of the Communist Central Bank who had just arrived from Hanoi, was to prevent the circulation of the new one-thousand-piastre banknotes[4] stockpiled in the National Bank's safes. Then he ordered the other banks to open up their wickets, but forbade them to give money to the customers. They were required to update their bookkeeping, to centralize the accounts of all their branches, to draw up inventory of all credit they had in foreign currencies, cash money, estates, and personal safes and those of the banks, and to demand the recovery of all outstanding debt and to entrust all this to the central state-owned bank.

Meanwhile, the *bô-dôis* were paid in kind by their units, and the population was forbidden to or prevented from withdrawing any money, even to cope with the most urgent need, such as food, medication, and the funerals in greater number every day. People then began to sell what they had and tried to survive on that.

That was only the beginning of the economic measures implemented by the communists. The governor of the central bank secretly distributed the banknotes to the cadres, with the express order to buy anything of value. With a population short of cash and all its assets frozen in the banks, the word spread like a bush fire, even before the cadres arrived in the streets with their bags full of banknotes. And they bought, a lot. They played the game of bargaining, for the sake or the fun of it, and had the merchandise taken away as soon as it was bought, then gathered to various places where they were loaded on trucks that would go to the North at night. They spend without counting or almost. The money was not too hard to earn, and after all it was an order, yes, sir! And the South Vietnamese sold like crazy all they could to these cadres who did not seem to know the value of what they were buying and of what they were spending. To obtain the same merchandise that otherwise would go to the black market, the cadres paid three, five, and even ten times their price downtown. Out in the country, things were slightly different: there was no competition, and the cadres bought the reserves of rice at the official rate of the day.

Then the South Vietnamese counted all their banknotes running through their fingers. Business had been good, one had to say. Never had so much sold so well. Then, the day after—September 20, 1975—they had to count again their cash. During the night, the communists had invalidated the money, period. The South Vietnamese realized, too late, that what they had in their hands was worth nothing. They had been had. They were just left with paper not even good enough to wrap the little that was left. They felt powerless, at the mercy of the North Vietnamese. All of a sudden they felt frustrated. Had the soldiers tried to take away the merchandise by sheer force, there would have been fights, struggles, and riots; people would have resisted the theft. Instead, people were left dumbfounded by such demonic calculation. They knew then that the occupation was real.

In twenty-four hours, what will be described by some as a mere "professional incompetence" on the part of Trân-Duong, was in fact a longtime planned maneuver and would allow the communists to impoverish the South Vietnamese almost at once. Then, after this invalidation, they put into circulation one-, two-, five-, and fifty-dông notes printed in China in 1960 without any value at all. In 1978, to top it all, a second invalidation would follow, to invalidate this already worthless money, and then later another one.

Prices and inflation skyrocketed from one day to the next, and paper was flooding the market. What was even worse was that the lack of goods killed. The population could witness it every morning at dawn, when night left its contingent of corpses on the sidewalks and on the waste grounds.

The following table gives an idea of the prices in general at that time:

	1976–80	1981–82	1983	1984	Since then
Monthly salary					
Worker	45 to 60 d.[5]	100–20	140–60	180	
Technician	120	140–60	200–20	250	
Rice					
Cadres and soldiers: twenty-one kilograms per month of first-quality rice					0.40 dông
Workers and farmers from North Vietnam: sixteen kilograms of second-quality rice					per kilo
Population: twelve kilograms (six for children) of third-quality rice					1976–84
Black market: Rice:	7 to 8 d./kg.	13–14 d./kg.	20–23 d./kg.	38 d./kg.	60
Pork per kilogram	40d.	110d.	150d.	320d.	
Beef per kilogram	65d.	130d.	170d.	350d.	
Duck egg	5d.	6d.	7d.	8d.	
Fish per kilogram	20d.	30d.	—[6]	150d.	
Vegetables	—	5d.	—	5d.	
Fruits one watermelon	—	—	100d.	—	
one grapefruit	—	—	50d.	70d.	
twelve oranges	—	—	200d.	300d.	

Sea salt per kilogram	5d.	8d.	10d.	20d.
Condensed milk: 1 can of three hundred millimeters	40d.	60d.	70d.	80d.
Gas per liter	30d.	50d.	60d.	—
Material: tetotron				
1.20m wide	—	140d./m	—	—
Jeans (CDN $5)	—	1,000d.	—	—
Medicine: 1 pill of				
Erythromycine	8d.	8d.	—	40d.
Ampicilline	8d.	18d.	—	40d.
Tetracycline	4d.	12d.	—	20d.
Pure gold: 1 tael of 27 grs.	38,000d. to 40,000d.	50,000d. to 60,000d.	90,000d.	300,000d.
Electricity: cadres and workers	—	—	0.15d./KWH unlimit quant.	—
population	—	—	1.20d./KWH if less than 60 KHW/month 3.50d. if over	—
Mail: 1 letter of 20 grams for a foreign country	1.50 d.	2d.	30d.	200d.[7]

The first step concerning the economy was to lay a hand on all the resources of the country and of the population, then to impoverish the South Vietnamese and destroy free enterprise. To appease a public opinion utterly crushed in this upheaval and before bringing the ax down for a second time, the Transformation of Crafts Committee of Ho Chi Minh City'' would proclaim the New Economic Policy. That term Lenin had already used it in 1921, to momentarily alleviate the catastrophic effects of war communism. In Vietnam, this ''new'' formula called ''patriotic economy'' rests on five elements:

•The state enterprises.

•The mixed enterprises (half private, half state-owned).

•The cooperatives.

•The private enterprises.

•The individual enterprises.

In fact, and under the cloak of ''management,'' this was the first step towards total control of the production by the state. The proof of it is that three years later, on March 24, 1978, an operation called ''inventory of the goods'' would wipe out all that. The only things left would be:

•The enterprises owned by the state, under the communist cadres.

•The mixed enterprises (partly private, but under control of the cadres). These enterprises would later be wiped out, too.

•The cooperatives under communist control.

The last two categories are said to be ''private.'' In fact, everything is under the control of the state: raw materials, funds, and management, as well as benefits, if any. By 1978 some twenty-eight thousand to thirty thousand private firms had been abolished and there were over one hundred agricultural cooperatives in the country.

Since there are practically no more jobs available, people are obliged to work for the state for a handful of rice. There are no free unions to ask for a salary raise or cost-of-living adjustment. Even small jobs that used to feed the people have disappeared: the tailor does not find any fabric or any sewing thread, the mason any bricks or cement, the carpenter any planks or nails, and the soup merchant has no rice and no meat to cook with. Yet, on the one hand, the textile factories are still operating, the cement factory of Hàtien is still producing—in fact, money has even been sent from foreign countries to build plants—there is still wood in the Vietnamese forests, and rice has not stopped growing simply because there has been a change of regime. On the other hand, nationalization and total control of the state have not made the leaders, the bureaucrats, the cadres, and the settlers from the North less greedy or more able as technicians and managers.

As far as the hydro-electric complex was concerned, the project of the Da-Nhim plant was elaborated by the former regime and was to produce two-thirds of the electricity needed in South Vietnam, from the Mekong Delta to Nha-Trang. The first stone of this Da-Nhim Krongpha plant was laid in 1957, thanks to Japanese money paid as World War II compensation. It was finished in 1960, under Ngô-dinh-Diêm. It was sabotaged several times by the communists during the war—lines cut, posts cut down, towers knocked down, and pipes blown open—but it was repaired every time. When they arrived in 1975, the North Vietnamese had no terrorists on their back. They were the saboteurs and should not have had any difficulty assessing the damages, since they knew what they did. They declared that the plant would be in working order again by the end of 1976. People waited in silence to see the bulbs lit in the dark of the night. Years have gone by; things went the same way they did with oil.

In textiles South Vietnam had acquired the reputation of having one of the Southeast Asian countries' best weaving and finishing industries for quality, quantity, and variety. All factories had been equipped with American help, and with modern machines from Japan, West Germany, and Switzerland. In 1974

South Vietnamese production was estimated to be able to meet the needs of the population for at least ten years. Today the Soviet Union buys cotton from Egypt, gives it to Vietnam, and takes most of the production. The USSR provided 80 percent or so of North Vietnam's arsenal during the war; it is said that the South is repaying it this way, among others.

With the economy in such disarray and with the suppression of traditional jobs, most of the cities were and are still flooded with jobless people. This unemployment was partly reduced with the preparation for the invasion of Cambodia. The youth were enrolled and quartered outside the country, in Laos and in Cambodia itself. As for older men up to fifty-five and women up to fifty, the North Vietnamese resorted to the old tactic of fatigue duty or forced labor. The cadres raided the houses and designated those who would go and for how long. In all South Vietnam, millions of people of both sexes, it is said, were mobilized and sent in long columns toward an uncertain fate.

In Ho Chi Minh City, the urban population work on fatigue duties on weekends. Out in the country, this work can last two or three weeks, even a month. There are many arms for few tools; besides, there are no more bulldozers, digging machines, or other machines. They have been sent to the North. Therefore, one thousand people thirty-five to fifty-five years old working twelve hours a day do not even achieve the equivalent of seven or eight hours of mechanized work. The spectacle is poignant. Old bodies, always hungry, clumsily try to raise shovels and picks that slip here on a soil too hard, and sink there into a muddy suction, in which bare, skinny legs are sucked down, slipping in a dirty, unhealthy water and losing balance under the weight of baskets filled with earth. When at times a balancing pole splits and becomes sharp as a razor blade, the bamboo slices the back to the bone.

The South Vietnamese people believe they date back to the third century B.C., when the Chinese emperor and tyrant Ts'in Thuy Hoang, of the Ts'in dynasty, set up the fatigue duty and forced labor to erect the Great Wall. Millions of people of all walks of life died. He buried alive the scholars and burnt their manuscripts; altogether, nothing new. It was more or less what was done in Tibet some years ago.

At night people sleep in the open on a mat of straw in dampness. During the day, it is work under a sun hot as melted lead or under heavy rains, depending upon the season. Flies and mosquitoes, carriers of diseases, and poisonous snakes have a field day. No drinking water, no medicine. Heartbreaking scenes take place: parents sell what little they have left to find replacements for their children, or children take the place of parents or grandparents, too exhausted to move. Accidents are numerous: feet cut off by too heavy picks or because the arms are too clumsy to direct the tool correctly. There is no emergency care; bleeding empties the body. Snake bites are deadly because there is no serum. Drowning has been the cause of death for instance, of PTV, engineer for the former French company CARIC. Bodies or limbs are blown off by hand grenades or booby traps that have not been detected. At times, like in Bên-Trê, the people's ire, the real true one, walks on its tormentors, tramples them, and crushes them into the mud of the forced labor. It happened.

In Central Vietnam people on fatigue duty or forced labor are used to repair the railways sabotaged by the North Vietnamese and to clear away the fences, hedges, and barricades of the strategic hamlets erected under the Ngô-dinh-Diêm government.[8] They also level off the graves, tombs, and vaults to transform the cemeteries into arable land. In the South, they build accommodation roads and dig out ponds for fish breeding. In the Mekong Delta, their work is to dig out irrigation channels and other channels to drain the aluminiferous waters. In the province of Minh-Hai (Ca-Mau) in the southern part of the country, forced laborers erected dams to contain the sea. In Ho Chi Minh City, they had to dig out channels to drain off sewage, waste, and marshland. The shortage of technicians and experts,[9] the lack of feasibility studies, and human beings treated like beasts of burden instead of using machines—at this point, the government is not talking about "inhumane and degrading" treatment anymore—and the incompetence and inexperience of cadres certainly more gifted in Marxist-Leninist ideology than engineering are responsible for the fact that practically all large-scale public works are a failure. In some instances, like in the province of Vinh-Long in the Mekong Delta, they became disasters; instead of bringing in sweet waters, the channels tapped a briny water that destroyed a huge acreage of rice fields and gardens.

Unremunerated fatigue duty and forced labor do not represent a creation of jobs. In 1976[10] only one hundred thousand workers of factories and enterprises owned by the State had a real salary, out of a population of 6 million people living in Ho Chi Minh City and the suburbs. These conditions are therefore conducive to crime of all sorts: theft, armed robbery, burglary, pickpocketing, and prostitution with its train of diseases accompanying every war since time immemorial, except that here no one hopes for a postwar recovery. For those who are "lucky" enough to work for the state, the situation remains precarious: no job security, limited employment, no social security, no union,[11] no right to strike. Work in these conditions is only a remission. After four months to consolidate the regime, workers are "regraded" and their salary revised, meaning reduced. There is a compensation, however: the worker can buy his sixteen kilograms of rice per month and staples a little bit cheaper, supplies otherwise not to be found anywhere else—except at skyrocketing prices on the black market—but at the factory's cooperative.[12]

The work week is forty-eight hours (six days of eight hours), instead of forty, and extra work is mandatory, though not paid. It is strongly advised to produce more, which may earn a good worker the title of "exemplary worker" and the right to drink the words of the cadres during the political reunions at the end of the week. When a team manages to go beyond the quota set by the factory, it has the right to keep the flag of honor for one month. Sunday is the only day in the week when workers can enjoy some rest and use it to do "voluntary" collective work in the fields, on the farms, or for the benefit of the Food Service. In the now state-owned factories whose former directors have been jailed, the workers are the bosses. As such, they are responsible for the good operation of the enterprise, its security (prevention of theft, sabotage, and other crimes), general maintenance, and the good use of raw materials. However, and so that these responsibilities do not go to their head, their salary has been reduced, and, in order to become good working bosses, they put into practice the motto of the Party: "Work more for the state and eat less" because "manual work is honor."

NOTES

1. A dông is a Vietnamese coin that has no value internationally.

2. According to *L'Etat du Monde 83*, Maspero. Paris.

3. As soon as the Khmer Rouge of Pol Pot entered Phnom Penh, capital of Cambodia, on April 17, 1975, the communists immediately abolished the monetary system, thirteen days before the invasion of South Vietnam by the North Vietnamese.

4. The piastre, unlike the communist dông, was quoted on the international market. Toward 1960, one U.S. dollar was worth thirty-five piastres, 60 in 1963, 125 in 1965, and 2,000 beginning April 1975. A few days before the arrival of the communists it was worth about five thousand piastres.

5. D stands for dông, equivalent to 1 U.S. dollar and 1.25 CDN dollar: In 1976–80 the salary of a worker was roughly U.S. $1–1.50 dollar a month, the equivalent of a kilogram of beef, if you could find and afford any.

6. — means prices were not available to us as of this writing.

7. Prices have gone that high because the person was "receiving help from abroad."

8. Erected to help farmers to protect themselves against communist guerrillas and inspired by the strategic hamlets in Malaysia created by Gen. Gerald Temple.

9. Some escaped; others died. Some of them rotted in camps while still others simply found themselves in the street.

10. Things have not changed since. In fact, they are worse.

11. Certainly not as we know them in the West.

12. In 1975 and in 1976, the population could only buy twelve kilograms of poor-quality rice per month in several purchases. In 1977 the quota fell to nine kilograms (often replaced by wheat flour and sorghum). There was only one basic item and no gas.

THE IMPOVERISHMENT AND THE LEVELING OF VIETNAMESE SOCIETY

Uniformity is the symbol of small minds. Life is not a succession of monotonous actions. Uniformity is to pass by the best things in life, and differences which, far from being logical, are human.

—Marcus Tullius Cicero

On September 20, 1975, in all the territory of South Vietnam, from the province of Quang-Tri, from the seventeenth parallel to Ca-Mau, in the southern part of the country, the security forces, the police, and contingents of cadres who came from North Vietnam, got ready in buildings chosen in advance. That day, no one was allowed to open shop or to do anything; for some it was not much different anyway.

The entire country was paralyzed, holding its breath. After having laid a heavy hand on all possible booty, on the banks and their funds, the communists "bought" almost everything of value, distributing money in profusion and then invalidating it the next day. But trouble was not over yet.

The heads of families are summoned, this very September 20, 1975, to bring all the money they have in order to receive, in exchange, notes without any value on the international market, like giving away real dollars for some kind of make-believe money. In exchange for, say, one hundred thousand of the old piastres they will receive two hundred dôngs per family, whatever the number of people. That is, the head of a family of eight who gives the equivalent of, say, U.S. $200,000 and the head of a family of three giving, for example, U.S. $200 would both receive two hundred dôngs. Now even if one accepts the notion of a nation functioning completely out of the international system, remember that at that time a worker was receiving forty-five to sixty dôngs per month and a technician 120 and yet, they had a very hard time making ends meet. Here two hundred dôngs will have to do for a man, a woman, and several children.

Now all these piastres and dollars are not burnt; they are collected by the state. Piastres that are not exchanged—in the hope that they might be useful for a good opportunity someday in the future—are invalidated the very same day. Dollars will be searched for in homes and even personal accounts and safes. In exchange for all that money, the North Vietnamese gave banknotes printed in China in 1960 carrying the stamp "Provisional Revolutionary Government of South Vietnam."

In hours the fortunes of the capitalist industrialists and big merchants are reduced to two hundred dôngs per family. This monetary unit, which sounds like an onomatopoeia, demonstrates the situation well: the blow of a gong. Farmers who have sweated all year long in the rice fields and have just received the income from their harvest undergo the same fate. Some die of a heart attack. This first campaign of impoverishment targeting at the big bourgeoisie was called "the campaign of destruction of capitalism." The second one was aimed at destroying the engine of capitalism: the entrepreneurs. Agents of the security forces helped by cadres and students armed to the teeth—they had been promised admission to the university—broke into the homes of the most important business leaders. Some panicked and threw themselves out the window. Those who were captured were jailed in narrow and empty cells, their feet in icy cold water. The only interruption is the interrogation: "Who are you?! Where is your money?! The gold?! The precious stones?! How much?! How many?! Where is your family?! How many people?! Who knows about them?! . . ." Silence brings torture. False answers bring torture, too. Those who are truthful are tortured because nobody is sure of their answers. Exact and verified answers bring tortures because they are correct and revealing. Then people like T.T. (head of T.H. Company, producing monosodium glutamate and Ramen instant soups) kill themselves.[1] A great number of them, like H.K.Q. (head of VIKIMCO and a senator) die under the torture.

Toward mid-1976 people who had not been able to get access to their safety deposit boxes for about a year are asked to go to their bank in order to pay the rent. They will finally recover what is theirs. Of course, they have to establish proof of their identity, and their ownership, and for that, they have to give a list of what is in their safe and sign a declaration. Safes are opened, but when their owners are about to stretch a hand to take their belongings, they are told: "From now on, all these articles—gold, silver, money, jewelry—are under the protection of the state and are considered to be war booty." Some people faint under the mischievous eyes of the cadres.

If this campaign is part of a combined strategy that consists of extirpating capitalism at the deepest level of society, it is also aimed at "unifying the country more." Indeed, it already had been unified militarily in April 1975, politically in May 1976 with the one-slate "elections" of the National Assembly representatives.[2] Now it is united economically, and since a misfortune never comes alone, treasury bonds, pension books, savings accounts, and the bank creditor accounts are declared void.

Two years later, on March 23, 1978, another groundswell will submerge the entire population and increase impoverishment in an egalitarian misfortune. This time, however, the masses were hit head on. The money given in exchange in 1975 was invalidated. Instead of two hundred dôngs per family, every man would receive one hundred dôngs, every woman seventy-five (nobody mentioned equality in that case), and each child twenty-five. Given the current value of the dông, what appeared to be an improvement later revealed itself to be another measure for further impoverishment. This new campaign directly targeted the people and would be run exactly the same way as that of 1975, but it would be called "the general inventory of goods." Exactly as before, the security and the police squads raided houses right in the middle of the night of March 22, 1978. Teams of five or six agents hustled people out of their beds, hitting the butts of their rifles all over the place to show them that they meant serious business. Then the search began: walls, floors, ceilings, toilets, flowerpots, table legs, beds, and other furniture were felt, touched, knocked, searched, and pierced to find gold, silver, and currency that may have escaped the previous measures. Moving out and talking to neighbors was forbidden so that no one could pass on the word of what was going on or smuggle valuable objects to other people.

Early in the morning of March 23, 1978, security and police forces, reinforced by the People's Army divisions, encircled all the flea markets. In Ho Chi Minh City the perimeter delimited by the Huỳnh-thuc-Khang, Tôn-thât-Dam, Tôn-thât-Thiêp, Hàm-Nghi, Vo-di-Nguy, Nguyên-Huê, Lê-Loi, and Lê-Thanh-Tôn streets was surrounded and all merchandise taken by force from their owners, in the midst of tears, cries, shouts, and blows from rifle butts, and loaded in trucks that drove away, rocking, round-bellied, full of fridges, TV sets, radios, ventilators, stereos, electric cooking machines, and materials, everything that thus far had helped little people to run their lives. In Cholon the perimeter delimited by the Tran-hung-Dao, Nguyên-tri-Phuong, Nguyên-Hoang, Hùng-Vuong, and Khong-Tu streets underwent the same fate. But this time, trucks carried away Chinese food. The entire country was raked. Be it coincidence or not, members of the Soviet delegation going back to their country were seen carrying TV sets, radios, and stereos looking very much like the ones seized at the flea markets.

To justify their action, the North Vietnamese authorities declared that these "merchants against their will" were not useful mouths and were lazy. They did not point out how these people came to be reduced to doing that. At least when they were doing business they were not depending upon anybody; now they have nothing at all, and they will depend upon the state. And that is the intention behind it all.

For the young people, numerous in these markets, since most of them no longer had family or, as is often the case, were supporting the entire family left by parents prematurely dead, they will from now on become "productive": they will break their backs in collective farms or in lumber camps, or they would be enrolled in the army to accomplish the "international duty" in Cambodia. Flea markets will then take on a new face.[3] Those who still have things for sale stand on the same spots all right, but they do not have any display in front of them anymore. They discuss the prices and describe the objects as best they can, and when the deal is almost struck, they take the buyer with them, go pick up the merchandise themselves, or go halfway with the buyer and bring the objects the other half of the way outside the marketplace; any trick will do to avoid being caught by the security forces. The authorities call this activity neo-colonialism—one might ask who the colonialist is this time—"seeking profits and even lewdness." Well, that is the only thing these people have to survive. They are hungry, and their children are dying. Since then, shops—particularly those the tourists are likely to see—have been allowed; they are part of the cooperative system run by the state.

In the North, where the economic conditions have always been more difficult, it has been relatively easy to impose drastic measures, but in the South, where the population knows what it is to work and to get results, the communists behaved in a particularly harsh and bloody manner to impose mediocracy and government by the stomach.

During the eighteenth, nineteenth, and twentieth centuries, the population of the South lived in opulence, thanks to the alluvium carried every year by the floods of the Mekong[4]; it is like the Nile in Egypt. From the monarchy (1720–1863) through the French regime (1863—1941), including the very harsh Japanese regime (1941–45), followed by thirty years of war against the communists, South Vietnam never suffered from hunger.

The communists arrive, and there is famine.

Rice is the basic food for the Vietnamese and the Southeast Asian people in general, the way wheat or corn is for the North Americans, sorghum, millet, or manioc for the Africans. To take away rice is to condemn the population to death. Yet the communists considered rice as booty, exactly like guns, ammunition, and the rest of it. All the reserves supplying the main cities, the provinces, and the Plateaux (Pleiku, Kontum, Banmethuot, Tuyên-Duc, and Lam-Dong) were sent to the North by huge convoys. The reserves of the State were seized *manu militari*—in every sense of the word—and the private reserves of the farmers, merchants, and companies were requisitioned without payment and sent to the North in exactly the same way. Big grain traders were arrested, executed, or at best then jailed, accused of speculation, capitalism, and all the usual fuss. The harbors of Saigon, Cân-Tho, and Rach-Gia were jammed with ships making their way between the South and Haiphong to the North.

For Westerners this may seem incredible, but it has been the same story for salt. The South Vietnamese shore, one thousand, seven hundred kilometers long (about one thousand, one hundred miles), streches from Quang-Tri to the Khmero-Vietnamese border and is ideal for developing huge salt pans such as those in Hon-Khoi, Sa-Huynh, Ninh-chu, Ca-Na, Duong, Phan-Thiet, Bà-Ria, and Bac-Lieu. All of them have been nationalized—you guessed it. The salt has been stored in warehouses of the state and distributed with a dropper, if one can say that.

For the people of the Plateaux who need the salt, its minerals, and its iodine more than anybody living on the shoreline to ensure their physiological and mental balance, this "shortage" rang like the toll of a passing bell. The FULRO[5] from the Plateaux rebelled against this, of course, and were massacred, which was part of the North Vienamese plan, as we shall see later. Control of the salt also means monopoly of the entire industry related to it, which is very important in Southeast Asia. Among other things, soya sauce and *nuoc-mam*, a fish sauce extremely rich in proteins and minerals essential for the body, are the most well known to Westerners.

After the rice and the salt, real staples, came meat and then, coffee and tea. Think of it—taxation of the last product triggered a war in New England some two hundred years ago. Right from the beginning of the occupation and without warning, all travelers were systematically searched by mobile units of the police and were dispossessed of their bags of rice, meat, and other staples as they brought them to their families in the cities. As early as July 1975, the food blockade began on the main roads linking the countryside with the cities and public and private reserves were confiscated.

When the cadres could buy twenty-one kilograms of first-quality rice per month at 0.40 dông per kilo, the population had to pay—when it could get it—8, 12, and even 16 dôngs per kilo on the black market; that is twenty, thirty, or forty times more than the official price. But then why buy rice on the black market? Once again, figures will enlighten more than a long speech. The monthly quota of third-quality rice (with sand) allocated by the Food Service was:

- Twelve kilograms per month or four hundred grams per day and per adult in 1975–76.

- Nine kilograms per month or three hundred grams per day and per adult in 1977–78.

•Nothing in 1979.

•Children under twelve always received half the quantity of an adult.

In terms of quantity, twelve kilograms per month is already barely enough; one needs a minimum of fifteen kilograms. With nine kilograms or less, health is definitely threatened. As far as quality is concerned, the government sells third-quality rice to the population, the type that was used before the fall of the South for poultry. It is mixed with paddy (nonhusked rice) and even sand. Very often, as a matter of fact, when there is no rice, the quota is replaced with sorghum, wheat flour, or sweet potatoes, which Vietnamese stomachs are not used to digesting.

The artificial famine aims at and is the consequence of the raids on large quantities of food. The blockade strategy aims less at preventing food going through the police controls, although it greatly reduces it, but on pushing farmers to bring out their stocks—some are well hidden—which will be confiscated. And believe this: this strategy extends the smallest details.

One example among others: at the crossroads of An-Lac, a few kilometers from the western terminal of Ho Chi Minh City, a security agent discovers a small piece of roasted meat in the betel basket of an old country woman a little bit hard of hearing: "Eh, what?! Oh, that? . . . It is a little piece of roasted meat for my son and his little children who have nothing to eat anymore," declares the poor woman.

"I can see it is meat," sneers the agent. "But it is forbidden; you have to throw it to the dogs."

No sooner said than done.

After orchestrating the famine, the authorities, who have laid hands on practically everything now, decide to make a "humanitarian gesture." In October 1975 the People's Committee of Ho Chi Minh City starts an operation to help the starving. On top of the quota of the ration card, every family will be entitled to another ten kilograms of rice; free! . . . Rotten. It comes from the war reserves hidden earlier in Cambodia in anticipation of the invasion by the North Vietnamese. On top of that, people realized that those who went to pick it up were spotted by the cadres as being the most destitute and were sent to the New Economic Zones.

On October 24, 1975, a triumphant official statement announced that the "South Vietnamese population had just been saved from starvation, thanks to the compatriots of the North who had fasted two days in a row in order to save 240,000 tons of rice intended to help the South out of famine." Indeed, the North Vietnamese were likely to have "saved" 240,000 tons of rice, but what they did not know was that the South got the war reserves. Then what happened to the 240,000 tons of rice? Sold? Sent to the USSR as repayment for the war debt?

While this event was taking place, Vo-Van-Kiet, president of the People's Committee of Ho Chi Minh City, bragged about having saved the urban population from starvation, which is proof that it was indeed starving in the first place. On the other hand, the North Vietnamese have been extremely discreet about the S/S *Vaico 16* affair. Around mid-November 1976, this cargo ship was loaded with one thousand, five hundred tons of first-quality rice at Rach Gia,[6] and various merchandise with a destination of Haiphong. But instead of going to North Vietnam, it went to the Philippines with 150 refugees on board. After eight months of negotiation with the Filipino government, Hanoi sent trusted envoys to Manilla to bring back the *Vaico 16*. No one ever heard anything about the ship, nor about the rice the fasting "compatriots" from North Vietnam had sent to themselves. That is a story we know of, but there are many we do not.

It happens that every year or two deliveries to the USSR and other countries of the COMECON are made and remaining stocks are near deterioration. The Ministry of Food in Hanoi then gives the order to clear the warehouses. It is a blessed period indeed when one knows that in three years (1975, 1976, and 1977) for instance every ration card entitled a family to two meters of cotton fabric and every person over sixty to two cans of condensed milk whose shelf time was over. It is an opportunity for the cadres to praise "the state, which always takes care of the population."

In an article published in *Le Monde* in November 1984, Claire Brisset describes the problems of deficiency in fats and vitamins—particularly A (blindness), and of the B group (beriberi)—and essential elements such as iron (anemia), iodine (goiter, deafness, et cetera.). "A chronic catastrophe," said a Swedish doctor stationed in Hanoi.

While this famine, this orchestrated "shortage," is evident, one can find absolutely everything in the state-owned stores, including imported luxury products. On the other hand, counters and stalls in the cooperatives for the people are empty most of the time.

NOTES

1. T.T. tried to kill himself several times without success. He died recently.

2. The Socialist Republic of Vietnam was proclaimed on July 2, 1976, and admitted to the United Nations as its 149th member on September 20, 1977, exactly two years after the first campaign of impoverishment started.

3. In Vietnamese these open-sky markets since then have been called standing markets.

4. The Mekong is 4,180 kilometers (about two thousand, six hundred miles) long. It has its source in China, goes through Yunnan Province, Laos (for which it serves as a natural border with Thailand), Cambodia, and South Vietnam, where it reaches the South China Sea through nine mouths; therefore its name "The Dragon with Nine Heads."

5. Front Unifié pour la Libération des Races Opprimées (Unified Front for the Liberation of the Oppressed Races).

6. Rach-Gia is an important harbor in South Vietnam, located on the Gulf of Thailand, near Cambodia.

CORRUPTION

He reigns like Indra himself; his sons are all obedient to him, and he has no grief. However, he is not content with this, but wishes more wealth and power.

—Elizabeth Seeger

Once the South was occupied, Hanoi would certainly have liked to see the nationalized factories and enterprises work as before. This would have been to its advantage and would have served its propaganda.

In fact, like an engine whose gas line has been strangled and cannot provide a maximum or even a normal output, people whose rations have been cut down are not likely to produce much. On top of that, these factories are essentially dependent upon the supply of raw materials and spare parts from capitalist countries that the communists have just thrown out. That is why a whole network for spare parts has been set up, whose intermediaries in Cholon are protected by the North Vietnamese. This same network also helps dispense merchandise and aid from free and even socialist countries. Of course, this could not be kept secret all the time. The engineer Hô-ky-Duc who studied in East Germany, became the director of the Raw Materials Department,[1] and Commander Tran-Doan,[2] chief of the Chemical Products Bureau of the Ministry of Economy, have been entrapped and jailed for corruption, probably because they did not have the right connections. But except for a few revealing cases such as these two, the North Vietnamese protect one another to give themselves as comfortable a life as possible.

Whatever the regime may be, it is always in the Chinese part of Cholon that corruption sets in first, it is said. After the spare parts and raw materials traffic, it is the food products: ginseng from Korea, sugar from Cuba, cigarettes from Great Britain, orange juice from Algeria, wines from France, beer from Germany, staples and also gadgets, great brand names as well as counterfeits—in short, everything, including the "family parcels" traffic, slipped through the Khmero-Thai border from Singapore and Hong Kong, via Cholon.

There are indeed parcels really intended for families, but others are supplying a real illicit industry, with warehouses and big, well-off suppliers. It is also Cholon that determines the daily gold and U.S. dollar announced the first thing in the morning on the BBC broadcast. Cholon is also the center for pleasures, riches, and opulence that attracts all cadres and leaders without exception. So when Western cameras cast a very chaste eye on the paddy fields in the middle of nowhere or on certain streets of Ho Chi Minh City where nothing is happening, one can see that this will not to even blur the image of reality.

It is also in Cholon that "greasy spoons" are mushrooming on sidewalks, on vacant lands, and even in private houses, beside the now nationalized and chlorinated former great restaurants. They are packed every evening with cadres and their families and the nouveaux riches of this business world, which looks more like booty markets of old time. Two streets away Vietnam dies of hunger and disease.

Cholon is, with the creation of the Import-Export Society and the Hoa community, in the central part of the triangle: Cholon, Singapore, and Hong Kong duty-free zones. It is there that cinnamon from Quang-Nam, rubber from the Red Lands, shrimp from the Mekong, et cetera, are being sold. According to a declaration made by Nguyên-co-Thach, foreign minister from Hanoi, the trade with Singapore was evaluated at U.S. $200 million per year.[3] This business is done by way of barter and is therefore unseen by the banks and the international system. The old trading methods are very much alive.

This corruption has pipelines to the outside world. Cadres can therefore enjoy imported luxuries and pleasures they could not even dream about in the North where they come from. Inside the country, other cadres and other soldiers of lower ranks are exercising another form of corruption. They use their uniforms, their weapons, and their means of transportation to organize the traffic of food. This, naturally, does not proceed without some trouble.

In December 1976 the security realized that these various forms of traffic were digging heavily into the state monopoly and began to stop trucks driven by the *bô-dôis*. Toward Christmas, as a matter of presenting gifts to one another, the two sides engaged in some shooting, which degenerated into pitched battles when the security tried to search the bags the *bô-dôis* hooked on their motorbikes at the Cu-chi post on the road from Tây-Ninh to Ho Chi Minh City. In January 1977 toward the Têt (Vietnamese New Year) a military truck from Cân-Tho, a large city on the banks of the Mekong River, went to Ho Chi Minh City. At the western terminal of Phu-Lam, the military police, warned in advance and "advised" by the security force of Cân-Tho, asked the driver to park on the roadside. He was caught with his load of meat "bought"—inexpensively as one can imagine—by the soldiers.

Another form of traffic has also been imported by the North Vietnamese. They[4] come to replace people who are dead, prisoners, and those who have been sent to the NEZ, and they receive a monthly ration of eighteen kilograms of first-quality rice per person, plus meat, fish, vegetables, and the rest, not forgetting what they get from the population. For these well-fed soldiers, it is easy to sell three to six kilograms of rice per month. One million newcomers proceeding in the same manner would represent three thousand to six thousand tons of rice per month, enough to feed decently two hundred thousand to four hundred thousand people with fifteen-kilogram rations per month or to improve the twelve-kilogram rations to fifteen kilograms for 1 or 2 million South Vietnamese.

Another traffic is offered on the black market: handling. The machines having been moved to the North, human beings have to pick up the rice, sort it out, bring it to the warehouses, fill up the bags, and then carry it to the cooperatives. At two hands per person, it is a lot of handling: a handful here, another one there, the rest of a bag aside, in short, and by the end of the day double or triple pay.

At the highest level of the hierarchy, corruption means all kinds of trafficking—why limit oneself?—and the visible signs of it are luxurious villas, shining limousines, vacations in Dalat, and pretty women. At a lower level of the hierarchy, corruption is maybe less visible but fierce all the same. A Bay-Sông-Lô[5]—his real identity is unknown—came back from the penitentiary of

Poulo-Condor toward the end of 1975 and assumed the responsibility of president of the People's Committee in Ho Chi Minh City's fashionable First District. He was replaced in 1976 by his deputy Duong-Van-Day, known for his opposition to the former regime, and the security force took the opportunity to search Bay-Sông-Lo's home. They found two thousand two hundred taels of pure gold. At U.S. $200 each, this represents the comfortable sum of U.S. $440,000 in less than a year.

Following the examples of their superiors, the lower ranks and the intermediary cadres see in the situation the golden opportunity to "live on the inhabitants." In 1975, for example, a militant just out of the underground and without any money, dressed in washed-out black cotton and wearing a black and white checked scarf around his neck, was in charge of searching the travelers' luggage at My-Thuan, about one hundred kilometers (sixty-two miles) away from Ho Chi Minh City. Five months later, this same militant was seen strutting about, wearing heavy bracelets of pure gold and around his neck not a cheap scarf, but a splendid gold chain worth ten taels or the equivalent of two thousand U.S. dollars.

Jobs are scarce. There is nothing one can do without having to pay for it. Corruption is practically a must if one wants to survive, but the scope of it is beyond what was there before, and in this society, far from being a classless one, the new elite is even more corrupted than the old one. Even if one accepts the notion that corruption is common practice in this part of the world—though nobody has the monopoly of it—nothing will be done unless you help it happen. Palm greasing indeed helps slip out favors held by those in charge.

In its January 1976 issue—not long after the fall of South Vietnam—the review of the Communist party, *Hoc Tâp*, was already denouncing the degenerated bureaucratic elements as devoid of seriousness and lacking virtue. It further stated that counter-revolutionaries and opportunists should be eliminated, as well as the old elements who were to be blamed for bureaucratism and corruption.

In 1981 journalist Tiziano Terzani[6] wrote that since the victory over the United States and despite the fine talks and the fact that the Communist party had all the means in its hands, the

Vietnamese people were plagued with famine, corruption, war, and oppression. The North Vietnamese, posing as the knights-errant in the South, have done even worse than the former regime.

More recently, Radio Hanoi stated that it was urgent to clean up the ranks of the Party, revive the militant spirit, and consolidate the confidence of the masses in the Party. On February 5, 1987, the French newspaper *Le Monde* noted that *Nhan Dan*, the Party's daily, had revealed that 190,000 militants had been expelled from the Vietnamese Communist party.

Beyond all this, there might be something to understand, too. Every time there is a communist takeover in the world, the first wave of revolutionaries represents the "indomitable will of the people"; their fire and their ardor are praised. Then they are eliminated because of their "serious mistakes" and replaced by more "moderate" elements. Then the people who have incarnated this spirit—ideologically hard to the core inside, but media wise outside—are also removed and replaced by others more in line with the permanence of the Party, which is to establish its control over the world and to present an image in accordance with its role. They can always say that mistakes were made by others before them and that theirs are only the result of these cumulative errors.

Violence and crimes are committed and then, as with Stalin for example, are "confessed" as "serious mistakes," justifying the fossilization of totalitarianism. After all, mistakes have been identified and admitted as such, and what is now in place can only be better, correct?

NOTES

1. Charter 78: *The Prison System in Vietnam*, Movement for the Defense of Human Rights in Vietnam.

2. Ibid.

3. Dân Quyen, *Review*, no. 75 (May 1984). This is only with Singapore, which is very difficult to evaluate with precision, a lot of trade being controlled, or done outside the international system, some "exchanges" being done at sea, et cetera.

4. Seven hundred thousand in 1979, according to Pierre Brocheux and Daniel Hemery, in *Le Monde Diplomatique* March 1980, 1,500,000 according to Hadji Khedoud in *l'Actualité* of April 1987. With a minimum average of three persons per family this would represent about 4,500,000 newcomers in South Vietnam.

5. Assumed name. *Bay*: means seventh, that is, the seventh rank in the Party; *Sông-Lô*: "Black River," branch of the Red River in North Vietnam, where the Vietminh won a victory against the French in May–June 1951.

6. In an article for the West German magazine *Der Spiegel*, quoted in the *Gazette* of Montreal, October 10, 1981. A well-known journalist, she went to Vietnam several times before and after the fall of the South. She also went to the Soviet Union to interview Premier Gorbachev.

"FREIHEIT DURCH ARBEIT"

Pronounce it "fryhight doorch arbite." For those who have never heard of the nazi concentration camps—yes, there are many—the title of this chapter was the welcoming formula for the prisoners entering those camps during World War Two: "Freedom through work." Another variant was "Arbeit macht Frei" ("Work makes you free").

One has to believe that the formula must have been wrong somewhere, since very few who worked there came out alive from these camps, unless we understand death as being a liberation. The key to freedom must have been momentarily lost. Now there is another formula such as "Arbeit ist Ehre" ("Work is honor"), and there you have the communist formula posted in the streets, out in the country, and in the Vietnamese camps, to be seen by all.

In fact, since the arrival of the North Vietnamese, the entire economic structure has been short-circuited and unemployment is appalling. Only a small percentage of the South Vietnamese people seem doomed to enjoy the glory of working in nationalized factories, where, however, the personnel are progressively replaced by North Vietnamese. The food blockade and artificial famine are aimed at controlling the entire population. Vo-Van-Kiet, president of the People's Committee of Ho Chi Minh City, arrived there to set up a plan elaborated in 1960. That is a long time ago.

Under his orders, the "Service of the Plan" must depopulate Ho Chi Minh City by reducing the population of 3.5 million to 1.8 million. This means that a "little" 1.7 million will have to disappear or skedaddle through the cemetery door or toward the New Economic Zones (NEZ) to make room for the newcomers of the North. This was, in a way, confirmed by Huỳnh-Tấn-Phát, president of the Provisional Revolutionary Government (PRG) when he declared that 3.5 million will have to clear out the cities of South Vietnam: 1.7 million from Ho Chi Minh City and 1.8 million from the other urban centers.

The other department of Vo-Van-Kiet is the Service of Transfer, whose duty is to send the ruined working class to the NEZ, where the people will be able to make a "new life" for themselves. In the cities, though, the deported will be replaced by a docile population who will give the tourists the impression that communism has taken control smoothly and in collective cheerfulness. Once impoverished, the South Vietnamese are expelled from the centers, particularly the capital, where it could become a dangerous, symbolic, and visible resistance nucleus. Therefore, people are sent to zones where malaria, typhus, typhoid, and other niceties of the kind deal with them severely. If they die, the North Vietnamese will not be offended, and if they survive it will be an extra percentage in production, complying with their propaganda as being the fruit of elaborated thinking and work done with the care of the people in mind.

Without work and income, thoroughly robbed, rationed, controlled, and card-indexed, their money invalidated, the people have no other choice but to go away. As if by chance, this is exactly the time when the North Vietnamese are "offering" the New Economic Zones:

- Hear ye, hear ye! . . . Five hundred dôngs for each voluntary urban family!
- Free transportation for all the people and their furniture (that is, what is left of them).
- A house!
- A plot and tools for gardening will be lent.
- Six months of rice for the entire family![1]

Given the circumstances, what could be better? In any case this is it, the "Ethiopianization." Neighbors and friends leave together to try to rebuild over there the cells they used to constitute here, to strengthen the links of friendship, and work together: a new beginning. A detail, though, before leaving: the family house. Some manage to sell it for a ridiculously low price. Others take apart the beams, the doors, the windows, and the pipes.

Once in the NEZ, the dream of settling down anew pops like a bubble. First, the NEZs are hard to reach. Then they are far from everything. The so-called houses are in fact just a bunch of straw huts open to wind and rain. No drinking water, no electricity, no school, no dispensary, no medicine. As for the plot for gardening, it is just fallow land. "Traps for Vietnamese, a dead land, a cemetery for children," a survivor will say. Indeed, without milk, poorly fed and without medicine or care, children are dying like flies, the first victims of a sinister farce.

The Lê-Minh-Xuan (name of a communist militant) NEZ is an experimental zone; the problem is that it is located on aluminiferous soil, unsuitable for agriculture. Drinking water must be brought in every day with a tank truck. One year after its inauguration the well-aligned huts are deserted. The Pham-van-Côi (name of another communist militant) NEZ near Cu-Chi is called the "bronze citadel of the revolution." It is located on an elevation. Wells dug by hand become real abysses before water can be reached. Water, also brought up by hand, is barely enough for the people, and the gardens will not make it. In the experimental collectivity of Bà-Diêm-Cu-Chi in the same region, it appears that in 1978 the water was also too deep and that proper means to supply this zone with drinking water have not been used.

The six-month ration of rice gone and agriculture having failed, the population of the NEZ return to the cities in the hope of finding something to eat. The survivors, haggard, famished-looking, take up residence wherever they can, since most of them have no homes. In one year, from May 1975, to May 1976, these comings and goings have displaced "only" five hundred thousand people, according to official figures. But to reach that number at least two or three times more must have been moving back and forth. To redress the situation, Vu-Dinh-Lieu, a fanatic militant from Nghê-An in Central Vietnam, was sent by Hanoi, as president of the Poeple's Committee of Ho Chi Minh City and of the NEZ, to replace Vo-Van-Kiet, fallen in disgrace because of his "lack of firmness."

Toward the end of 1976, however, a battle took place right in the middle of the night between Kiet's people and those of Lieu. The shootings riddled the perimeter delimited by the Doàn-Công-Buu, Nguyên-dinh-Chiêu, Yên-Dô, and Nam-ky-Khoi-nghia (formerly Công-Ly) streets. The entire region of Tân-Dinh-Phu-Nhuan was seized with great fear. It seems that Kiet showed more firmness than others had believed possible, since Lieu, at his post for only two weeks, did not show any sign of life. It was rumored that he was evacuated to Moscow to receive medical attention.

Yet in two weeks Lieu had not remained inactive. In the dead of night, the security forces and the police gathered the famished people in rags, who had left the NEZ, and sent them back to where they came from. Some simply disappeared. At the same time, the jobless, most of whom had been working in flea markets, were "invited" to go to the NEZ. In Biǹh-Hoa, former Chief-town of the Gia-Dinh Province (a new district of Biǹh-Thanh), the families designated for the NEZ began to panic when they saw the skeletons coming back from the zones. To help them there as ordered, soldiers came with bulldozers kept for the army and razed their houses, leaving them no choice.

Beginning 1978, near the Têt celebration of the new year, families deserting the NEZ—where three-fifths of the children had died—were so numerous that the People's Committee could not manage to repel them. With no money, no shelter, in rags, with ballooned bellies, disease- and vermin-ridden, without rationing cards, they settled on the sidewalks, under the verandas of deserted houses, to wait, for the end.

This invasion of bodies began in Nguyên-cong-Tru Street, the part of Saigon where the stock exchange used to be, then spread to other streets of the city, leaving every morning its contingent of corpses, those who had passed away during the night. No camera, whether from the East or the West, was invited to film this disaster. At this point of the tragedy, the population refused to move. No more departures for the NEZ. Fields were cleared and huts built. The population refused to leave. After all, why did people have to wait for so long and suffer so much instead of the government doing what was necessary, right from the beginning? Most of them had taken refuge in the capital city and towns of a certain importance to escape the atrocities, abuses, and injustices of the communists during the war. This time, no one moved; after all, if it was so great in the NEZ, how come the North Vietnamese themselves were not going there? Some people, however, took their authorization to move—which at other times was forbidden—went near the shores, and then left the country.

The authorities tried to send the farmers back to their villages. But those who had known the land for so long knew that going back there would not help them tie up again the thread of centuries, broken by arrogant people pretending to know everything better than the earth itself and those who had been working it for so long, the history of peoples and nations engraved in its furrows or in its paddy fields. The infrastructure was dismantled, the material stolen; the mainspring was broken. The worst was still to come.

And what about the millions of North Vietnamese who took refuge in the South in 1954–55? Where were they supposed to go? Up north? Where they were forbidden to go back to their ancestral towns and villages? This appeared to be too much of a contradiction. In fact, they were prevented from going back to the North so that they would not tell how things were in the South before the arrival of the North Vietnamese, but more than that, the Party had something else in mind: if it was sending people from the North to the South, it would not bring back some of them.

NOTE

1. This shows that the State has the reserves to "invest" in advance in projects such as this.

COLLECTIVIZATION AND LIFE IN THE COUNTRY

The principal reasons for starvation are man-made: wars that disrupt the pattern of food production; economic disincentives for farmers; poor distribution systems; and political corruption. There are also natural disasters that temporarily interfere with yields. But droughts and earthquakes do not last forever.

—Herbert I. London

While reducing the population in the cities, the communists proletarianize and collectivize the country by force; exactly what Stalin did to the Ukrainians in 1933.

In Central Vietnam, the High Plateaux dominate the narrow coastal strip where a chaplet of little paddy fields and some crops adapted to the region run along the shore. All strategists know that to hold the Plateaux is to control Vietnam, with a hand over Cambodia and Laos. They form the Anamitic Cordillera, covered with very dense tropical forest and spread over eight provinces: Kontum, Pleiku, Phubôn, Darlac (Banmethuot), Quang Duc, Tuyên Duc, Lam dông (Dalat), and Phuoc Long. Eight mountain ethnic groups live scattered on these Plateaux:

•The Sedang: 50,000.

•The Bahnar: 58,000.

•The Djarai: 134,000.

•The Rhades: 80,000.

•The M'nong: 14,000.

•The S'tieng: 36,000.

•The Koho: 43,000.

•The Cham: 32,000.[1]

A total of 447,000 people to which one must add 3,000 Nung, Man, and Thai from the high region of Tonkin, who took refuge there in 1954, and 350,000 Vietnamese. A grand total of eight hundred thousand people very, very independent-minded.

The communists know this strategic imperative and for a good reason: the Ho Chi Minh Trail goes from North to South through the entire region, and has been the starting point of their campaign since World War II. It was also the center of the United Front for the Liberation of the Oppressed Races (UFLOR) movements, then infiltrated and controlled by the communists themselves.

The war against the American forces over, these very independent-minded populations turned against the new oppressor. Hanoi will eliminate them by force indeed, but mostly through the food blockade: starvation. With these mountain people not having direct access to the rice of the Mekong Delta or to the salt and the sea products from the coast, it does not take a Ph.D. in political science to know how the North Vietnamese will eliminate them.

On the Plateaux, the mountain ethnic groups lived in the dense forest and in the bush regions bordering the streams. The Vietnamese live in villages spread over on the moutains, and they take care of the trade and commercial activities and administration. The jungle, suddenly silent, hides corpses of those who died from artificial famine. But nearby the little towns, the Vietnamese begin to see the skeletons of these mountain people who, in a final effort, tried to come closer in the hope that they would find some food. Their destiny, it seems, was to die. Some Vietnamese ventured to follow their trail, and that is how Minh Hiên, during one of his visits in the region, got to learn about what was going on. The South Vietnamese understood even better when, later on, these populations began to be replaced by North Vietnamese settlers and militants coming from the Red River Delta in North Vietnam.

We do not know precisely how many died, because the food blockade is silent, takes place in Vietnam, and therefore does not make the front page of any newspaper. But what we do know, is that it all started in 1954 with the signing of the Geneva Conference ensuring the neutrality of Laos and Cambodia within the peace treaty between North Vietnam and France. In 1956 the

"Civilian Irregular Defense Group" was created, then trained by U.S. military advisers, and about one hundred posts were established along the Lao-Khmero-Vietnamese border in order to maintain the neutrality of Laos and prevent the North Vietnamese from keeping in touch with their sanctuaries in these countries and from functioning in Vietnam and the region. In 1962 the neutrality of Laos was confirmed by the Vienna Conference. The Soviet and U.S. forces there withdrew, but not the North Vietnamese. Therefore, some two to three hundred U.S. advisers came back to help the Laotians protect their border and their neutrality until the Paris Accords were signed in 1973. We will see later why it is that behind all the peace talks, treaties, and accords, the North Vietnamese never ceased to violate them to suit their purposes, and also when they began to do this.

The extermination of the mountain populations by the communists has beheaded the resistance movement of the United Front for the Liberation of the Oppressed Races. Even today, in 1987, resistance commandos in Laos and elsewhere are being hunted down by the North Vietnamese.[2] Since the mountain people have always been demanding their independence from any central government and knowing how they have been using them against the former regime, the North Vietnamese did not want to keep such a force in their backyard. In November 1986, according to one of these moutaineers who found refuge in Thailand: "out of the population of a town of 4,000, only 206 have survived": 5.1 percent.

We also know that on the Plateaux in Northern Laos, the communist Yellow Rain[3] has killed 78 percent of the Hmong (Meo) population. From a population of five hundred thousand—a figure similar to that of the Vietnamese Plateaux—5 percent are still on the spot, fifty thousand are in Thailand, and thirty-five thousand in the West.[4] According to the French newspaper *Le Monde*, Mr. Gorbachev announced in Prague on April 10, 1987, that the USSR will cease to build chemical weapons.[5] Not long ago the Soviet Union was denying the presence of such plants on its territory. Victims examined by Canadian and American scientists are the unmistakable proof that Yellow Rain has been used in Laos since 1975, in Cambodia since 1978, and has been used in Afghanistan, despite the Geneva Protocol on chemical warfare of July 20, 1925.

These tribes having been decimated and the region—part of the Golden Triangle—having been flooded with yellow, red, blue, and blue-green rains, the cultivation of poppy had to be transplanted to the east. As of today, it is still in the mountain region, its natural habitat, but inside Vietnam, where there have been no rains, and is cultivated in the region of Diên-Biên-Phu[6] —a way to restore a very, very lucrative business, known to be financing international terrorism, among other things.

What is also certain: rain has drained the contaminants from the Plateaux to the Mekong Delta. In 1979–80 the waters of the Mekong were so contaminated that entire shoals of fish were floating belly up, which is—to our knowledge—not their natural way of swimming. We will talk about this pollution in another chapter.

In South Vietnam alone,[7] which covers sixty-four thousand square kilometers (roughly twenty-five thousand square miles), paddy fields, market gardens, and kitchen gardens represent more than forty-five-thousand square kilometers (roughly seventeen thousand square miles), that is, three-fourths of the total surface of good arable land, enriched every year by the alluvium of the Mekong, abundantly watered and basking in a generous sun. Of the twenty-two provinces of the South, twelve agricultural ones border the branches of the Mekong: the Bassac and the Transbassac, which form the Delta, a real cornucopia throughout the centuries, whatever the circumstances or wars there may have been. Two other provinces border the river Donai, the Eastern Vaico, and the Western Vaico. In the country, where very strong bonds with the soil are well known, farmers have been bowing in sweat to work. But since Marx and Lenin farmers are considered by the communists to be the "last capitalist class";[8] they must be eliminated, while the communists trumpet around the world that the soil should belong to those who toil on it.

In fact, there is no more private property; everything must belong to the state, which by the same token becomes the largest "private" owner ever: everything which was yours is ours, and since the State owns it, we—the minority who so decide, profit from it and represent what was yours, the people in whose name we have been maneuvering all along—own it and are the rulers of the land. This is centralized and pyramidal feudalism on a wide scale.

As in the Ukraine in 1933, the communists will use collectivization to fight and control the farmers. The South Vietnamese, less austere and more naive than their northern counterparts because of the generosity of the soil, believed that the communists would be grateful for their work and for feeding the nation. Not so: what is important is not the harmonious efficiency based on individual and national freedom, but the implementation and maintenance of socialism at all costs.

To reduce the farmers, the North Vietnamese will first ruin them. They are strictly forbidden to do private business or to carry rice anywhere. The state controls the entire commerce of rice, sets the price at which farmers have to sell it to the Agricultural Service, runs campaigns of impoverishment, and imposes the invalidation of the money obtained for the harvests. The Agricultural Service forces the farmers to sell the paddy at two hundred piastres per gia,[9] cleans the rice, and sends it to the North, while the population gets only a third-quality rice mixed with paddy, rice husks, and even sand. To eat decently, South Vietnamese in the cities have to buy the first-quality rice on the black market at three thousand piastres per kilo, bought for ten piastres per kilo from the farmers. Therefore, when the North Vietnamese say "the state must maintain an official price and ensure the trade of rice to help the needy population and prevent speculators from selling it on the black market," it sounds right, but it hides the fact and reality that rice is monopolized and sent to the North and that farmers are driven to get rid of their crops, "sell" their land, and get into the collective system.

For instance, over a period of two years, a farmer could have recovered from a bad harvest with the next crop—a farmer can make two of them per year. But on top of the fact that the North Vietnamese are monopolizing all the rice, they are also asking the payment of all taxes in kind, per crop, whether the harvest is good or not. Some say it represents an increase of 50 percent of the taxes. Moreover, the North Vietnamese are playing with the figures: the agricultural tax is equal to two gias—forty kilograms of rice—per công[10] of arable land. This means that farmers have to pay, in rice and whatever the outcome of the harvest, for 45 million côngs of cultivable paddy fields and for 19 million côngs of market gardens and kitchen gardens, a total of 64 million côngs. This tax of forty kilograms of rice—not paddy—per công of cultivable land is calculated in terms of harvest returning 18, 21, and even 22 million tons of rice,[11] which means that farmers had to pay a maximum of taxes with a minimum revenue. After calculation of other taxes and deductions of the state, it has been evaluated by those who have been through the experience that farmers were left with only one-fifth of their harvest.

Another fraud is the extension of the first scheme. The Agricultural Service accuses the French colonialists and former governments of having surveyed the paddy fields incorrectly. Therefore, the representatives of the service are arbitrarily increasing recorded surface by 20 percent and are, of course, making the farmers pay the taxes in consequence. Even if they are bound to the land, rice growers cannot afford too heavy taxes, and one by one, they have to yield their paddy fields to the state, and then their land. When the farmers have no more land of their own to cultivate, the state imposes collectivization: "instead of working and reaping the benefit of your work for yourself and your family, do it for me." It took six or seven years to bring the farmers down "legally," through state policy.

Then there is the vicious cycle of meanness: one has to beg for authorizations and gas-oil coupons needed to husk the strictly limited quantities of rice. It is forbidden to use the traditional grindstone or the wooden leg, just to make sure that everything going on is controlled by the state. It is also forbidden to raise ducks, "because they eat rice." Nothing could be further from the truth, since they eat snails, small fresh-water crustaceans, and everything they can find in the ponds they clean up, maybe some paddy, but that is what they find on the ground and which would be lost anyway. The point is that ducks give eggs—six dôngs apiece (today eight) or twelve to thirteen times the price of a kilo of rice at the official price,[12] meat and down. Enough to start a small enterprise, and that's what it is all about.

The calculated failure of this type of economy is blamed on the weather; it has worked for seventy years and still does. Up north in 1976, it was said that a wave of cold froze the seeds; the South had to send aid in a hurry to help their "compatriots." On the other hand, toward the end of the same year, in the South this time, it was said that drought faded all the ears of paddy.

There was also the war debt. In 1977 China required the entire payment of the debt of rice borrowed during the war of "liberation" and the South bore the cost of it. We will see a little bit later how in fact these weather fluctuations are used to form public opinion.

Now there are still a few general facts we need to examine. It is not that people and nations cannot or do not know how to produce what they need. They have done so for hundreds and even thousands of years. And after the dark years following World War II, we all thought—that is, those of age to do that—that this time we were on our way up. Everyone was going to get his or her fair chance to make it decently in this world and ensure a better future for their children.

Many nations have proven this to be true. Japan, destroyed by the war, is now a leading country in the field of economy. Taiwan, which was very poor in the sixties, is very competitive today. So is South Korea. So was Vietnam. The fact is that these countries were not using their best energies for ideology, but to learn, to create, to adapt, and to count. And it worked. It is not free enterprise that ruins this world; on the contrary, but more and more human flaws are used to discredit it and help establish another system.

Droughts and earthquakes are indeed terrible, but wars are even more disastrous and despicable. In a book—now out of print[13]—a little section titled "War Has Ruined the World" tells the whole story: World War II cost $375 billion in gold. With that money, every family in North America, Europe, and the Soviet Union could have had a house with all the furniture going with it and enough money to live comfortably. On top of that, every city with more than two hundred thousand people would have received a fat present to build schools and hospitals. By the way, taxes during World War I were supposed to be a provisional measure for the duration and the financial support of the conflict. The maintaining of these taxes must have been an oversight on the part of the warlords, busy preparing for World War II.

Nations do not need to be enslaved. There is no need for Vietnams, Laoses, Cambodias, Afghanistans, Ethiopias, and others of that sort. The questions, though, remain: if all the war matériel went up in smoke, where did the money go? Who benefited from it? Who lost from it? We must not forget that World War I and some forty-five or so other "local" conflicts have also cost a great deal of money. Just as an example, the Iran-Iraq war alone has cost, thus far in 1988, $450 billion,[14] and even if the value of the dollar is not the same, it is still a lot of money.

We believe it was Montesquieu who wrote: "I love farmers. They are not erudite enough to reason crookedly" or something to that effect. Even if today they are as erudite as anyone can be, the fact remains that they cannot lie to nature, but others have done it for them, and Vietnam, for that matter, is more than simply the lesson of a "lost war."

NOTES

1. From the last available statistics of 1967.
2. *L'Express*, November 27, 1987. Two-hundred resistance fighters were caught by the Vietnamese army, which, having been underground before, did not want to see any underground force against itself.
3. Also used in Afghanistan.
4. From Jane Hamilton-Merritt's article "Génocide au Laos" ("Genocide in Laos") in the French version of the *Sélection du Reader's Digest* of October 1980.
5. April 15, 1987.
6. See the economic map of Vietnam, p. 134.
7. Here Central Vietnam is not included. All of Vietnam covers three hundred thirty-five thousand square kilometers.
8. Raymond Aron, "De Marx et du Marxisme" ("Of Marx and Marxism"), *l'Express*, May 13, 1983.
9. Gia: is a former measure, still in use, of forty-two liters of paddy or twenty kilograms of clean rice. We are talking about piastres because this was before the first invalidation of money on September 20, 1975.
10. A công is about ten metric ares (one thousand square meters) or 10,764 square feet.
11. *L'Etat du Monde 1983*, Maspero.
12. According to Pierre Brocheux and Daniel Hemery, in *Le Vietnam exsangue*, a duck's egg was worth five dôngs in Ho Chi Minh City in February 1983, when the average salary of a worker was one hundred dôngs. Refugees have revealed that a duck egg cost seven dôngs in Ho Chi Minh City in 1983, eight in 1984, apiece of course, not a dozen.
13. *La France et sa Littérature, guide complet dans le cadre de la civilization mondiale* (*France and Its Literature, a Complete Guide in the Context of World Civilization*), by Pierre Bornecque (les Editions de Lyon), p. 618.
14. "Table Rase" ("Tabula Rasa"), Radio-Quebec, January 13, 1988.

THE FIVE-YEAR PLANS

With artificial famine, concentration and re-education camps, the New Economy Policy, and the New Economic Zones, here they come again, the five-year plans "producing 13,000 pairs of sunglasses so dark that you could not see the sun through them even when looking directly at it, and manufacturing thousands of children's plastic balls that burst like soap bubbles as soon as they were kicked."[1] They also build on paper tractor factories by the thousands that do not exist in reality and whose funds allocated for their construction have disappeared between the decision making and the absence of realization.

In "reunited" Vietnam the first five-year plan of 1976–1980 had set as objectives to:

•Eat one's fill of exquisite food.

•Dress oneself warmly and nicely.

The goal of the second plan of 1981–85 was not to give every family a Volkswagen, as Hitler had promised to the Germans, nor to produce more, bigger, and larger than the United States, as Khruschev roared, but to equip every house with a television set and a refrigerator. One wonders why, since before the arrival of the North Vietnamese and their pillaging, everybody already had all that at home, unless, of course, they took them away to replace them with other ones.[2]

For the first plan, the North Vietnamese had all the cards in their hands: the crops, the food, and all the goods, the means of production, in one word everything, including the textile industry, one of the most modern in Southeast Asia. During the first days of the occupation of the South, hosts of cadres from Hanoi swarmed over the country, satchels on their backs, paper and pencil in hands, establishing without respite, like ants, statistics for the five-year plan of 1976–80. In December 1976 Lê-

Duan, secretary of the Party, praised the plan in front of the National Assembly in Hanoi: Vietnam was going to be happy; statistics were proving it. They were even posted on huge advertisments hanging on one of the Unions'[3] House walls, formerly the Sporting Circle of Saigon, on Xô-Viêt-Nghê-Tinh Street: within five years, that is by 1980, Vietnam would have to produce for the entire nation and per year:

•Twenty-one million tons of rice, the equivalent of the best years.

•Sixteen million tons of pork, to which one must add beef, lamb, poultry, and the products of the sea.

•Four hundred and fifty million meters of fabric.

•Two million tons of cement.[4]

•One million, three hundred thousand tons of fertilizers.

•Five billion kilowatt hours of electricity.

With these figures in mind, applying an equal sharing of the goods—as has never been in force in any communist country—every person out of a population of 52 million at that time[5] should have received:

•Four hundred kilograms of rice per year or thirty-three kilograms per month, one kilogram per day and per person, without distinction of age—children under twelve usually receiving half an adult's ration. For the time being, adults were receiving four hundred grams per day, children under twelve, two hundred.

•Three hundred and seven kilograms of pork or twenty-five kilograms per month and per person, eight hundred grams per day for each individual, without distinction of age, to which beef, lamb, poultry, and products of the sea should be added.

Tea, coffee, and rubber—an extremely important export—were not mentioned in the five-year plans. The seventy-five thousand hectares of *heveas* (rubber trees) that formerly did belong to the

Société des Plantations d'Hévéas (SIPH) and the Société des Plantations des Terres Rouges (Société des Hévéas de Tây-Ninh) have been nationalized, but the yearly production of one-hundred thousand tons of rubber is entirely bought by the USSR.

Early in 1981, that is, at the beginning of the second five-year plan, Hanoi rectified the statistics of the first plan, specifying, in case the population did not notice, that "the cadres made beautiful reports, but that their work was not exactly all what it should have been." New rectifications, some modifications, new objectives, and again way off target.

Grains for instance: the quota was set retroactively, believe it or not, so that the figures would get a chance to match the production, set at 16.5 million tons for 1979 and 21 million tons for 1980, which, on the average, is still the equivalent of the good years: 18.75 million tons. In reality, Vietnam produced 13.5 million tons of rice in 1979, according to local sources, 15 million tons in 1980, and 13 million in 1982, according to *l'Etat du Monde 1983*.[6] But even with these figures, and if we remove discreetly the people who have died in the meantime, that is, if we still keep the same figures as before in terms of population, every person should have received:

- Two hundred and fifty-nine kilograms of rice in 1979 or twenty-one kilograms per month, seven hundred grams per day.

- Two hundred eighty-eight kilograms of rice in 1980 or twenty-four kilograms per month, eight hundred grams per day, without distinction of age.

Instead of that, the ration per person per month in 1975–76, when the communists had the hands on all the reserves, was twelve kilograms per month and per person, then nine kilograms in 1977–78, and 0 kilograms in 1979–80. The ration of pork and fish was set at one kilogram each per family and per month during the first five-year plan and five hundred grams at the beginning of the second plan. This must have been the time when people appreciated having a single-parent family with only one child.

With a normal production of four tons per hectare, and with 4,500,000 hectares of paddy field in the South, the crops should have been indeed 18 million tons of rice per year. On top of that, propaganda was announcing that new paddy fields had been added to the existing ones.

As far as energy is concerned, the North Vietnamese had planned a production of 5 billion kilowatt hours of electricity, coming mostly from the hydro plant of Danhim. A huge project, it was supposed to provide energy for all of South Vietnam and half of Central Vietnam and feed the TV sets and refrigerators promised by the second plan. This hydro complex, located near Dalat, comprises a dam built at one thousand, two hundred meters altitude feeding through two pipelines of three kilometers at forty-five degrees the power station Krong-Pha (Da-Hoà), near Tour-Cham in the province of Phan-Rang. Two hundred and seventy electric towers support the high-voltage lines meandering over mountains and through valleys of Da-Hoà to the distribution center of Thu-Duc. This complex was financed and erected by Japan as a compensation for war damages done during World War II. Built and finished under Ngô-dinh-Diêm, it operated for a while and then was sabotaged by the communists. Finally, the North Vietnamese were controlling the country. The only thing they needed to do was to repair the damage they had caused to the plant. What they did, instead, was to cancel the rural electrification program of South Vietnam. People could get electricity only between 6:00 P.M. and 9:00 P.M. Beginning with the second five-year plan, Saigon, which had the reputation of being "the pearl of the Far East," was gradually left in the dark once it became Ho Chi Minh City. At the beginning of 1982, the city had four power cuts every week: two during the day, two during the night, by shifts of two sections of the city at a time.

After the fall of the South (mention has already been made about it earlier in the book), the North Vietnamese claimed they would bring the electricity to working order within a few months. For years now the South Vietnamese have been waiting to see the bulbs lighting darkness.

NOTES

1. Michael Binyon *Life in Russia* (Hamish Hamilton), p. 15. London.

2. In the South, at least, since every home had all that and more.

3. It is called a "Union" but has nothing to do with what we know in the West.

4. It should have been easy: millions of dollars have been sent to Vietnam by Western nations to build various kinds of plants and factories.

5. North and South.

6. Maspero. Forget about people; save the plan.

THE TRANSFORMATION OF THE VIETNAMESE SOCIETY

Totalitarian governments are those whose rulers see the whole of society, economy, culture, and personality as appropriate fields for government regulation.

—Jeane J. Kirkpatrick

One of the priorities of Hanoi in South Vietnam is to privilege the section of thc population that is ready to support and maintain the communists in power and then to transform the entire nation into its image. Children are the prime target of the regime. Here, as anywhere else, they represent the future, whatever that may be.

Soon after the arrival of the *bô-dôis* in South Vietnam, one could see children and adolescents wearing shorts gathered under the lambent streetlights or in schoolyards when they were spared by the power cuts. Young cadres were teaching them Eastern European songs while clapping their hands. Two or three months later, however, there were no more songs.

To distract the attention of the adults, the North Vietnamese ask them to stage plays or to go into sports, particularly soccer, thereby renewing with the Youth and Sport Movement of Colonel Ducoroy in 1940–45.[1] The two soccer teams from Hanoi and Haiphong were sent on a mission to the South to meet—in all friendship, of course—the teams of Saigon-Ho Chi Minh City and Cân-Tho. The two teams from the North were so sportively booed, hissed, hooted, and called names by the crowd of spectators that meetings of this kind were forbidden until the South became socialized, believe it or not.

Cadres also organize "spontaneous" meetings between young singers and dancers and "informal" meetings of small groups coming to fiddle around with a balloon on the sidewalks under the streetlamps. That too soon came to an end: hungry bellies do not listen well.

The North Vietnamese want to indoctrinate the population, who do not want to be manipulated. In the middle, the artists act, like the teachers, as a transmission belt between the two. They do not want to be unemployed or, worse, sent to the NEZ. Knowing that, the Party:

- Nationalized all theaters.

- Organized indoctrination courses for the artists, authors, and composers at the Vung-Tàu camp.

- Sifted all the plays with a fine-tooth comb.

- Showed all the old movies from the Eastern Bloc countries and even produced one on the fall of Saigon in which the roles of the Americans were played by Soviet actors.

Movies from the West are labeled "capitalist and reactionary propaganda." The "new" theater following the Party's line, playing under the direction, surveillance, and strict control of the cadres, naturally deals with the class struggle, the liberation of the people, and the revolution. Actress Phung-Ha, more than seventy years old, was pulled out of her thirty-year retirement to produce herself, unsteady and husky, in the role of Lu-Bo, which she immortalized during her prime years.[2]

Finally, the people decided that they had been manipulated long enough and deserted the theaters, henceforth visited only by the cadres and their family. Movie theaters were just as successful, but on the other hand, forbidden Western music, such as jazz, for instance, drew crowds, including the cadres. The leaders realized that they had also lost on cultural ground and the arts were required to keep a low profile.

Meanwhile, in the street, people who had nothing to eat had to resort to theft, prostitution, and rummaging garbage in order to survive. Adolescents who in the past were selling newspapers, shining shoes, and eating with the street merchants were left with nothing, the only daily being distributed within a restricted circle of communists. As for the shoe-shiners, the *bô-dôis* were wearing espadrilles. Children, therefore, end up in the garbage dumps. Others, also in rags, now style themselves as pickpockets, bag stealers, beggars, or procurers.

In the beginning, the North Vietnamese arrested these offenders, executing some in public places as examples, and published their pictures in the Party's daily. Since these shootings were looking too much like political executions, it was decided that arrests should be limited to a minimum. Prisons, however, being filled in no time, arrests of this kind were stopped.

Women without income, whose husbands had disappeared in camps or in prisons, began to prostitute themselves on the street or at home. Their clients: the occupation troops, of all ranks. The North Vietnamese tried to clean up Ho Chi Minh City through raids and arrests, but nothing changed. People did not need to be arrested, but to be fed.

During the American presence—and probably the French before—prostitutes were attracted by money and imported goods. Under the communist regime, even mothers had to sell themselves in order to survive and try to feed their children or support elderly parents. Prostitution tripled, then quadrupled. When Ho Chi Minh City tried to open up a little to tourism in 1979,[3] the People's Committee of the city fitted up House 18—a former bordello for soldiers—in the harbor and recruited its most beautiful prostitutes. Now, during the former regime, when prostitution had not reached such proportions, Mrs. Ngo-Ba-Thanh, a lawyer, and Huynh-Lien, a woman Buddhist priest, launched the movement for the "right to life for women," organizing public demonstrations, and throwing discredit on the government, thus favoring the communists, who found in this, material for their propaganda. Since 1975, strangely enough, no one has heard anything about the right to life for women.

During the invasion of South Vietnam, the North Vietnamese used Laos and Cambodia as sanctuaries, but more actively as penetration and withdrawal zones, or as rear or forward bases, according to their needs. After the fall of South Vietnam, Hanoi controlled Laos in 1975 and invaded Cambodia in late 1978. Now, whoever lays hands on Laos or at least part of it is grabbing a share of the Golden Triangle.[4] In that country, expeditionary forces of sixty to seventy thousand Vietnamese were confronted with the fierce resistance of the Meo (Hmongs), mountain tribesmen who were growing poppy in the highlands. They were eliminated through food blockade and chemical warfare.

Once the regime was in place in Laos in August 1975, the trading of opium and heroin, interrupted during the hostilities, was reorganized and got going even stronger than ever before, but this time under the control of Hanoi. In South Vietnam opium would reach a price of twenty-eight thousand to thirty thousand dôngs per kilo.[5] Ten percent of the women and 90 percent of the men among addicts consume twenty to thirty dôngs' worth a day.[6] This means that a worker who would indulge in that could smoke his or her salary in three to five days.

As early as 1976, Ho Chi Minh City was flooded with drugs. Everywhere retailers, dealers, and go-betweens of all caliber were heavily involved in the trade. Even former fashionable intellectuals are "surprised to find themselves doing this sort of work." Then, forgetting that they are being occupied by "compatriots" with a brainwashing ideology, the young people in particular, also the dealers themselves who want to forget the morass into which they slid to survive, use drugs and dream that they are in a Western country and that the communists have finally understood the monstrosity of their policy; in one word, everything is fine in a brave new world.

Right in the heart of the city, on the sidewalks of Nguyên-công-Tru, Vo-di-Nguy, and Hàm-Nghi streets or on the docks of Chong-Duong, small retailers inject a kind of brownish liquid with unclean syringes into the veins of the addicts. Others are using their kilo of heroin as an investment, "in case the Reds invalidate the money once again," which they will. Still others organize parties during which everyone can get stunned with as many puffs as he or she wants.[7]

All these people will have to wake up to a harsh reality. The communists themselves feel the youth slipping through their fingers. True enough, no one has ever really been able to control desperate people. They tried to set up clinics where traditional medicine and the experience of those who have been through the ordeal attempted to help the youngsters, sent later for re-adaptation to the NEZ.[8] Not that it changes anything in their illicit trading, but the North Vietnamese—and we understand it is spreading to others communist countries—are becoming aware that this weapon used against Western youth can blow up right in their face, without any foreign meddling.

The production, consumption, and trading of drugs are on the increase today, since hashish and opium poppies are also being grown in Dalat, South Vietnam.[9] According to the UN annual report of 1986 concerning the Vienna Convention on drugs and narcotics, of the 185 countries and territories in the world, five have refused to divulge any information on the subject: Bolivia, Cambodia, North Korea, Liberia, and Vietnam.[10] However, the Dainam Press Agency (DNTT, Thailand) reported in July 1988 that a cargo ship flying a Panamanian flag was hailed by the U.S. Coast Guard. On board were three Americans, one Briton, one New Zealander, and a crew of thirteen Thais, Indonesians, and sailors from Singapore. Seized: seventy-two tons of marijuana, loaded by the bô-dôis in Danang Harbor, under the supervision of a cadre dispatched from Hanoi. On September 6, 1988, the same source reveals that FBI agents and the police of Massachusetts have arrested four Vietnamese and seized 300 million dollars' worth of cocaine. The drug had been sent from Hong Kong to the United States.

Another danger is overflowing the streets of the country. After the North Vietnamese invasion in 1975, alcohol of all sorts from the export counters, boutiques, the American PX (post exchange), closed for two years, and local distilleries flooded the place, and the *bô-dôis*, like the cadres, did not ask twice for the privilege of trying them all. The production of beer by the only French firm (the Brasseries et Glacières de l'Indochine) was largely sufficient for a population with little liking for that sort of drink. Since 1975, the North Vietnamese have been sending the reserves and almost all of the production to "Big Brother," who does not mind trying his throat on anything drinkable, if one can judge by the real problem of alcoholism in the Soviet Union. It is common knowledge that the Soviets drink imported vodka (the best, it is said, and therefore only for those who can afford it), local vodka, alcohol made of potatoes (this must be more like German war production of fuel during World War II than a beverage), alcohol made of beets, alcohol made of anything you can find, wine, and beer. Some even say they drink antifreeze.[11] It must be cold indeed out there, but it sure keeps the throat and the pipes clean.

Economy of Vietnam

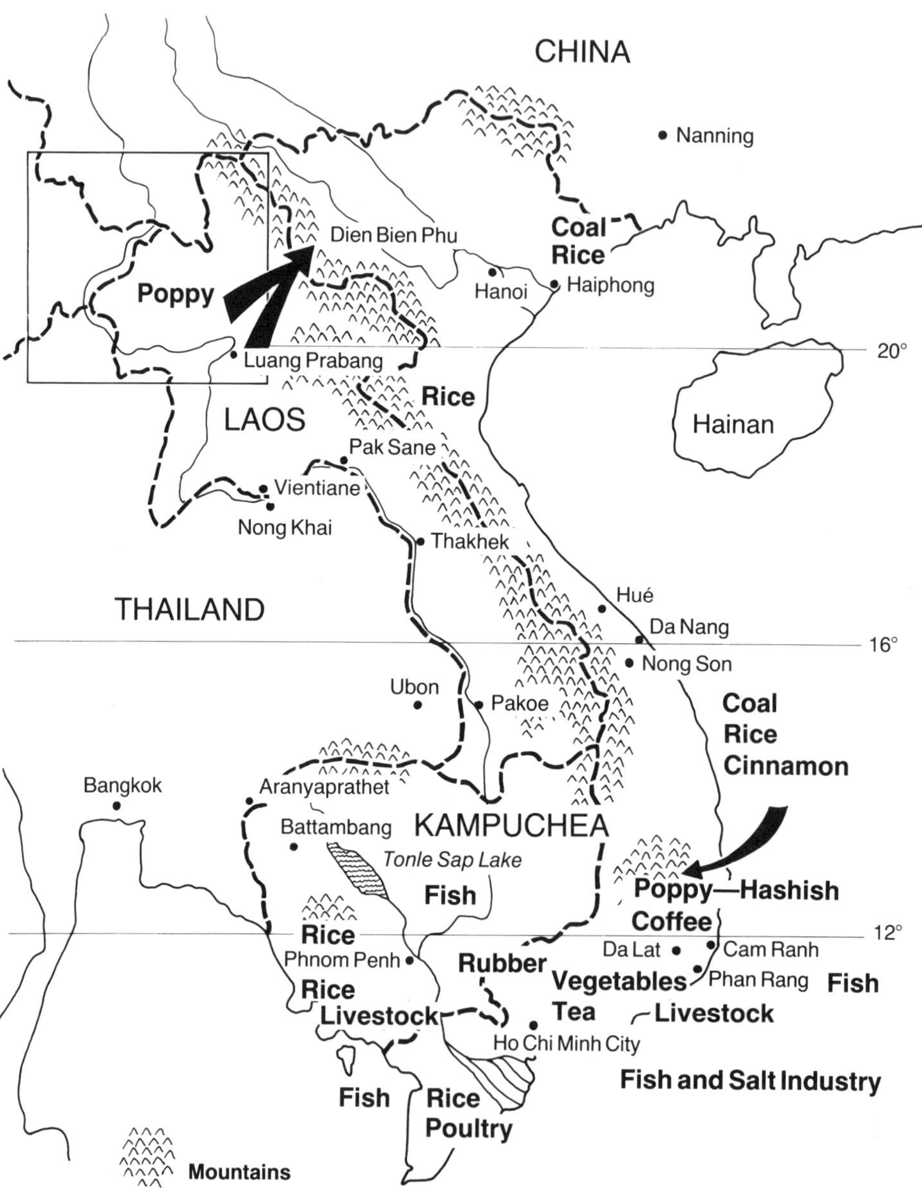

Today in South Vietnam it is rice alcohol, or *tchum-tchum*, that is devastating, particularly in the countryside; of course farmers can hide some rice, or believe they do, and distill it. In fact one would be surprised, since ducks are forbidden because they eat rice, to find people brewing moonshine alcohol. First, it is cultural, traditional. *Tchum-tchum* is to Vietnam what moonshine is to the Americans, ale to Great Britain, wine to France, whiskey to Scotland, and beer to Germany. Second, it is indeed difficult to control absolutely everything in the delta, since rice is produced there and a good part of the black market of that grain is done in the countryside. Third, it pays good money to local authorities who collect a handsome "provincial tax." And last, but not least, it is another way to keep the population under control. According to Minh-Hiên, it is another form of opium, encouraged by the system.

It is so real that whereas in the olden days commerce was flourishing at the western terminal of Ho Chi Minh City—travelers were getting out of the buses right in the middle of stands overflowing with all kinds of rice, raw and roasted meats, lard, fruits, and vegetables—today the entire place smells of *tchum-tchum* and *tchum-tchum* only. And the authorities do not say anything about it, as if Soviet alcoholism had arrived in Vietnam with the Marxist-Leninist manuals.

The poorer a nation is, the more people will try their hand at gambling. In Vietnam people who refuse to give a few dôngs to the state's "saving account"—this despite the cadres' warning—do not hesitate to buy lottery tickets sold by the local People's Committees. They even sell the few remaining goods they may have, borrow, or even steal in order to do that. Owners of clandestine lotteries, being watched over by the cadres who manage the official gambling industry, had to close their "boutiques." Under the former regime, the management of the lottery for the National Reconstruction made weekly draws for all of Vietnam. Under the North Vietnamese regime, because of the transportation problems—they are not an accident, are they?—and also because of the way communism separates, and isolates everything so that people cannot get a general perspective of what is going on, each branch of the communist administrative sections organizes its own lotteries. No one ever hears about the eventual winners.

NOTES

1. He created the Physical Education High School of Indochina at Phan-Thiêt and organized numerous championships.

2. Famous play inspired by the intrigue of the romanticized history of China's Three Kingdoms (A.D. 220–65). It was "renovated" by the North Vietnamese. Actor Thanh-Duoc, well known in South Vietnam, defected to the West on February 17, 1984, the evening of his very first show in West Berlin. He had to leave his wife and his children in Ho Chi Minh City.

3. Today one can see once in a while tours advertised in Western newspapers.

4. Laos, Burma, and China.

5. The price of thirty thousand dông has been confirmed in a report filmed by Australians and broadcast by Radio-Quebec on September 9, 1985.

6. Same source: "1984: The Year of the Mouse."

7. A puff of opium is the size of a pencil's tip.

8. From "1984: The Year of the Mouse," Radio Quebec, September 9, 1985.

9. *Van-Nghé-Thên-Phong (VNTP)*, no. 261 (December 15, 1986).

10. AFP, Vienna, published in *La Presse* (Montreal), November 20, 1986.

11. This was said on a TV program some years ago on the American and the Soviet armed forces. A Soviet pilot revealed that he had drunk some of his plane's antifreeze.

PUBLIC OPINION AND INTERNATIONAL AID

Hornets do not suck the blood of eagles, but pillage bee-hives.
—Shakespeare

The radical and rapid transformation of a prosperous society such as South Vietnam into a disastrous human, social, and economic situation, throwing out refugees by the hundreds of thousands, shook the world's public opinion, that is, those who still have an opinion of their own.

After having invaded the country, put into place their police network, ruined and starved the nation, sold part of the population, and liquidated another part of it, the North Vietnamese would blackmail the West to get international aid, ransack the refugees who are now nationals of their host countries, and cover up for the failures of the regime.

People for diametrically opposed reasons—some out of genuine generosity and charity, others to support the communist regime, others still to further the cause of internationalism no matter what—were in favor of sending all possible aid to Vietnam, as if feeding the monster would keep it quiet. This is ancient Greek policy, based on the legends of gods being appeased by the sacrifice of virgins once in a while. Today the West lets a country be devoured by the communist hydra every time it feels hungry, in order to keep it hushed for as long as possible. One can predict, however, that it will stop only when there are no more countries to be swallowed up.

Other people thought that since the communists are responsible for the disasters they create, they should repair the damages themselves. They are mature enough to perpetrate chaos; they should be mature enough to control it and to reverse a trend they initiated. But, like many other countries dying because of their totalitarian regime, the North Vietnamese used blackmail: "West without heart," "the inhumanity of democracies," et cetera. And mind you, the West had better not point out to them that they have massacred millions of people since 1917! "What?! You are meddling in the internal affairs of our countries! We will not let the revolution be belittled." In short, how does the West dare to talk about human rights? For the communists they are only a *vue de l'esprit.* As for freedom and liberties, they are simply a different subject. Indeed, if one looks into their semantics the same words have a totally different meaning.[1]

Therefore Hanoi cheerfully sends messages for international aid, not considered as meddling in its internal affairs anymore. And here is probably one of the keys concerning this subject: receiving aid from other nations is fine and deserves a little bit of theatrical footwork, but the distribution of it is indeed an internal matter. The North Vietnamese deal with it on their own terms and according to their plans. It boils down to making wealthier or more generous countries work for their system. They are not concerned with the fact that these nations may have worked on themselves to achieve freedom, democracy and liberty; socialism should be the new center of the world, and other nations are supposed to act according to this vision. The rest is only a matter of tools, means, and tricks:

•In early 1976 Radio Hanoi announced that "bad weather" had destroyed 50 percent of the winter/spring crops[2] and that the cold wave had frozen all the seeds. However, Hanoi did not state—probably an oversight—that in South Vietnam, where most paddy fields are, it practically never freezes, and up north, where the temperature does not go under seven degrees Celsius in general, four degrees in extreme cases, the seeds do not freeze either. The weather is rigorous only on the Plateaux, but there, there are no paddy fields. What is interesting, though, is that Europe had just experienced a cold wave at that time, and Hanoi may have hoped it could draw a parallel between the two situations and that the world would soften at Vietnam's fate.

•Early 1977, Hanoi announced that the summer/fall crops had been 70 percent destroyed, this time by drought and insects. It is true again that Europe had also experienced a heat wave. But as a matter of fact, droughts are unknown in the Mekong Delta's tropical weather. As for the insects, if the North Vietnamese had supplied pesticides as promised, that probably would not have happened. Now it is also true that many countries in the Third World and in the West alike are concerned with the use of pesticides. And Vietnam had a beautiful opportunity to develop more natural ways of growing food without chemicals; any ecologist would tell you that.

- In September 1978 Hanoi announced this time that the early floods of the Mekong had destroyed 70 percent of the crops. Mind you, one year earlier it was saying that the region had suffered drought in a region of flood. But here the problem is different. The floods of the Mekong are like those of the Nile in Egypt: they are nature's way of depositing fertile alluvium on their banks, which is why the harvests are so good in that region. Oh, a last point: Hanoi also forgot to say in September 1978 that these floods only occur after the August harvests.
- Early 1979, Hanoi accused China of having provoked a war with Vietnam and therefore prevented it from harvesting its crops. This was also the time Hanoi chose—just a little earlier, in December 1978—to start the costly campaign against Cambodia, in order to put in place a pro-Hanoi/Moscow government in Phnom Penh and to reinforce, on the threshold of China, a Soviet-Vietnamese zone.

All this allowed Hanoi to ask for international aid while keeping the Vietnamese population in a state of famine: the ultimate justification to control conquered nations and to allow the communists to pursue their policy of expansionism that will cause other genocides.

In 1978 Pol Pot declared that if the Vietnamese expeditionary forces—which established the pro-Hanoi Heng Samrin—stole practically all the food in Cambodia, it was because Vietnam was hungry. Whose fault was it? Instead of attacking Cambodia, Vietnam would have been better off growing its crops and would therefore have had no reason to invade and pillage a neighbor.

At the UN in October 1979, Prince Norodom Sihanouk asked free nations to send enough food so that Vietnam could withdraw its occupation forces—in short, to feed the ogre so that it would keep quiet for a while. That is exactly what the communists were hoping for: that the West would provide for the needs of the red troops storming the democracies. Learning about the massacre of Cambodians,[3] countries of the free world sent all they could. But it was the North Vietnamese who laid their hands on the international aid, and only a small fraction of it made it through to the victims.

Along with the war booty, this newly arrived aid in Cambodia was loaded on trucks leaving for North Vietnam via Ho Chi Minh City. It is in this city that the South Vietnamese discovered the shady side of this story, while the West believed it was helping the victims of this plunder.

In terms of foreign aid, Nguyên-Van-Canh writes that between the end of 1973 and mid-1976, France has sent about U.S. $363 million to North Vietnam.[4] That includes sums not used by the former South Vietnamese government.

There were also many agreements for offshore oil exploration, construction of plywood and paper mills and a cotton factory among others. In 1978 two joint French-Vietnamese companies were formed. According to *Paris-Match* of April 3, 1987, and in an article concerning the *Ariane* space program, these joint companies, often under a "cultural umbrella," are nests of spies, of all communist countries working for Moscow.

Nguyên Van Canh also writes that Sweden, Holland, Italy, Denmark, Belgium, Finland, Norway, and Austria sent at least 631 million U.S. dollars' worth of aid in loans and grants for hospitals, a paper mill, irrigation projects, oil exploration, a cement plant, harbor and dockyards development and equipment, fertilizers, medical drugs, fisheries and oceanic research, and agricultural development. These two figures alone represent nearly a billion dollars. And that is only part of the overall aid program.

As far as we know:

- In 1977 the FAO (Food and Agriculture Organization) dispatched as first-aid 350,000 tons of wheat flour to Ho Chi Minh City. Overpopulated India, which certainly has no food to throw away, lent one hundred thousand tons, too, discreetly, modestly. On the other hand, the representatives of the World Council of Churches (USA) made sure they were being photographed in front of the ten thousand tons of wheat flour they brought along with them. The North Vietnamese unfolded flags and streamers of thanks, and all this was published in the Party's daily, to make people believe that the American public was in favor of Hanoi against the "hostile" government of the U.S.

•In 1978 the same FAO granted aid again worth U.S. 2.5 million, to buy 11,380 tons of wheat flour and 250,000 dollars' worth of pesticides. What else? The last crops, it was said, had been destroyed by drought and insects.

•For the implementation of the green belt project, instigated, by the way, by the former government to help Saigon become self-sufficient, the communists cashed in a loan of $U.S. 57 million, granted by the IMF in 1979.[5]

•As for Japan, it lent 57 million yen, the Federal Republic of Germany 25 million Deutschmarks, Sweden 40 million Krones, without interest, and the CEE sixty thousand dollars and five tons of grain in 1977.

Meanwhile, what happened to the international aid? Before the wheat flour—sent for free—was put up for sale, the cadres gathered the members of their cells and told the people:

•Wheat and rice have about the same amount of proteins and are equally nourishing. This does not seem quite right, since white wheat flour has a protein value of nine against six for white rice, whereas whole brown wheat flour has a value of eleven and whole brown rice thirteen. However, they did not argue about the color of a given horse. This time, people just hoped their stomach would be able to accept a food to which they were not accustomed.

•Foreigners need rice and Vietnam barters it at the rate of one ton of rice for three tons of wheat. This was absolutely untrue, since the flour was sent for free. But in order to sell it to the South Vietnamese, they needed to make it look like it was trade, and mind you, they were that sharp; they could exchange one ton of rice for three of flour.

•The state hopes to make a good profit out of this. And it did. The flour was sold at the official rate of 0.40 dôngs per kilo, and 140 million dôngs must have been cashed in by the North Vietnamese Treasury for the 350,000 tons of flour sent for free by the FAO alone.

•The green belt project did not take off, and the IMF has not seen the interests on the $57 million loan it made and is probably not going to see the repayment of the loan itself for quite some time. Yet the South Vietnamese would certainly have benefited from the extra food it could have produced.

•Among the various religious denominations, some groups have helped Vietnam out of genuine charity; others did not even know that they were helping the communists. In *The Coercive Utopians* Rael Jean Isaac[6] and Erich Isaac explain how David Jessup, an AFL-CIO official and a member of the United Methodist Church reports that "most Methodist churchgoers" would be shocked and even outraged to learn that their contributions have been used to help Cuba, Vietnam, the PLO, and pro-Soviet movements in Latin America, Africa and even certain groups in the United States. Twenty-nine pages later, the same authors are pointing out that leaders of the Church World Service, through the World Council of Churches, have sent half a million dollars for two New Economic Zones in the Plateaux region in Vietnam, where Hanoi is sending North Vietnamese people.

This did not trigger any "Vietnamgate" then. Nor is there any "Sandinistagate" where in the United States one hundred thousand people are ready to infringe the law, if need be, in order to help the communists in Nicaragua and El Salvador.[7]

Testimonies from widespread sources are now beginning to mesh, and we shall see, later, how they shed light on plans of the communists.

In June 1978, facing a "disastrous situation," Hanoi announced a cabinet shuffle, as if it wanted to start anew. The vice prime minister, Vo-Chi-Cong, was "relegated" to the rank of vice minister, and the five ministers responsible for resources, construction, steel and engineering, ocean and sea products, and foreign trade were dismissed from their functions. The reason: "The weather and the insects have destroyed the seeds, therefore causing famine." There must be something peculiar about communists: for centuries South Vietnam was harvesting beautiful crops in the very same climatic conditions as today. They take over, and the nation starves. The same goes for any other country where they implement their system.

On the other hand, the minister of agriculture and the minister of the Food Department—without being responsible for the weather, by the way—should have been the targets of the Party's ire, if indeed heads had to roll, but they were not touched by the change of cabinet.

However, internal theft or external aid, which at times is just plain wheedling, squeezing money out of other nations, cannot result in development, which requires freedom, real democracy, creativity, research, and exchange, not monopolization plagued by bureaucracy, corruption, nepotism, and fear. Besides, there is so much aid can give, and with the current demographic explosion in particularly affected nations it represents less and less per capita every year.

Obviously, if socialism trains people, through fear or otherwise, against free enterprise and development, it cannot require production from them, even with the most pressing arguments and persuasion. One can at times, like Stalin for example, use war and patriotism against an invader and require extra efforts. But after forty years of waiting for another invader that never comes, the trick does not work anymore. Therefore, it will have to be invented, if not provoked, somewhere else: in Asia, the Middle East, or Latin America, with the risk of a World War III, or with local conflicts that distract internal public attention while ensuring an outdated expansionism that flatters the national ego?

Finally, even nations that were destroyed during World War II but had as much freedom as possible have not only survived, but recovered and prospered, like Japan for example, and opened up the way to others in the region, while those restricting freedom and real democracy are falling further behind every day and at all levels, be it spiritual, human, social, or economic.

NOTES

1. Raymong S. Sleeper (ed.), *A Lexicon of Marxist-Leninist Semantics*.
2. The first crop is ripe in February, the second—generally less important—at the end of August.
3. In his book *Le Cambodge*, Jean Delvert writes that, despite overwhelming testimony, the crimes of the Khmer Rouge have been denied for years—that is, as long as Pol Pot was a friend. When he was out of line, Hanoi conveniently denounced him.

4. *Vietnam under Communism, 1975–1982* (Stanford, Cal.; Hoover Institution, Stanford University), pp. 236–37.
5. *Le Monde*, December 19, 1986, stated that Vietnam had failed to repay its debt for two years.
6. Rael Jean and Erich Isaac, *The Coercive Utopians* (Chicago: Regnery Gateway 1983), 1 and 30.
7. *National Review*, March 4, 1988, p. 12.

THE GENOCIDE

Today, we do not shoot you anymore, but we have other different methods to make sure that you will never get out alive from here.
—*Commander Shorin*

With the arrival of the *bô-dôis*, those who knew what communist hell is like killed themselves, from Mr. Tran-Chanh-Thanh, ex–minister of information under Ngô-dinh-Diêm, and generals Pham-van-Phu, Nguyên-Khoa-Nam, and Lê-Van-Hung, to the privates who had fought bravely on the battlefields and in the rice paddies, or, for instance, Colonel Cân, who shot himself in the head in front of the statue of the Fusilliers Marins (Marines), standing across from the National Assembly: he decided to be with his companions in arms, in honor and by choice.

The more the regime was consolidated, the more suicides were committed. Toward the end of 1976—that is, a year and a half after the invasion of the South by the communists—a dozen Buddhist priests and nuns immolated themselves at Cân-Thô, where their pagoda had been desecrated by the North Vietnamese. In the Montreal *Gazette* of February 21, 1987, Harvey Sheperd reported the story of Buddhists whose situation has been intolerable since 1975 with continued persecution, imprisonment, forced labor, and temples being destroyed or turned into market-places or stables.

This is the real face of socialism, contrasting with "Saigon's persecution of Buddhists," which was in fact a communist disinformation scheme. The *American Spectator* of May 1985 reveals that many of the accusations against former president Diêm were not only false, but were invented by radical Buddhists controlled by the NLF. Some of them, picked up in the provinces, were told horror stories about Diêm's people burning pagodas and disemboweling priests. They were then pressed to immolate themselves by the "suicide promotion group," which provided them with garb already soaked with gasoline. Letters of protest were distributed to the media in the name of these "victims," and locations in Saigon were chosen to attract a maximum of onlookers. And that is what we saw on television, without knowing the entire story.

Meanwhile, in Nepal, "agitprop" groups in an effort to prepare a revolution are saying that Lenin had nothing against deities (they do not say that he had nothing for them either), but that he also told people to stand on their own feet.[1] And, of course, communist propaganda agents are there to explain in detail what this means in revolutionary terms: the same old routine, applied and adapted over and over again, every time it is needed.

Other people—entire families—kill themselves to put an end to the anguish of famine, humiliation, and bad treatment. Old people do not see the necessity of having to wait till the end of this misery. Suicides are skyrocketing so alarmingly that the North Vietnamese set up a "tax on suicide," believe it or not, evaluated according to the means of families whose members have put an end to their life.

In the main cities, execution poles are erected on public places: the state arrogates the right to kill, but individuals are not allowed self-determination on the issue. Men are shot by firing squads without anyone knowing exactly why: were they enemies of the regime, gangsters, or simply victims of personal vengeance? Their picture is published in the Party's daily, the *Liberated Saigon*. Even for those who do not know how to read or write, one can understand that with their hands tied behind their backs, and their heads bowed on their chests these victims were not counting ants marching past their feet.

People's tribunals are also devastating smaller communities. The population of the neighboring counties is "invited" at dark (it is always more impressive then) to partake in the shows. Cadres in civilian clothing stir up the crowd, who administers brutal verdicts: "Guilty! Must be executed!" At Vi-Thanh, chief-town of Chuong Thiên, where fierce combats had taken place between nationalists and communists, Col. Ho-Ngoc-Can, chief of the province, was captured and brought, tied up, on the soccer field, "judged," and condemned to be beaten to death with wooden sticks. Executions take place on the spot. They are numerous, and often people do not even know why they are perpetrated. One kills; that is all.

Meanwhile, during this collective fever, the North Vietnamese cadres harangued the crowd, got it caught in praise to the memory of Ho-Chi-Minh and the deeds of arms of the People's Army—in full action, as one could see—and deafened it with invectives against the leaders of the former government, the Americans, and the "rebels."

Then, all of a sudden, the poles disappeared: no more public executions, no more insults, and bloody acts are deemed "detrimental" to the nation. One would even say that after a violent attack of fever, the sick nation is at last calming down and will recover. Rumors were beginning to circulate about "clemency of the state" and "tolerant government," and the term *rebel* was being replaced by *misguided, misled*. It is only a pause during which the disease will incubate; the "misled" will be eliminated as such anyway, instead of being eliminated as "rebels."

From being apparently disorderly and feverish, the genocide will become cold and calculated.

In every medical cell—one can hardly call them clinics—one finds personnel of doubtful training, more acquainted with Marxism-Leninism than medicine. Some have no adequate university training at all. Others have acquired their title by "seniority," that is, by the number of years they spent in a fighting unit. No medicine, no medical equipment, since everything had been sent to the north and to Eastern Bloc countries. The cadres decide which women will have an abortion and designate them the "specialized services." The two big maternity hospitals of Tu-Du in Saigon and Hung-Vuong in Cholon, previously delivering an average of two hundred babies per day, are now, under the North Vietnamese, mostly used for abortions. Every morning women sent there by the cadres of their medical cells come to squat in front of the hospital's main entrance and wait their turn to get an abortion. A woman doctor from the South, transferred to Hanoi in 1955, then assigned to the Tu-Du Maternity Hospital of Saigon in 1975, bragged about being able to perform between 150 and 180 abortions in eight hours of work without anesthesia.

Children who are unlucky enough to survive are condemned to deficiency. The two milk factories of FOREMOST and CO-SUDA at Thu-Duc and the NESTLÉ Society at Bièn-Hoà were nationalized early in 1975, and all their production has been sent to the North: "to oblige South Vietnamese to use local products made of soja," a woman doctor will say later. If so, why is it that the North Vietnamese and their leaders are not doing likewise? Pregnant women and young mothers are confronted with a basic problem: when they go to the "milk provisioning cell," similar to the "rice provisioning cell," the cadres in charge ask them to display their breasts, then to breast-feed their children. With what, when the mothers themselves do not even have enough food to eat? They do not need to be told what to do with their breasts and milk; they have known that since the beginnings of mankind. What they need is food. One cannot help but notice that the lawyer Mrs. Ngo-Ba-Thanh and her movement for "the right to life for women" did not show up on that occasion either.

Sure enough, some women can get milk; the population of Hanoi, in North Vietnam, was offered milk coming from South Vietnam. But not many people were used to it anymore, or maybe they saw in it a good opportunity to make a few dôngs: for a good price the North Vietnamese sold their cans of milk to the cadres going to the South. It was then discovered that the milk sent from the South was sold at three dôngs per can, the official price in North Vietnam, and it was sent back with the cadres leaving for the South, where it was sold again for forty dôngs on the black market when the salary of those who could get work was ranging between 45 to 60 and 120 dôngs per month.

Right after the fall of Saigon, all the imported and locally produced medicines, the reserves of the military commissariat of the health services, and the equipment of the private, public, and military hospitals were sent to the North. Drugstores and warehouses were closed down, pharmacists sent to re-education camps, worked in the fields, or simply left unemployed. Every bit of high-quality and efficient medicine was kept exclusively for the North Vietnamese leaders and the high-ranking officers.

This lack of medicine, particularly antibiotics, was severely felt by the population, especially in the NEZ, where three-fifths of the children sent there died of malnutrition and disease. For three years (1975, 1976, and 1977) medicine that escaped the communist seizure was sold on the sidewalks at very high prices, and without any guarantee of quality—many were placebos, had been tampered with, or were outdated. Since 1978 and the "general inventory" campaign aimed at the population medicine is in even shorter supply and prices are astronomically high. It is sold secretly in front of hospitals, like porn pictures offered on the run, hospitalized people being required to bring their medications as prescribed by the doctors. If one cannot afford it, well, one will have to do without.

In his book, *40,000 enfants par jour (40,000 Children a Day)*,[1] Dr. François Rémy, who lived in North, then in South Vietnam between 1975 and 1977, reports an infant mortality rate of children of thirty per one thousand in the North and 200 per one thousand in the South, due to the food blockade and shortage of medicine.[2]

People who escaped from the NEZ but were weakened by malnutrition and disease were dying on the sidewalks of the cities they returned to, some diseases being more lethal in the cities than in the countryside, like tuberculosis, for instance.

The children's hospital of Ho-Chi-Minh City, which in the olden days saved the lives of babies, was now the place where one helplessly witnessed their death. According to a doctor working at this hospital—a Boat Person who left Ho-Chi-Minh City early in 1979 and is now established in Toronto, Canada—an average of thirty children per day died for lack of medicine. With this situation, the communist authorities enjoined the population "to resort to traditional medicine." Here again, the Vietnamese pharmacopoeia based on plants and herbs did not last long. It could not be renewed for lack of supply and means of transportation. And why should the North Vietnamese have to use "capitalist medicine" and not the South Vietnamese as well? Charity was certainly not a motive.

Speaking of children, we cannot forget the tens of thousands of orphans in South Vietnam. We cannot forget the twelve to fifteen thousand Amerasian children left behind. In the book by Gen. Henri Jacquin, *La Guerre Secrète d'Indochine (The Secret War in Indochina)*,[3] he writes that in 1953 Lê-duc-Thô[4] drowned three hundred Eurasian orphans in the Red River—an ironic name under the circumstances—on orders of the Revolutionary Committee in Hanoi. Yet it was one of his fellow revolutionaries, also in power, the well-known former prime minister of Vietnam Pham-van-Dong[5] who told Claire Brisset in an interview for the newspaper *Le Monde*[6] that Vietnamese children—who when not under the Party's grip for indoctrination are a little bit ours—must not be held responsible for what is happening in Cambodia. He even complains that some people have said that the aid sent by UNICEF has been diverted for the North Vietnamese soldiers fighting in Cambodia and therefore ask if these people are human—a good question, that three hundred Eurasian orphans were probably asking at the time of their death in the Red River. Were they condemned like all the children and the adults massacred because they had been in contact with the West?

It has also been proved since then that foreign aid—not considered to be a stigma when it comes to cashing it in—has been diverted from Vietnam and Cambodia. South Vietnamese have seen it being sent to the North.

In the re-education camps, those who are condemned without trial to hard labor die from starvation and are executed for the smallest "mistake." About 30 percent of these detainees are said to have died in these camps. Those who survive do not have the right to citizenship in their country and therefore do not receive a ration card for rice. The investigation of Jacqueline Desbarats and Karl Jackson[7] with 831 Vietnamese refugees established in France and the United States was published in *Asia Week* of June 1985. It revealed that sixty-five thousand detainees in these camps have died in front of a firing squad or were stabbed, disemboweled, or buried alive. These figures have been established from testimony from eyewitnesses, no hearsay having been accepted as proof. Dead: sixty-five thousand; witnesses: eight hundred. What are we going to discover if we manage to interview all the survivors?

The communist security force was and is probably still looking for the seventeen thousand agents who worked with the Americans, particularly the CIA, and eliminates them as they are discovered. The Adventist Mission of the Protestant church has also been accused of having worked for the American agency. Everybody dreads the tag "CIA agent," for everyone knows that the security's motto is identical to that of Lenin: "rather one thousand condemnations than to let one guilty person escape." Needless to say that when the United States admitted that they left agents in the country it must have been buzzing in the Vietnamese "Loubiankas."[8] We must add to this toll all the agents of the Counterespionage Service, the former National Security, and the leaders of any rank in the former ministry for the rallying of the country and those of the former ministry for the rural reconstruction.

According to Trần-vān-Thái, in his book *The Camp of the Dùn Lagoon*, and to Trân-trung-Quân in *Behind the Lines*,[9] captured secret agents are made to starve like anybody else, but they are also electrically tortured, shocks being applied to sensitive parts of the body. They are also locked without food or water in steel boxes exposed to the rays of the sun, or hung by their feet, swung in all directions, and beaten at random with wooden sticks. They are also blinded with powerful spotlights while their eyes are kept open by pincers, or they have their head submerged in a pail of excrement until they run out of breath.

During the war in South Vietnam, some 220,000 guerrillas and militants left the ranks of the Communist party and joined the free South. They are not to be confused with the nine hundred thousand or so North Vietnamese who fled to the South in 1954–55. Of course, along with them there must have been agents true to their cause, infiltrators, but when the South fell in 1975, most of the "traitors" were arrested and condemned.

Before 1975, people were only talking about the defection of lower-ranking militants. After 1975, however, people were talking more and more about higher-ranking officers defecting to the other side:

- Hoǹg-van-Hoan, vice president of the National Assembly of Hanoi. En route to Moscow, where he was to be hospitalized, he defected in New Delhi and took refuge in Pekin in August 1979.

- Truong-nhu-Tang, an aristocrat by birth and an engineer. He left France, where he had studied, and became director of the Sugar Company of Vietnam. During the Têt Offensive of 1968, he joined the Vietcong and became honorary minister of justice with the provisional government. In May 1975 he left Hanoi to go to Saigon, where he was rather coldly recęived by other intellectuals. After several failed attempts, he succeeded in fleeing the country in September 1980 with the Boat People and found refuge back in France.[10]

•Nguyên-cong-Hoan, nominated for the one-slate elections in May 1976 for the province of Phu-Khanh. He also fled the country with Boat People and found refuge first in Japan and then in the United States in 1979.

These are a few examples among an intelligentsia as unhappy with the new regime as with the former government. There are also people who manage to be discontented with the former government, the communist regime, their country of refuge, and again the communist regime they join for a second time.

There is the couple NTP and HTVT, for example, both from South Vietnam, well known in Canada—Montreal in particular—where they studied and got their university degrees thanks to a bursary from the Colombo Plan, communist militants since then. Toward the end of 1977, they decided to go back to Vietnam "to serve their homeland." There was a big going-away party at Mirabel International Airport (north of Montreal), on which occasion they expressed their discontent with Canada. In 1979 they escaped from Vietnam with the Boat People and found refuge back in Canada; Toronto this time.

And then there are those who are helped to find refuge in death:

•Dinh-Ba-Thi (Ung-Van-Khuong was his real name), Hanoi's ambassador to the UN in 1976, declared persona non grata in the U.S. in 1977. Back in Vietnam, he visited the little town of Tourcham in the province of Thuân-Hai. He was found dead behind the wheel of his booby-trapped car. It is said that, while supposedly en route directly from the United States to Vietnam, the imprudent man had made a stop at the embassy of the People's Republic of China in Paris.

•Mai-vān-Bô, born in Long Xuyên in South Vietnam, Hanoi's general delegate in Paris, until the end of 1970. He, along with Mr. Etienne M. Manac'h, the French ambassador to Peking from 1969 to 1975, actively participated in the negotiations on Vietnam in early 1968. Called back to Hanoi in 1970, he was run over by a military truck under mysterious circumstances, on January 20, 1985.[11] His recall may have had something to do with the fact that his twin brother had joined South Vietnam in 1970. Since then, no one has heard of his twin brother either.

- •Ta-công-Bang, a militant since his youth, graduated from a Canadian university, and went back to Vietnam "to serve the freed homeland." One year after his return, he was found in his native province of Quang-Ngai, floating in the Tràkhuc River, whose flow at its deepest hardly reaches chest height. He was probably drowned when, tired of the regime, he began to regret leaving Canada.

There are also those who do not belong to any political party but are eliminated all the same:

- •Prof. Nguyên-ngoc-Huy,[12] the famous cardiologist, was run over by a jeep in front of the faculty of medicine. He had just said good-bye to his students and was about to go into exile in France.

- •Actress Thanh-Nga, also very well known, was shot with several handgun bullets in front of her house for having interpreted a role incompatible with the Party's line.

- •Astrologer Huynh-Lien, famous since the thirties, was shot in his home with several handgun bullets. One must say that astrology is not exactly appreciated by the Marxists. Can you imagine an interpretation of Nostradamus predicting the end of communism in the world? The communists do know the power of legends and prophecies, for they have resurrected quite a few of them and modified others for the needs of their cause.

- •Former professor Nghiêm-Xuan-Thâm, of the literature faculty, was assassinated by hammer blows for having refused to surrender his priceless collection of books to the Party.

As far as the Chinese community established in Vietnam for centuries and having Vietnamese nationality since 1955 was concerned, the Party has been particularly harsh. During the war years between 1945 and 1975, Hanoi kept more or less quiet, probably because China was providing weapons and food. But when the relations began to sour, the Vietnamese Communist party expelled all the militants of Chinese origin. Then, using the conflict with the People's Republic of China, Hanoi began to despoil the Hoa (the Vietnamese of Chinese origin), thus beginning the trade in of human lives.

In the North, according to the UNHCR figures, 272,000 Hoa were expelled by the North Vietnamese security at the Chinese border. Mrs. Bang, living in Canada since 1982, declared that she was summoned by the security of Hanoi to "voluntarily" leave her country with her family, but on the condition that she pay one tael of gold per person. To leave, yes, because the North Vietnamese want to get rid of the Hoa anyway, but so long as they pay for it.[13]

In the South, the Hoa will be "authorized" to leave, provided they pay between ten and thirty taels of gold per person, because they are richer than their northern compatriots. Still, according to the UNHCR figures of May 1985, four hundred thousand Boat People died at sea, among whom one hundred thousand (one-quarter) were children. Among the victims, two thousand three hundred women and girls were raped and seven hundred taken away by the Thai pirates and sent to join the thirty thousand or so Bangkok prostitutes.

To these figures, one must also add those of the Land People,[14] about whom we have heard little indeed. To find refuge in the border camps of Thailand, packed with Laotians and Cambodians, the Vietnamese must cross a Cambodia occupied by the communists of their own country. Women are less likely to be shot on the spot, but they risk being raped by their wardens, ten, twelve, and even more in some instances. When free at last, the Vietnamese who find deserters of the communist army in Thai camps where they too have found refuge, keep away from them. They are considered by all to be infiltrated agents, which some certainly are.

When the lucrative expulsion of the Hoa was in full swing, one could see corpses on the beaches of Vietnamese, rolled over by waves, and on which flocks of security agents were pouncing, looking for gold, jewels forgotten on the dead, or in ripped open wrecks, now motionless and already conquered by the sands. Today still long lists of missing relatives are published in numerous reviews in the United States, Canada, Great Britain, France, Australia, Japan, West Germany, and some ten other countries around the world.

The "emigration" campaign of the Hoa ordered by the North Vietnamese was in many cases a death sentence. Except for the cargo ships such as the S/S *Hai-Hong*, *Tung-An* and the *Sky-Luck*, for instance, the old tubs and the fishing boats happened to be just floating coffins. Firstly, they were overloaded: fugitives of all ages—from the very old to the newly born—were jam-packed deep in the hold and had to stay squatting for a journey of one, two, or three weeks or, even one month, short of food and drinking water. Secondly, many of these tubs with a very low draft were sent out to sea right in the middle of the tropical monsoon season (from May to October) without any concern about weather conditions.

L.M.H., a former second class petty officer in the navy established in Antony, a suburb south of Paris, says that he had to pay in gold the passage for his wife, their two children, and himself, then for a false Chinese identity card for each member of thc family, and finally for the North Vietnamese police authorization to go from Ho Chi Minh City to Rach Gia. Once in the harbor, the four of them were allowed to embark at daybreak on May 23, 1979, on a little boat that was part of a flotilla of five nutshells. Between their starting point and the river's mouth—about five hundred meters (roughly 550 yards)—the already packed boat had to stop twice to pick up two other loads of passengers who lowered the tub's waterline to thirty centimeters (about one foot) below the deck. After three hours at sea, the flotilla faced a monsoon. By chance, the boat, on which L.M.H. and his family were, managed to find refuge in a little bay of the island of Hon-Chuôi. After a journey of five days, part of the flotilla arrived at Pulau Bidong, an island situated some ten kilometers east of Trengganu in Malaysia. Three boats out of five had sunk apeak with their human cargos. Only in L.M.H.'s boat, three people suffocated to death in the hold, without anyone realizing it was caused by overcrowding. His eyes lost in his memories, L.H.M. concluded by saying, "Normally, our boat should have loaded 200 people . . . on a calm sea; we were 559."

Another example of which we heard more about: the case of little Tran-Hue-Hue, thirteen years old, the one and only survivor out of a cargo of fifty-one people. Their boat had run aground on a coral reef in the middle of the China Sea. Out of food and drinking water and after an ordeal of 120 days (four months), the survivors ate the flesh of the dead, and died, in turn, a few days later. Little Tran-Hue-Hue alone survived, and was taken out of this hell by the little Filipino fishing boat, the *Sittirazma*.[15]

Another tragic case among others was that of a small coast vessel, sunk with one thousand people aboard, blown up by a time bomb set in the engine room. Among the victims, were L. and T., a couple of doctors from Phuoc Kien Hospital.

As in all communist countries, the Party monopolizes power and eliminates all other competitors. There is nothing really new about this in Vietnam; since the early thirties all existing nationalist parties had a bone to pick with the communists. Again, after the invasion of the South in 1975, the scenario was the same: victims of disappearances, executions, and imprisonment accumulated. Among the best known: Trân-van-Tuyen, lawyer, secretary of the Nationalist party (VNQDD), imprisoned in a reeducation camp in the South, then transferred to the North, where he died in 1976, and Dr. Phan-Huy-Quat, former president of the Anti-Communist League in Asia, who was arrested and died in the central prison of Chi-Hoà in Ho Chi Minh City.

Priests, whose ideals are considered superstition by the communists, are also reduced through starvation and are the object of false accusations and libel. Their groups and congregations are infiltrated, as was the case with the Buddhists and others during the war, and then dispersed. The members are arrested, then sent to the NEZ. Religions of "foreign origin" with a few adepts, such as the Baha'i, the Evangelical Mission, the Adventist Mission, and the Theosophic Mission, for example, are simply forbidden, like religious sects or meditation groups. In the case of the priest Nguyên-Thanh-Nam,[16] his thousands of followers were dispersed and sent to the NEZ. The Protestant church was accused of having worked with the CIA; its churches were closed, its priests hunted down, just like agents of other groups. For the Catholic church and its millions of believers and based in the Vatican, repressive measures were taken by diocesan centers. The vicar apostolic[17] was "invited" to leave his position in Saigon immediately, after having been "spontaneously" decried by a crowd manipulated by communist agents in civilian clothing. Bishops and priests were constrained to house arrest; there were no free sermons or unauthorized movements and limited contact with the faithful. Schools and seminars were closed. They were used by the North Vietnamese to teach Marxism-Leninism instead of the Scriptures.

As far as Buddhism is concerned with its 7 or 8 million faithful in Vietnam, but with no particular links with other nations, the regime took tougher measures. Novices were sent back to civilian life or to the NEZ, priests and nuns were incarcerated, the pagodas desecrated and put under the regime's control. Some of them have been turned into produce markets or stables.

The two politico-religious sects of the Hoà-Hao and the Cao-Dài from South Vietnam numbered some 5 million practicing members whose majority were farmers from the Mekong Delta. The Hoà-Hao sect has its birthplace in the town of the same name—Hoà-Hao—in Chomoi, a region in the province of Long Xuyên. The Cao-Dai sect was born in Tây-Ninh, one hundred kilometers north of Saigon, and in Bên-Tre, eighty kilometers west of the capital city. These two sects have had bloody precedents with the communists: especially the Hoà-Hao whose prophet Huynh-Phu-So disappeared in an ambush set by the communists in 1947. Vengeance has been terrible and triggered a never ending spiral of violent clashes: disappearances, murders, executions, et cetera. When they took power, needless to say, the North Vietnamese had nothing more urgent to do than to wipe out both sects.

As far as the population of the Plateaux is concerned—we already wrote about them, mostly in the chapter on collectivization and life in the countryside—we just want to remind the reader that they comprised eight ethnic groups totaling about half a million people, to which one must add 350,000 Vietnamese. These Montagnards have always fought for their independence against any governmental authority. When the North Vietnamese strove to seize power, these Plateaux were of use to them, but since 1975 they have become more of a danger. Hanoi has eliminated these ethnic groups without mercy through the food blockade, since they depend for 95 percent of their needs on the rice of the delta and for 100 percent on the salt and sea products controlled by the communists. Vietnamese witnesses have revealed that they saw corpses of people who died from hunger lying on the outskirts of the forest, up on the Plateaux. As soon as 1976, contingents of farmers from North Vietnam came to replace them.

The story of these minorities is in many ways similar to that of their Laotian neighbors. The Hmongs of Laos fought with the Americans to prevent the taking over of South Vietnam and ultimately of Laos. According to Jane Hamilton-Merritt,[18] there were five hundred thousand Hmongs in Laos in 1960—there were about four hundred and fifty thousand Montagnards on the Plateaux of Vietnam. In 1976 thirty-five thousand of them had found refuge in the West, fifty thousand were in refugee camps in Thailand, and only seventy thousand were left in the country, running the risk of being exterminated, gassed. We thought this word to be buried in the trenches of World War I. No. The red rain is the most lethal; it kills on contact. Then there is the yellow rain, also used in Afghanistan, sticky like ointment. Then there are the green and blue-green rains, which have no immediate fatal effects. The local population ingest a little bit of opium, used for centuries as a medicine for gastro-intestinal illnesses, in order to get out "only" with dizziness, vomiting, and nose bleedings.[19] Jane Hamilton-Merritt also reports that, between 1975 and 1978, the communists have killed fifty thousand people in the Phu Bia region alone, and that forty-five thousand others have perished on their way to Thailand.

As we stated earlier in this investigation, these deadly rains have been drained by real, natural rain into the Mekong. It so heavily polluted the river that in the delta entire shoals of fish have been found belly-up, scales puffed out as if attacked by Scab. Scales of these fish and shrimp have been sent to Montreal, Canada, to determine the cause of death and the degree of toxicity—shrimp in particular because they could be dangerous for exportation. In 1986, however, shrimp from Vietnam were for sale in a Montreal store.[20]

Speaking of yellow rain, one cannot avoid the link and parallel with the American agent orange used in Vietnam during the war as a defoliant. The North Vietnamese said that it was responsible for pollution, birth defects, abortions, and premature births. And they showed glass jars from the maternity hospital of Tu-Du, containing deformed fetuses, to Australian cameras.[21] According to some Americans themselves agent orange is said to have provoked marrow cancer.[22] Thus far, things seem to be clear. They cease to be when a Vietnamese woman now living in Canada says, "I studied at Tu-Du from 1948 to 1951 to become a midwife, and the deformed fetuses kept in these glass jars shown in the Australian report are the very same. Generations of doctors and nurses have used them for their studies at the maternity hospital. I recognized them." This raises, at the very least serious questions. Now if agent orange was still dangerous at the time of the Australian report—although it has been used long before the Soviet-made yellow rain used by the North Vietnamese—why were Vietnamese shrimp up for sale in Canada a little bit later? On the other hand, if this defoliant had all of a sudden become harmless, which would have permitted the sale of shrimp, how come the public was not informed about it in a similar and spectacular manner?

To trap those who are discontented with the regime, the North Vietnamese have set up false resistance groups and false "passeurs."[23] First, rumors are circulated, something like: "Yes, yes, I know an absolutely ready clandestine organization; . . . an underground force supplied by helicopters; . . . Buses stopped by *maquisards*; . . . frogmen of the resistance; . . . a submarine spotted along the coast . . . " Many such tricks are known today to have trapped many Vietnamese; groups of young and old who paid with their lives for trusting such rumors, and groups of refugees, caught and jailed while going to their meeting point on the border of Laos or on the shores of Vietnam:

- Mrs. M.V.A., a Boat Person today established in California reports: "After failing a first time, we tried a second one with my three still very young daughters [her husband was held prisoner in a re-education camp in the South first, then in the North, since 1978]. We went to the agreed rendezvous, and we embarked with 200 other people. After 20 minutes at sea, the boat came back towards the shore. The crew, guns in hands, rushed out of the cabin, and invited us to line up . . . and to go directly to the prison." Boat and crew were soon ready to pull this trick again.

- Dr. Phan-huy-Quat, former prime minister and president of the Anti-Communist League of Asia (already mentioned) was contacted by a so-called passeur. A car from the organization picked him up as agreed and drove him directly to the central prison of Chi-Hoà, where he died two years later.

•Textile engineer Pham-vân-Hai, former director of the SICOVINA textile company, had to accept the position of vice president of the Patriotic Intellectual Society established by the communists as early as 1975. He fell three times into the trap of false passeurs, but was cleared, it seems, because he was protected by an influential member of the People's Committee of Ho Chi Minh City.

We shall not forget the young who tried to join in the resistance and fell victims of false undergrounds whose recruiting men were agents of the communist security disguised as "anti-communist resistance fighters"; they disappeared. Even their parents did not dare talk about them, for fear of reprisal. They just mentioned their absence to the concerned services, which cut out the rations they controlled. The former *maquis* zones the communists left during the Ho Chi Minh campaign, such as Le-hong-Phong, Rùng-lá (in Phan-Tiêt), Binh-gia (Baria), the iron triangle,[24] Boi-Loi (Tay-Ninh), Nam-Càn (Camau), and Dilinh on the Plateaux, are examples of false undergrounds, traps for *maquisards*. A farmer living nearby the Binh-gia region told M.T.H., resident in Canada since 1983, that this false underground has been the theater of at least two major slaughters in which hundreds and hundreds of young people were massacred. On November 27, 1987, *l'Express* revealed that resistance fighters caught in Laos by the Vietnamese army would be tried, probably in December. The most important of them would be Hoang-Co-Minh.

There is nothing new about this. During World War II, the communists infiltrated the resistance groups to fight, after 1941, the Nazis who had attacked the Soviet Union. It is to be noticed that since then the communists have said that the Nazis (also socialists) were a trick of the West, when in fact both ideologies were at war for supremacy and to impose their view of the world. They had been allies for several years, including two during the conflict against Western democracies. This strategy was also aimed at controlling the underground toward the end of the war. It has been witnessed that in many instances they used them to take over the country right after the end of the hostilities. In some other instances, as in France for example, some real, true patriots paid with their lives for their refusal to go along with them.

Understandably, should the coup have been successful, the communists would have had these resistance fighters on their back, fighting them as the new invaders, the new enemies. Control was necessary not only during World War II, but also afterward. Today this remains true of all freedom fighters. The tragedy, however, is that some Westerners as well consider them to be embarrassing in view of the great coming together of East and West.

Another form of genocide consists, of sending young people to die in expansionist wars abroad, like in Cambodia for example. Starved, they enroll in the army's ranks. The regime does not like them, but it uses them, then eliminates them on the battlefields. They all know the slogan: "Born up North, dead in the South," which has become for all Vietnamese the "international duty." The figures of the dead are never released. The bodies of the fallen are buried in haste, never restored to their families. That is bad publicity for the Party, particularly in small towns where everyone knows everybody. If, per chance, a family is notified of a death it will be much, much later.

The Vienna Accords of July 23, 1962, concerning the neutrality of Laos have not been respected, since the communists established their sanctuaries in that country. The Paris Accords of 1973, on the neutrality of South Vietnam, have not been respected either. The plan for communist hegemony in the region goes back to 1932, but the four phases of its implementation were instigated in 1953, just few months before the signing of the Geneva Accords of 1954, putting an end to the war between France and Vietnam and establishing the neutrality of Laos and Cambodia:

- A. Domination of Laos before occupation of part of the Golden Triangle and control of the wealth it provides: protection of the Ho Chi Minh Trail.

- B. Occupation of South Vietnam: the horn of plenty in the region, equipped with a modern industrial complex, but most of all, access to warm waters and first-class strategic position.[25] In 1974, there would also be the oil potential, all lost to the Soviets, who did not even have to fight for it.[26]

- •C. Invasion of Cambodia: for its wealth certainly, but mostly as a springboard to Thailand. Combat is already taking place.

- •D. Invasion of Thailand: opposed by China and the United States and postponed by the dismantling of the Thai Communist party in 1976.

The Vietnamization of Cambodia is in full swing: food blockade, pillage, imposition of the Vietnamese language, transfer and establishment of cadres and farmers from North Vietnam, five hundred thousand according to Prince Norodom Sihanouk who declared in 1985, at Dong-Rek, on the Khmero-Thai border, that should this continue, there will be 1 million North Vietnamese to vote in 1990 for Heng Samrin, Hanoi's puppet regime in Cambodia. In short, Cambodians are being eliminated, replaced by well-indoctrinated North Vietnamese who will vote for a puppet regime set in place by Hanoi, and the entire world, ignorant of what is really going on, will believe the process "democratic."

Likewise, Hanoi has been deporting South Vietnamese to other socialist or friendly countries since 1980. The *London Times*[27] has revealed the figure of half a million people deported to Siberia to work in factories, in coal mines, and on the gas line planned to forge trade links with Western Europe; three hundred thousand have been sent to other Eastern countries (East Germany and Bulgaria), one hundred thousand of them in Czechoslovakia. Small contingents are also said to have been sent to work in Angola, Mozambique, and Algeria. When Siberian workers, stouter and used to the harsh climate—they are also offered three times their salary and allowances to go there—hardly manage to keep going, the Vietnamese, used to another climate, are dying like flies. In the best of cases, they are happy when they are able to survive, that is to eat and keep warm enough. To give you an idea of how it is out there, during World War II, of the tens of thousands of Germans of the Von Paulus army taken prisoner in Siberia,[28] only one-tenth of them came back alive, usually with frozen fingers that had to be amputated.

In its report on disappearances, Amnesty International defines them as the "new technique of repression," applied in certain countries under given political regimes, whatever their place on the political spectrum. In his article "Les Droits de la Personne au Cambodge" ("Human Rights in Cambodia"), Mr. Buddhi Klok writes that under any totalitarian regime, anywhere in the world, disappearances are a very efficient way of oppression and that Vietnam has become a leader in the field in Cambodia.[29]

In Vietnam this technique is not new at all. The population of the South experienced disappearances as early as the forties due to the Communist party, particularly during the troubled years of 1945, 1946, and 1947. More recently, just remember the Têt Offensive of 1968: The People's Army of North Vietnam invaded part of the city of Huê, among others, and within three weeks thousands of people disappeared from the region. Arrests, liquidations, and disappearances are perpctrated at night in general, and the kowledge of it remains therefore very limited among the people.

In his book *A Vietcong Memoire*,[30] Truong-Nhu-Tang writes that it is impossible to evaluate the number of people arrested by the government agencies and the military authorities in 1975–76, to which must be added the three hundred thousand people imprisoned in re-education camps in June 1975. Several books have been written in Vietnamese—and not yet translated—on this particular subject. Their titles can be given in English as:

- *Reeducation Camps,* by Pham-quang-Giai.
- *The Red Carcan*, by Pham-quôc-Bao.
- *Deep Down in Hell,* by Ta-Ty.
- *Bloody University*, by Ha-thuc-Sinh.
- *The Reeducation Years in North Vietnam*, by Tran-huynh-Chau.

These books describe the abominable, inhumane character of these camps in which about 30 percent of the prisoners died from physical and mental torture, hunger, and disease.

In these very camps, information is available, but it seldom reaches the public, unless a survivor manages to escape the country and write a book about it. In Vietnam it will be undercover;

in the West it will face the language barrier. In *The Dun Lagoon Camp,* for instance, Trân-van-Thai, who passed away during the fall of 1988 in Australia, unveils the atrocities and torture inflicted by the communists who preferred to see their victims agonize rather than shoot them.

Out in the countryside, the massacre of the farmers has been directed like maneuvers. The targeted regions were encircled by "unknown armed forces" at curfew time, as usual, and everybody or almost everybody was shot. The massacres were attributed to "resistance fighters"—when most of them have been liquidated by false undergrounds—or to the Khmer Rouge. Not that the Cambodian communists would not be able to do such things, but in his book *Que sait l'humanité de l'enfer du Vietnam (What Does Mankind Know about the Vietnamese Hell)*[31] Lê-tân-Trang mentions the testimony of two survivors, one at Thât-Son, in the province of Chau-Doc (west), and the other at Tay-Ninh (east). The villages were encircled and taken by surprise, and the population was massacred with side arms and firearms. The murderers uttered few words: it was Vietnamese with the accent of the North.

In 1977, at the terminus of the Dông-Thap province, right in the middle of the Mekong Delta, a terrified countrywoman, with her clothing in rags and covered with mud, told Minh-Hiên himself, "Last night, the village was encircled by men with arms who shot everything that moved. After that, they set fire everywhere." The poor woman escaped because she fell in a ditch, where she remained hidden until everything fell still.

In Christmas 1977 the diplomatic body of the nonaligned countries, in Hanoi, was invited by the minister of foreign affairs to acknowledge the damages cause by the alleged incursions of the Khmer Rouge into the Mekong Delta. Asked about it by Minh-Hiên himself, one of the diplomats[32] visiting Ho Chi Minh City said that he saw, indeed, the distressing spectacle of villages burnt to the ground; no more, no less.

Thus the Khmer Rouge had the audacity to provoke the Vietnamese army on its own territory when two hundred thousand *bô-dôis*—that is eight hundred men per kilometer and ten times the strength of the Cambodian forces—are massed on a front of 250 kilometers, only 80 kilometers away from Phnom Penh, the Cambodian capital? Khmer Rouge speaking with the accent of

North Vietnam would have raided Vietnam, and Hanoi would have the damages assessed by an interposed diplomatic "notary"? Peculiar, or is it that Vietnam was looking for a good opportunity to invade Cambodia? And that is what it did a few months later anyway.

This situation allowed Hanoi to:

•Liquidate the farmers of the Mekong Delta who were refusing collectivization and blame the Khmer Rouge, who have a bad reputation according to international opinion. This being said, had Pol Pot remained faithful to the Soviet Union, Vietnam would have concealed his crimes for as long as possible.

•Replace them by more docile and more indoctrinated farmers from the Red River Delta of North Vietnam.

•Clean up the Khmero-Vietnamese border region where the religious sects' resistance units were entrenched—especially those of the Hoà-Hao and those of the Cao-Dai—and therefore to protect the rear of the Vietnamese expeditionary forces. For all we know, refuges of the Hoà-Hao sect near the Cambodian border[33] have been flattened by shells of the Vietnamese artillery and bombs of the Vietnamese air forces; some say MIG-23 jet fighters. The practicing farmers of this sect living in the quadrangle delimited by the towns of Tân-Chau, Cho-Vàm, Nang-Gù, and Hoà-Hao—birthplace of the sect—have been encircled and liquidated. These eliminations have been extended to neighbouring villages. This allows Hanoi to

•send contingents of young, discontented Vietnamese boys and girls, listed for five years, to die in the campaign set up to get even with "the Khmer Rouge's intervention in Vietnam," but mostly to ensure Vietnam's control over the region.

•install in Phnom Penh the Vietnam educated Heng Samrin and to evict the "cruel" Pol Pot and his Khmer Rouge denounced by Hanoi, which seems a worthy cause, but very clever as far as international public opinion is concerned. It gives Hanoi full credit for "denouncing" Pol Pot. Now Vietnam is invading Cambodia and will perpetrate its own massacres.

•Vietnamize Cambodia—according to plan C—and build bases to continue the conquest of Southeast Asia and extend Vietnamization to the region.

In August 1977 the Vietnamese general Vo-Nguyên-Giap exhorted his troops massed on the Khmero-Vietnamese border since the beginning of the same year, and in December war broke out between Vietnam and Cambodia. Hanoi was supported by Moscow, and Phnom Penh by Peking. On December 25, 1978, when international public opinion was celebrating Christmas, Vietnam launched a great offensive that resulted in the fall of Phnom Penh on January 7, 1979. The day after, at the UN, Prince Norodom Sihanouk denounces the Vietnamese aggression. Hanoi, then, takes the opportunity to reveal Pol Pot's crimes, and the Soviet veto prevents a vote for the withdrawal of the foreign forces in Cambodia.

Thus Soviet-made tanks and the Vietnamese infantry are two hours away from Bangkok, Thailand—plan D. Hanoi is practicing the divide-and-conquer strategy with the ASEAN countries. Incursions are already taking place in Thailand, and the little stability that may have been left in Southeast Asia is threatened. The UN, aware of the situation, has requested the withdrawal of the foreign forces from Kampuchea on several occasions, but to no avail.

As in Vietnam, Hanoi has been and is still implementing the same policy of pillage, military repression, famine, impoverishment, torture, elimination, corruption, and diversion of international aid, while hand-picked journalists are taken for a walk where there is nothing to see, especially not the genocide.

In Vietnam figures are hard to come by—as in all communist countries—but various evaluations are coming close to what Sir Robert Thompson predicted in his 1972 report, one year before the signing of the Paris Accords, that should South Vietnam be invaded by the troops of the North, 3 to 5 million South Vietnamese would be doomed to be massacred.[34] In his book *l'Indochine Rouge (Red Indochina)*, Gen. Raoul Salan estimated that nearly 3 million South Vietnamese would disappear.[35] In his book *Vietnam, qu'as-tu fais de tes fils? (Vietnam, What Have You Done with Your Sons?)*[36] Pierre Darcourt writes that the communists had planned to evacuate 3.5 million people from the cities—1.8 million from Saigon alone—and send them to the New Economic Zones. These figures have also been forwarded by the Party itself. One cannot speak of elimination per se, of course, not directly, that is.

The then prime minister Pham-van-Dong said that it would be stupid and criminal to invade South Vietnam: "Come on . . . never on your life has there been any bloodbath in Vietnam!" added Hà-van-Làu, Hanoi's representative at the UN and ambassador to Cuba. The figures we have been able to submit generally come from the West—official organizations or media—and some come from the Communist party itself. Others have come from Vietnamese refugees themselves. I also asked Minh-Hiên to forward his most conservative figures, according to his own experience.

Do you remember, in the introduction, Minh Hiên's impressions about Vietnam just before 1975? Here is the rest of them: "In 1972–1973, I could not accept Sir Robert Thompson or Gen. Raoul Salan's forecasts, that 3 to 5 million of my people, on an estimated population of 27 million, would be eliminated in the event of a communist takeover. A few thousands . . . certainly; it was inevitable. But millions . . . "

And these are very conservative figures. One day, maybe, more precise figures will fill in the blanks with numerical certainties. For the time being, we know that Hanoi has sent a minimum of 1,500,000 North Vietnamese cadres—with their families it goes up to 4 to 4.5 million people—to the South. To that one must add the farmers of the Red River Delta of North Vietnam, who are replacing the population of South Vietnam, Laos, and Cambodia.

In his book *From Colonialism to Communism*,[46] Hoàng-vàn-Chi[47] writes that in his report to the second Congress of the Party, which took place in February 1951, in Tuyen-Quang (Tonkin), Truong-Chinh, president of the National Assembly of North Vietnam, explained the plan for the agrarian reform that was to be the blueprint for all other countries where it would be applied later. First, the elimination of the landowners in North Vietnam—at least fifty thousand—to implement the communist system, then the transfer of 10 million farmers of the overpopulated Red River Delta toward South Vietnam, Laos, and Cambodia. That was already in 1951, three years before even signing the Geneva Accords in 1954, putting an end to the conflict with France, and the formulation of plans[48] for the domination of Southeast Asia. In his article "Les Vietnamiens aux prises avec la paix" (which could be translated "The Vietnamese Wrestle

		DESCRIPTION	NUMBER		DEAD	
A.		Civilian and military who escaped before April 1975	135,000		NFA	(37)
B	1.	Suicides and summary executions			5,000	
	2.	Reeducation camps	800,000		240,000	(30%)
	3.	Unemployed	5,000,000			
	4.	Women and children without support (malnutrition, no medicine)	4,000,000		800,000	(20%)
	5.	Agents who worked with the CIA	170,000		17,000	
	6.	Deserters, "traitors"	220,000		220,000	
	7.	Capitalists (1975)	2,000		—	(38)
	8.	Bourgeois (1978)	40,000		—	
	9.	Religious (Catholic: 3 million; Buddhists: 7–8 million; Hoa-Hào: 4 million; Cao-Dai: 2 million)	NFA		NFA	
	10.	Militants of opposition	NFA		NFA	
	11.	Boat People (1975–Feb. 1985)	969,000		400,000	(39)
		Killed at sea by the pirates			1,500	(40)
		Raped women	2,500	(40)		
		Kidnapped women and girls	700	(40)		
	12.	Land People: North	272,000	(40)	—	
		South	14,000		3,500	
	13.	ODP	70,674	(40)		
	14.	Victims of false "passeurs"	NFA		NFA	
		Victims of false resistance groups	NFA		NFA	
	15.	Farmers opposed to collectivization	NFA		NFA	
	16.	Ethnic groups of the Plateaux	450,000	(41)	400,000	
	17.	Abortions (planned)	150 to 180 per day		(42)	
	18.	Victims of drugs and alcoholism	NFA		NFA	
	19.	Orphans and war amputees	NFA		NFA	
	20.	New Economic Zones (1975–80)	3,500,000		1,400,000	(2/5)
Total: (some figures being not available)					3,487,000	
C.		Troops				
		In Laos	60,000		NFA	
		In Cambodia	200,000		NFA	
		Against China	300,000		NFA	

DESCRIPTION	NUMBER	DEAD
D. Deportations		
In USSR	500,000	NFA
East Germany, Czechoslovakia, Bulg.	300,000	NFA
Angola, Algeria, Mozambique	5,000	NFA
E. Replacement of the populations by North Vietnamese		
In South Vietnam (cadres)	1,500,000	(43)
(farmers)	6,000,000	
In Laos	100,000	(44)
In Cambodia	500,000	(45)

with peace)''[49] Hadji Khedoud writes about smuggling, prostitution, drugs, austerity, ostentatious luxury next to sordid misery, and corruption. Some bureaucrats manage to divert, and misappropriate aid from even the Eastern Bloc countries and the USSR. He also writes that the transfer of population is to erase the cultural differences between the North and the South and that this "North-malization" is aimed at suppressing the sense of identity of the southerners, who resent any form of authority, to transform people into a controlled, brainwashed mass.

Before yesterday, it was the Ukraine: twenty five thousand dead per day, more than one thousand per hour. This sound barrier of horror was smashed with 10 million victims, of which 3 million children, dead of artificial famine in the midst of one of the most productive wheat cornucopias of Europe.[50] It was brought to an end in three seconds: the time it took Stalin to sign the decree ending the tragedy. Yet when Canadian prime minister Brian Mulroney spoke of these events for the fiftieth anniversary of this planned massacre, the Soviet ambassador denied the evidence. The bigger the lie, the more Westerners are likely to swallow it up. Yesterday it was Hitler. Today it is Laos, Cambodia, Vietnam, and Ethiopia, among others. Tomorrow . . . but that is going to be the subject of our next chapter.

NOTES

1. From a French documentary, "Il était une fois le pouvoir" ("Once upon a Time There Was Power") broadcast by TVFQ 99 on September 12, 1987.

2. Robert Laffont, *Vivre la Cause de l'UNICEF (To Live the Cause of UNICEF)*, p. 155.

3. Olivier Orban, p. 167.

4. Dr. Kissinger's interlocutor during the Paris Accords in 1973, twenty years later, and until recently Politburo leader in Hanoi. Both Lê-duc-Thô and Dr. Kissinger won the Nobel Peace Price in 1973. The Politburo forbade Lê-duc-Thô from going to Stockholm in order to receive his prize. He left the Politburo—or maybe was not re-appointed—in June 1987.

5. Pham-vang-Dong is still indirectly in power, as an adviser, since June 1987.

6. November 4, 1984.

7. Berkeley University, California.

8. Building in Moscow of sinister memory, which Solzhenitsyn often refers to in his writings and where the Soviet secret police—whatever its name, since changed several times—tortured political prisoners to death. Today, according to John Barron's *KGB Today* (Reader's Digest Press), these activities are taking place at the prison of Lefortovo, in downtown Moscow, in camps outside the city, and in psychicatric hospitals.

9. In Vietnamese; another translation could be *Life in Enemy Territory*.

10. He published *A Vietcong Memoir* (New York: Harcourt Brace Jovanovich, 1985), also published in French by Flammarion.

11. *VNTP*, no. 218 (February 28, 1985); *LV* no. 11 (July 1985).

12. Not to be confused with the author of *A New Strategy to Defend the Free World Against Communist Expansion*, Thanh Phuong Thu Quan, five years younger—Minh Hiên recalls—than the cardiologist, a perfect example of homonymy.

13. Several thousand of them (from North and South) have been "authorized" to leave Vietnam through Hong Kong for one tael of gold.

14. Five hundred and forty-eight thousand and seven hundred and eighteen Vietnamese, Laotian, and Cambodian refugees all together.

15. Peter Townsend, *The Girl in the White Ship* (Glasgow: William Collins Sons and Co. Ltd., 1981).

16. Nicknamed the coco priest, not because of his political persuasion, but simply because his diet was mostly composed of coconuts. He was jailed in the prison of Cân-Tho until his death in 1976 or 1977.

17. His Eminence Henri Lemaître.

18. From her article (in French and in English) "Genocide in Laos," *Reader's Digest*, 1980.

19. According to Minh Hiên, the yellow rain has been used in Laos in 1977–78, after other chemicals, and as a result of new developments in the field of chemical warfare. Still according to Minh Hiên, the yellow rain would have been used in Cambodia in 1980, and early 1981, and through the same process of natural drainage, the chemicals have been found later in fish from the Mekong.

20. During the summer of 1987, Vietnamese shrimps were not on display in the same shop anymore. According to Minh Hiên, there are, however, shrimp

that come from the South China Sea. But who can tell the difference? Besides, after having used all kinds of rains to kill people, selling heroin and hashish to kill Western youth, why would these people care anyway?

21. "1984: The Year of the Mouse," broadcast by Radio Quebec on September 9, 1985.

22. A comprehensive study from the Center for Disease Control on over fifteen thousand Vietnam Veterans published in the *Journal of the American Medical Association* of May 13, 1988, shows no difference between soldiers who have been exposed to agent orange and those who did not even serve in Vietnam, or more birth defects in the children they fathered (AIM, June-B, 1988).

23. Passeurs are farmers or smugglers who, having a particular knowledge of a region, help people pass the border between two countries in wartime.

24. The iron triangle is south of Le-hong-Phong.

25. Cam Ranh has always been a formidable, natural harbor and an advanced position on the Pacific.

26. We know that even the North Vietnamese are not allowed to come close to this now Soviet base. One of the lessons of Vietnam is that without shedding a single drop of blood, the Soviets have managed to be the real winners of this conflict.

27. *London Times*, October 29, 1982, and the *Yomuri Shimbum* (Tokyo) *AFP*, April 21, 1982.

28. In his book "The Unknown War," Harrison E. Salisbury mentions 200,000 Germans. A French army archive movie "39–45" broadcast by Radio-Quebec on March 4, 1987, mentions 91,000.

29. *Le Devoir*, Montreal, January 7, 1984. Mr. Buddhi Klok was an administrator during the government of Prince Norordom Sihanouk.

30. Truong-Nhu-Tang, *A Vietcong Memoir* (New York: Harcourt Brace Jovanovitch 1985).

31. Published in Vietnamese, in California, in 1982, pp. 127–36. This book should be and already may be translated into English. The author, former deputy of the National Assembly, escaped Vietnam and arrived in the United States in 1981.

32. For obvious reasons, his name and country are not mentioned.

33. South of the Seven Mountains region, with difficult access.

34. Minh Hiên read the report in the *Chinh-Luan* (*Impartial Opinion*) in 1973. Despite this very accurate prediction, we now know what happened. The question remains: why people, and particularly those in charge, did not know better and act accordingly?

35. General Raoul Salan, *l'Indochine Rouge* (Paris: Presses de la Cité, 1975), p. 13.

36. Pierre Darcourt, *Vietnam, qui'as-tu fais de tes fils?* (Paris: Albatros, 1975). The title could also be translated as *Vietnam, What Have You Done to Your Children?*

37. NFA means "No Figures Available."

38. — means "We do not know."

39. According to W. R. Smyser, an American diplomat working with the UNHCR (see note 5, p. 74) 1,500,000 refugees have been relocated and 150,000 are still in transit camps. According to Richard Nixon in *No More Vietnams* (p. 222 in the French version, *Plus Jamais de Vietnams* [Albin Michel]), six hundred thousand refugees have died at sea.

40. Lowest figures from the UNHCR.

41. According to recent news (Review "Avant-Garde" No 263, November, 1986) out of 4,000 Montagnards, only 206 have survived, and managed to flee to Thailand, then to the US.

42. Only for the maternity hospital of Tu-Du in Ho Chi Minh City (in eight hours and without anesthesia). These are not figures for the all of Vietnam. One hundred and fifty children per day means 54,750 children per year. According to Dr. François Rémy ("40,000 children per day," Robert Laffont), the death rate was 30 o/oo in the North, 200 o/oo in the South due to the "shortage" of medicine, while cadres, farmers, and of course members of the Party are well fed, and well taken care of.

43. With an average of 3 people per family: 4,500,000.

44. According to the Nhan-Ban review (*Review Humanism*), No 31 (October 1, 1979), one hundred thousand North Vietnamese have been displaced to Laos in 1979.

45. This figure is according to Prince Norodom Sihanouk in 1985. There are probably more today. The total number of victims in Cambodia has been set at 3 million people, in 1985, by François Chalais ("7/7" program broadcast in Canada by TVFQ 99, April 20, 1985).

46. Hoàng-vàn-Chi, *From Colonialism to Communism* (London: Pall Mall Press, 1964).

47. Former communist diplomat in New Delhi, defected, and found refuge in Australia.

48. See pp. 161–162.

49. *L'Actualité*, April 1987.

50. According to a PBS report on Ukraine, broadcast on September 5, 1985, and a PBS program "Harvest of Despair," broadcast in September 1986. Some have raised this figure to 14 million victims.

THE RED OCTOPUS

> *But war, organized war, is not a human instinct. It is a highly planned and co-operative form of theft. And that form of theft began ten thousand years ago when the harvesters of wheat accumulated a surplus, and the nomads rose out of the desert to rob them of what they themselves could not provide.*
>
> —Jacob Bronowski

According to the Australian report "1984 Season: The Year of the Mouse":

> Since 1979 the economic disaster is even worse. . . . Today in a Vietnam which will have a population of 90 million people by the year 2,000 . . . a woman worker or a mechanic still works 48 hours a week . . . earns 800 dôngs per month . . . and a little civil servant 250 . . . when 1,000 are needed to make ends meet.[1]

In his book *A Vietcong Memoir*, Truong-Nhu-Tang writes that his salary as justice minister from 1975 until 1979 (before he escaped) was 210 dôngs.[2]

A refugee freed from Vietnam in 1985 told us that the average salary of a middle-rank employee working with the state-owned bank in Ho Chi Minh City was:

> . . . 250 dôngs: 50 as basic salary, to which are added up various fringe benefits" such as the cost of living, etc. A person with a basic salary of 50 dôngs receives 13 kgs of rice, and 400 grams of meat per month; . . . and, a person with a basic salary of 60 dôngs receives 15 kgs of rice, and 600 grams of meat per month. So much for equality. Doctors are earning a little bit more, whereas . . . teachers and secretaries receive between 180 and 200 dôngs per month. Rice at the official price is still non-edible, and the one suited for consumption costs 60 dôngs per kg on the black market (the equivalent of a basic salary). Pork meat costs 320 dông per kg, and . . . 1 duck egg 15 dôngs on the black market.

The gap between the figures of the Australian report "1984 Season: The Year of the Mouse" and those available as of December 1985 may come from the fact that the money has been invalidated for a third time since 1975, on September 14, 1985. Yet if the figures vary a little, the situation remains disastrous. When we read that the Vietnamese authorities are concerned about the nutritional situation of their country,[3] we are tempted to believe it—anybody would—but the fact is that stores for the privileged are packed with food, while the population is still run and controlled by the stomach; it is not mismanagement or "terrible mistakes," but intentional, planned policy.

The same authorities, it is also said, are trying to teach farmers how to socially manage the state-owned lands when for centuries they have been successful, individually or in families, with their fields and rice paddies. What they refused, though, like those in the Ukraine or today in Ethiopia, is the collectivization, the political and mass displacements of the population, leaving a trail of dead behind them. The earth has no other strategy than creation, and to respect it is an act of faith, not exactly in the Party's line.

It also seems that the communists simply cannot cope with the enormous needs of the nation, despite Vietnam's assets. It is like "forgetting" that they had these resources at their disposal, absolutely all of them. The point is that you cannot run a liberal economy with a socialist system.

It is also said, at times, that the North Vietnamese were taken by surprise by their independence. The hero and model of Vietnam, Ho Chi Minh, posed as a nationalist. However, he established, as early as 1930, the first communist cells in Indochina, whose admitted purpose was to establish communism in all of Indochina. Independence occurred officially on September 2, 1945. When someone wants it, thirteen to fifteen years for leaders who are said to have vision are not a surprise anymore.

We have seen the results in North Vietnam. The plans of the fifties for the conquest and Vietnamization of the neighboring countries confirm what the communists intended to do with independence, and we do not see in them the failure of a leadership taken by surprise. In the seventies, Pham-Van-Dong's lie was also part of that same long-term strategy: invasion, pillage, elimination of the population, its impoverishment, and colonization by well-indoctrinated elements from North Vietnam. The same pattern is applied everywhere. In Cambodia, for instance, and still according to Mr. Buddhi Klok, the Vietnamese soldiers sell the rice and the international aid they have recovered to the Cambodians, who use whatever is valuable left in their family to survive.[4]

When it is also claimed that international organizations are sending thousands of tons of food and millions of dollars' worth of aid, it is also like "forgetting" that the population does not see a single penny of it in a country that was producing 18, 21, and even 23 million tons of rice every year, before the arrival of the communists, plus the rest of it, because there was no starvation in South Vietnam.

When people are moved to tears by the fact that these same organizations are obliged to build factories to produce milk and food for children, it is, once again, like "forgetting" that this structure of production with the required raw material existed before, but that the communists dismantled it and sent up north all that they could. By the way, one wonders why the West keeps doing it.

When people pretend that money is short, it is like "forgetting" that the clean sweep of currency, money, gold by the ton, jewelry, and precious stones—real ones, not the 0.1 carat supermarket ring—private and public goods, factories and reserves, plantations and businesses, farms and herds, and the trade of human life in gold—even today—meant more capital than many governments could have ever hoped for to start with. Where did all this go? Financing invasions of neighboring countries? Certainly. Paying debts to the USSR and China? Definitely. But some say that at least part of it is being stored away to build reserves in case of a larger conflict in which the survival of any country will depend upon these reserves. But that is not meant for the population.

Communism is like an army of warrior ants: once they have eaten what was on the spot and since they do not produce much to replace it, they have to roam around to survive. We have always thought of espionage as a political or strategic technique. We now know it encompasses far more than that: high technology, money, information, and control of refugee groups in the West, whose families are kept hostage back where home was.

As far as the activities of Vietnam in the West are concerned and outside the relatively small number of "diplomat comrades" enjoying diplomatic immunity, we have to point out that a fairly important number of agents had settled down in the West before 1975. Remember, most communist parties have been activated in the West since the early twenties. This represents a superstructure. As far as Vietnam is concerned, the communist security forces infiltrated a first wave of Vietnamese agents between 1975 and 1979, especially with the "semi-official emigration." Their job was to establish contact with the media, to infiltrate all possible refugee organizations, peace movements, and the like, to meld into the hosting community's way of life, and to recover refugees as soon as they land, by blackmailing them about members of their families left in the motherland.

This was around the time when the West was stunned by the discovery of the Boat People. Refugees at that time could send aid to their families left in Vietnam without any problem (currency, medicine, clothing, et cetera) by parcels of ten kilograms. It was also the time when the smuggling of parcels arriving in Cholon was flourishing.

The second wave of agents was somewhat different from the first: better indoctrinated to resist "the temptations of the West" and professionally better trained in the USSR and in the GDR, in order to be more "attractive" to Western emigration services. Their task was different, even if the bottom line is the same. They are instrumental to the next step in exploiting the West.

In 1979, however, the whole thing was curtailed by some countries; the infiltration did not go unnoticed. Hô-Xuan-Dich, second secretary of the Hanoi Embassy in Ottawa (Canada), was declared persona non grata and sent back back to Vietnam within forty-eight hours by the Foreign Ministry of Canada. In the United States, Dinh-Ba-Thi (Ung-van-Khuong was his real name), Hanoi's ambassador to the UN, was also declared undesirable and would complete his career in an "explosive" manner—behind the wheel of his booby-trapped car, while driving in the middle of nowhere in Vietnam. That was also the time when some agents coming to the West, supposedly to make a better life, could not hide their leaning toward communism.

In July of this same year, 1979, delegates of fifty-seven nations gathered in Geneva decided to bring some order into the Boat People exodus, set up and manipulated by the communist security forces. It was the Orderly Departure Program, ODP for short. After 1979 a new strategy was devised for the communist agents of the new wave: Western countries are like milk cows. Therefore, their role was to be to milk the refugees the way it is done for international aid and this, thanks to the native Vietnamese population held hostage in Vietnam. They intend to play the sensitive string of charity and family ties, but in a very organized way. Today they are tapping people who are now nationals of their countries of adoption.

Communist agents have simply established an international network of economic, political, and diplomatic activities, dealing above the head of the host governments. In his report published in the *Hamilton Spectator* of July 13, 1985, Wayne Mac Phail cast some light on the shady side of the Vietnamese network in the United States, Canada, and France. We shall see that Australia, Japan, Hong Kong, and Singapore must be added to the list.

Since 1982, when the Vietnamese government established the network, mapped out the year before, the communist hydra had three important heads outside Vietnam: Montreal, Paris, and Hong Kong. In 1987 Singapore gradually replaces Hong Kong. Japan, which has a small community of refugees (a little over six thousand), is very important due to the fact that it has invested heavily in Vietnam. Another head has grown in New York (on Wall Street) with a branch, Canal Express Cargo, located on 210–212 Canal Avenue, New York, NY 10013. Covered in Canada by the Union Générale des Vietnamiens (General Union of Vietnamese in Canada),[5] these communist business companies such as Vietimex Inc., Vinamedic Inc., and Laser Express on 1444–1446 Beaudry Street, and QTK[6] on 1700 Berri Street—all four in Montreal—and Vina Pharmacy in Toronto were used as relays between the United States and France. Transaigon, strangely enough not named Trans–Ho Chi Minh City, is the terminal in Vietnam. Today it seems that all these companies in the world are more independent, yet working still with one another toward Vietnam.

What do these businesses do? As far as we know, in the

United States for instance, orders were placed on paper—before the opening of the New York branch—and then sent to Montreal, cosmopolitan city "par excellence," and turn-table of an America itself at the crossroads of the five continents. Asia and Europe are part of the same continent, but have access to North America, either by the eastern or western coast. Orders were then sent to Paris, another turn-table in Europe located between the East and the West. Then they were, and still are, sent to Vietnam, via Hong Kong or Singapore.

Parcels going through the mail were limited by the communists to three per family and per year. In order to enrich the business companies of the network, most parcels "got lost," were ripped open, or were delivered half-empty—or half-full if one is an optimist. Their contents were often confiscated or "bought" very cheaply by the communist Customs.

Parcels that were flown directly to Ho Chi Minh City were distributed at the Tan-Son-Nhut airport warehouse, three kilometers away from the city. It is difficult to reach, since state buses are in limited number. The taxes levied by the Customs are very, very high: a pair of jeans bought for five Canadian dollars[7] were taxed one thousand, five hundred dôngs; that is the equivalent of six to eight months' salary for an average cadre, more for a worker: four to five times the price of the pants themselves. Vietnamese living in the countryside are obliged to pick up their parcels in Ho Chi Minh City after having obtained the police authorization to do so, bought their ticket in an indescribable mob, and gone through all the checkpoints punctuating a journey that lasts the entire day to reach the city. Then they have to go all the way back with a probably ripped open parcel whose contents have been partly, at the very least, levied by the Customs agents. Among other things, quantities of more than one hundred pills are simply confiscated.

On the other hand, parcels going through the companies arrived faster and without any problem to the Hanoi and Ho Chi Minh City branches. Taxes, however, remain the same, and people have to travel all the same to pick them up unopened. Today the refugees have got the message: most parcels are now going through the companies of the network.

Foreign currencies sent by the refugees to their families—who in most cases have only this to survive on—are not handled as such. The government receives them through the state-owned bank and gives in exchange, to the addressees, small amounts of local currency without any international value. In some instances, instead of money the Vietnamese receive bonds exchangeable in several years. In some other cases, even the local currency is frozen in a "saving" account, and the holders have to submit a special request to the authorities with the hope that they will be allowed to make a withdrawal and not all of it in one time, mind you.

Foreign currencies are so badly needed that refugees who want to send medicine to Vietnam are requested to give a certified check or money order to the branch they are dealing with, which in turn will send it to its destination. Then the same scenario takes place: the government keeps it and gives the local currency in exchange, et cetera, and the addressee will have to buy his or her medicine on the black market, if he or she can find it, and pay for it.

According to Wayne Mac Phail's report, families left behind the Vietnamese "Bamboo Curtain" have been "strongly invited" by the communists to solicit money from those who have fled the regime and are now living in the West. As we can see, Hanoi indeed welcomes aid from overseas. Refugees living in North America were sending—in 1985, that is, at the time of this report—an average of U.S. $140 million per year, the amount winding up in the safe of the Democratic Republic of Vietnam. The U.S. Treasury even puts forward the figure of U.S. $216 million, half of it transiting through Canada. This matches, more or less, the figures for trade between Vietnam and Singapore, according to Nguyên-co-Thâch, Hanoi's foreign minister.[8]

We must point out that amongst these businesses, QTK Express accepts only U.S. dollars, whereas other companies accept Canadian currency on which they levy a tax of 76 percent for the exchange rate. These companies are mainly used to channel the very lucrative trade of medicine, parcels, and goods, and most importantly foreign currency. The addresses of those dealing exclusively with money are at the end of this chapter.

Vietnamese refugees here in the West are sending merchandise badly needed by their families kept hostage in Vietnam, and the Vietnamese government takes away most of it. It is particularly the case with money—the regime keeps the foreign currency and gives worthless paper—and with medicine. Goods are also very heavily taxed. For example, Japanese motorbikes have been traded for some years now. A Vietnamese refugee in Canada, who wants to send a Honda C-70 to his family in Vietnam must place his order with Laser Express in Montreal and pay U.S. $850 (in 1987, price unchanged since 1985, we were told) for the motorbike.

In 1985–86 the sender was also required to send the equivalent of $300 U.S. for the tax. Laser Express would then call its Hong Kong or Singapore branch to order the motorbike in Japan, which in turn would deliver it in Vietnam, through one of these branches. Today, in 1987–88, the sender is required to send a tax of $800 U.S.—practically as much as the motorbike itself. We also learned that since more and more Japanese firms are being established in Vietnam, orders are placed directly with them.

By the way, it was when placing an order of this sort with Laser Express in Montreal that Vietnamese refugees were able to become acquainted with the Vietnamese file concerning the causes and effects of pollution on the fish and shrimp of the Mekong River, loaded with yellow, red, and other chemical rains of the sort, dumped over Laos, and which in the long term have poisoned the Vietnamese waters.

This network has several goals:

- To undermine the life of any host country accepting refugees.
- To drain all that is needed by Vietnam.
- To keep track of all the Vietnamese established in host countries and their connections in Vietnam, since both have to divulge extensive lists of personal information in order to send or to receive even a small parcel.
- To impose the monopoly of these companies created by the communists.
- To use them as unofficial consulates.

•To transfer money from one country to another without using the usual international channels.

•To establish highly efficient secret services working for Big Brother.

This structure in place, the next line of products planned to go through these companies will be computers and high technology. There is nothing new about this, since all Eastern Bloc nations have been doing it for a very long time, but it is an extension of Hanoi's activities.

Why is Canada, and Montreal in particular, a favorite place for this kind of trading?

Well, let us have a look at where the refugees are located in the world:

•824,000 in the United States.

•122,964 in Canada.

•108,481 in Australia.

•101,432 in France.

•23,246 in West Germany.

•17,391 in Great Britain.

•9,428 in Switzerland.

•7,369 in New Zealand.

•5,835 in Holland.

•5,135 in Norway.

There are also over 6,000 in Japan, and some 250,000 or so in other countries, for a grand total of 1,489,100 in the world. As one can see, the United States, Canada, Australia, France, and Japan are the most strategic countries, and this shows in the network's activities. Next in line are West Germany and Great

Britain (technology) and, yes, Switzerland, but not necessarily for its cheese.

Canada is bordering the United States, both representing two thirds of the refugee "market" and both rich countries. There are no exchange controls, as in France for instance, where it has been momentarily suspended, probably for the 1988 election campaign. People know still little about communism as it really is and how it proceeds. A Canadian woman back from a visit to the USSR even said, talking about Soviets, "But these people are free." She choked when asked why 140 dissidents had to be released if they were supposed to be free in the first place. Many political, educational, media, union, and social organizations are easy to infiltrate and some just want to cooperate.

Why Paris?

- It has been France's and Europe's most important crossroads for Asians and this for decades.

- From an economic point of view, Vina-Paris, one of the companies of the Vietnamese network, supplies a very large amount of medicine ordered even in Canada and the United States; transportation fees were paid, at least thus far, through Laser Express in Montreal. Now that every branch in various countries is becoming more independent, things may be different. Orders from other European countries are also placed with Vina-Paris.

- From a diplomatic point of view, legation being full-fledged, agents and militants working in North America stay in Paris for a while before going to Vietnam. People who left that country and later decided to go back, even momentarily, have been able to do so because they got a favorable backup from the agents in their host countries—acting as unofficial consuls, but known in Vietnamese milieux—and thanks to a visa from the Vietnamese embassy in Paris. For example, T.T.T. went into exile in Switzerland in the sixties, married a Swiss-German woman, then decided to go back to Vietnam to pay a visit to his mother. It was the embassy in Paris that delivered the visa. This, by the way, took more than a year. In Brussels, D.T.S., a well-known militant, transmits the requests for entry visas with favorable or unfavorable decision for the Vietnamese living in Belgium to the Vietnamese embassy in Paris.

Why Australia?

•Since the Labor party took over, Canberra follows a moderate policy with Hanoi.[9]

•Important financial transactions in U.S. currency go through Australia: in 1985, for instance, L.N.D., living in the United States, admitted to having paid all the family's savings to the "intermediaries" in Australia, in order to get the fifteen remaining members of his sisters' families out of Vietnam. At $4,000 U.S. per person, this amounts to U.S. $60,000. This shows two things: First, that prices have gone up. In 1978–79, U.S. $2,000 were required to escape the country, today U.S. $4,000 are needed. Second, the network is working well, since both families have reached the Philippines in August 1985.

Hong Kong, at the doorstep of the ASEAN countries, the second most important duty-free harbor in the world—but soon to be handed back to the People's Republic of China and to be replaced by Singapore—plays a preponderant role for Vietnam. Each month, Dalat Express, one of the companies of the Vietnamese network located on 19–21 Hennessy Road, sends three cargos with six-thousand-ton loads of supplies requested by Hanoi: machines, home appliances, Japanese motorbikes, but also raw material, among which is sulphur for the manufacturing of ammunition.

The Dalat Express branch is also of the utmost importance for the transfer of money for Hong Kong Chinese who already fear the eventual communist control and are moving their fortunes, out to the West. This is how it works:

•Vietnamese refugees in the United States or in Canada, for instance, want to send merchandise and/or money to their families in Vietnam. They place their orders with one of the companies, such as Laser Express in Montreal or Canal Express Cargo in New York. They pay in U.S. dollars only. Then, the company they are dealing with informs Dalat Express in Hong Kong (19–21 Hennessy Road) that trading is going on, but the money remains in the United States or in Canada.

•In Hong Kong—which is going to be recuperated by the People's Republic of China in a few years—Chinese who want to transfer their money to the West pay on the spot for the orders placed by the Western branches and the same amount of money is credited to them in the United States or Canada or possibly elsewhere. For example: twenty Vietnamese refugees in Montreal order for twenty thousand dollars' worth of merchandise to be delivered in Vietnam through Dalat Express in Hong Kong. They pay that amount of money in Canada. In Hong Kong, a Chinese wants to transfer funds to North America. He is informed that in Canada Laser Express has twenty thousand dollars available in Montreal. He pays that amount of money, plus the fees to Dalat Express, which in turn informs Laser Express by telex to credit the money to this Chinese in Montreal. This practice is very handy when money needs to be transferred outside government regulations and exchange control and establishes a system that avoids the current international way of trading.

The U.S. dollars milked from the Vietnamese refugees, now nationals of some twelve countries or so, are transferred through:

•**Japan:** Vinaseko Co. Ltd. 3.6.14.406 Nishinippori, Arakawa-Ky, Tokyo 116.

•**USA:** Vinamex, 40 Wall Street, Suite 2124, New York, NY 10005.

•**Canada:** QTK Express, Inc., Berri Street, Suite 209, Montreal. Vinamedic, 1446 Beaudry Street, Montreal.

•**France:** Vietnam Diffusion, 146 Bld. Vincent Auriol, 75013, Paris.

•**West Germany:** Asico Handels GMBH, Eichentra B 59, D 6230, Frankfurt, Main.

Other branches whose addresses have been mentioned along the way are used for transferring merchandise to Vietnam. The communists ask their agencies to acquire everything essential for the military and the police (clothing, medicine, even old tires for the shoes, et cetera) and then whatever they can get for the economy, such as pesticides for example. The Soviet aid only consists of the military equipment of the forces of occupation in Laos and Cambodia and those facing the Chinese army.

Reimbursing the IMF is certainly not Vietnam's priority. Twice already—in 1986 and in 1987[10]—have the IMF and the World Bank refused to further loans to five countries: Vietnam, Peru, Guyana, Liberia, and Sudan.

After the third invalidation of the money on September 14,

1985, with the urgent need for dollars—and any foreign currency for that matter—the communists have increased their exchange rate.

Before September 14, 1985, one U.S. dollar was worth 180 dôngs. After October–November 1985, a "new dông"—worth ten old ones—was put on the Vietnamese market. Therefore, a U.S. dollar was worth "only" eighteen dôngs.

	Dôngs
December 1985–January 1986	20
February 1986–September 1986	30
October 1986	220
November 1986	260
December 1986–April 1987	300
May 1987	360
June–August 1987	500
September 1987	504
October 1987	600
November 1987	700

Early in 1988, the Vietnamese refugees also discovered another network, another way money is being transferred to Vietnam, which in turn uses it according to its needs. For example, a refugee wants to send money to his or her family in Vietnam. He or she will go to a certain local bank in his or her country of adoption:

United States—San Francisco:	International Banking Group 420 Montgomery Street. CA 94163
Australia—Sydney:	Anz Banking Group Ltd. CNR Pitt Street Martin Place
Melbourne:	Anz Bank 388 Collins Street
Canada—Vancouver:	Bank of Montreal 595 Burrard Street, B.C.
New Zealand—Aukland:	Anz Banking Group Ltd. CNR Queen Victoria Street
Singapore—(ASEAN):	Banque Française du Commerce Extérieur 50 Raffles Place
Switzerland—Lausanne: (Europe)	Union des Banques Suisses 1, Place St-François.

and the central banking institution of all this:

Lausanne:	Fortrade Finance Corporation 38 Chemin de Mornex, 1001

Most of the time, when these banks are too far away or when the entire network was not yet in place, refugees use the companies to send their money to their relatives in Vietnam. These companies then contact one of the banks closest to them to do the transactions. They all send their transactions to Fortrade Finance Corporation in Lausanne, which deals directly with Vietnam and distributes the money to the interested, the way we described it earlier in this chapter. Thus far, the money has not been transferred from one country to another, but when Vietnam needs financing for whatever trade it may have to do with one of the concerned countries, it has available funds kept on the spot. As far as the Vietnamese refugees know, and although there is no formal proof at this point, it seems that the money is being used among other things for the upkeep of their delegates to the UN and the Vietnamese embassy in London. Part of it is also used to buy whatever is needed for the maintenance of the Vietnamese army and bureaucracy, such as medicine, for instance.

Since 1987, Minh Hiên has learned about other banking institutions trading directly with the state-owned bank of Vietnam:

Canada:	Royal Bank of Canada Bank of Montreal (already mentioned) Canadian Imperial Bank of Commerce (Toronto)
France:	Banque Commerciale pour l'Europe du Nord (Paris)

In his book *Le KGB en France* (*The KGB in France*), Thierry Woltan reveals that the BCEN is a Soviet bank established in France since 1924.

Australia:	Commonwealth Bank of Australia (Sydney)
Hong Kong:	Hong Kong and Shanghai Banking Corporation (Hong Kong)
	Vietnam Finance Company (Hong Kong)
Singapore:	Banque Nationale de Paris (Singapore)
	Banque Française du Commerce Extérieur (Singapore)
	Moscow Narodny Bank (Singapore)
Great Britain:	Moscow Narodny Bank (London)
Japan:	Mitsubishi Bank (Tokyo)

This list has been published in *Dât Viêt* in August 1987, a magazine obedient to the communists.

NOTES

1. Broadcast in French by Radio Quebec on September 9, 1985.
2.Truong-Nhu-Tang, *A Vietcong Memoir* (New York: Harcourt Brace Jovanovitch), 1985, p. 302.
3. Article by Claire Brisset, in *Le Monde*, November 10, 1984.
4. *Le Devoir*, Montreal, January 7, 1984.
5. This organization is also using several other names: Union des Vietnamiens au Canada, Union des Vietnamiens du Canada, and others, including the Association des Vietnamiens au Canada (the Association of the Vietnamese in Canada), the largest noncommunist Vietnamese organization in Canada.
6. is the Vietnamese abbreviation for Saving Bank.
7. In 1979 and with a small defect.
8. *Dân Quyen Review*, no. 75 (May 1985.)
9. There are diplomatic exchanges, the opening of an Australian embassy in Hanoi, and Vietnamese students sent to Australia and Australian journalists to Vietnam.
10. *Le Monde*, International Edition, no. 1977 (September 18–24, 1986), and no. 2029 (September 17–23, 1987).

WHAT'S NEXT?

Mischief has been created by the logical mind.

—Chuangtse

In terms of projection, the Vietnamese regime—which has inherited the sum of communist experiences since 1917 and is applying them in the most subtle manner—has its business network implanted in the West and in Southeast Asia, the Pacific being the place where things are going to happen next. It also has advisers in Central America, Africa, and the Middle East and of course troops in Southeast Asia, where the slogan "Asia for Asians" is becoming more and more "Asia for communists."

According to Jean-Claude Pomonti, the third five-year plan of 1986–90 is projecting to send 12 million North Vietnamese farmers and settlers from the Red River Delta to the Plateaux region, to replace the massacred ethnic populations,[1] unless, like many others elsewhere, they have been wiped out to make room for the northern population whose transfer was planned decades ago: in the 1950s, before the signing of the Geneva Accords that were to ensure peace in Vietnam and the neutrality of Laos and Cambodia, 10 million North Vietnamese were scheduled to be transferred to South Vietnam, Laos, and Cambodia.

Even though this Plateaux region has good arable land it is not able to support more than 2 million people. Therefore, the questions are: What is going to happen to the other 10 million North Vietnamese, and where are they going to be resettled? In Laos, where underground Soviet missiles are said to be aimed at Thailand? In Cambodia, where Hanoi is already transferring North Vietnamese "voters" and "Vietnamizing" the country? In Thailand, later,[2] and in the rest of Southeast Asia? This would be indeed the application of the plan A, B, C, and D. Understanding that, we too will know our political alphabet and see clearly what is going on in the world.

Even distributed all over South Vietnam, 12 million newcomers would represent the equivalent of an injection of 115 million immigrants in the United States, twelve in Canada, twenty-eight in Great Britain, twenty-seven in France, thirty-one in West Germany, fifty-nine in Japan, one hundred and thirty-five in the Soviet Union, or five hundred in the People's Republic of China. And mind you, Vietnam expects to have a population of 90 million by the year 2000. What is it going to do with them, and, most important, what for?

This North Vietnamese population transferred to Laos, Cambodia, and South Vietnam is well indoctrinated and certainly does what it is told to do. Can one imagine if one day communist Vietnam decides to hold "democratic" elections? All these imported people would "vote" automatically for the puppet regime put in place by Hanoi, and most Western journalists would rejoice about this "democratic process." Meanwhile, the North Vietnamese are eating the bread of the South Vietnamese.

Once again, it is possible to transfer all these people, only if there is room to do it, unless one makes room in order to do it, which in the end comes down to pretty much the same thing. And the more room you need . . .

It is to be feared that Sir Robert Thompson and Gen. Raoul Salan's forecast of a genocide in South Vietnam—3 to 5 million victims—is an accurate figure. It may even become an underestimation in the long run, especially when one knows that the economic system, the production, and the crops are absolutely unable to sustain the existing population, even less demographic increases. Once again Vietnam will have to feed on others. It already has, and it will again.

On May 26, 1987, Tran-Van-Hung, ambassador to Britain was visiting Canada and gave a conference in Montreal. Among other things he promised that:

- The re-education camps would be closed, which proves, if anyone doubted it, that they are still open.

- More visas shall be delivered to Vietnamese refugees, and they will be able to bring as much foreign currency as they want to Vietnam, and deposit it in Vietnamese accounts. Withdrawal, however, will only be done in dôngs. And wait until the next invalidation of the money or a crash, as will be the case on October 19, 1987. Also in an attempt to get some shares of the market with the West, Canadian enterprises that want to do business with Vietnam are invited to contact the Vietnamese embassy in London.

It is interesting to note at this point that in June 1987, soon after Ambassador Tran-Van-Hung's visit to Canada, twenty-three Vietnamese were prevented from coming back to Great Britain and were charged with espionage. They had indeed been invited to go on a tourist trip to visit Vietnam and had obtained a visa from the Vietnamese embassy in London, on a loose leaf, not on their passports, so that they could travel to Vietnam without British authorities knowing about it. The fact is that they did and the British police were waiting for them at Heathrow Airport.

Beside the business network in North America and in Europe, Vietnam wants to create an image of "normalization," being confident that its trade with Southeast Asian countries will help project itself in the West, and to some extent it already has. In 1986 Vietnam exported $U.S. 20 million to Japan—whose investments in that country are said to be on the increase—primarily salt, white sand for glassware, and coconut fiber. It also imported 272 million U.S. dollars worth of motorbikes, steel tubes for bicycles, and household appliances (refrigerators, and TV sets), and textile equipment, probably to replace or rebuild those stolen in the seventies and sent up north or to Eastern Bloc countries. Its trading does not seem to be what pays for all this, although there has been another $U.S. 130 million of exchange with Singapore in 1986, mostly shrimp and shirts.[3]

In August 1987, *l'Actualité* reported that behind a mask of normalization, the Vietnamese are establishing terror in Cambodia: torture, hard labor, terrible sanitary conditions, absolute state control, delation, children dying at the rate of 160 o/oo,[4] without any foreigner, or almost, to report about it, some journalists going as far as saying that refugees exagerate their account of the situation. Yet practically none of them is going there to check it out. Would they be allowed and then why reject systematically what the refugees have to say? To keep silent about the whole thing and disinform the West, in the name of getting together?

Meanwhile, also in August 1987, a Canadian network[5] was still airing the series "Vietnam," showing the way it was some twenty-five years ago, probably forgetting that the world has turned a lot since then and that during half that period of time Vietnam has been under a communist regime and that there is a lot more to tell now than ever before.

In early September 1987, a large Vietnamese delegation was present at the francophone summit held in Quebec, Canada: Nguyen-Huu-Tho, seventy-seven, ex-president of the National Assembly, vice president of the Council of State, official ombudsman; Ha-Van-Lau, ex–ambassador to Cuba and to the U.N., ambassador in Paris, expert in international relations; Vo-Van-Sung, ex–ambassador to Paris, deputy-director of the international relations committee, in charge of aid, trade relations, and foreign investments; and Pham-Giang, political commissar with the Culture Department, secretary of the delegation. Yet, like Laos and Switzerland, Vietnam was at the francophone summit only as an observer. And yet again, French has not been spoken in North Vietnam since 1945—forty-two years ago—and in the South, since 1954, although some schools teaching French are said to have been authorized until 1975. Vietnamese have also witnessed the fact that anything French has been destroyed or has disappeared.

Why this heavy "cultural" artillery? At the end of July 1987, Prof. Gérard Hervouet, of the Political Science Department of Laval University and director of the review *Etudes Internationales* (*International Studies*), was invited through the Union Générale des Vietnamiens au Canada (General Union of the Vietnamese in Canada) in Montreal, by the International Relations Institute of Hanoi, to study the economic situation for the Department of International Relations of Quebec.

Beginning August 1987, Mr. Denis Ricard, Quebec's international relations deputy minister, went to Hanoi in order to proffer an official invitation to the francophone summit. The Department of Foreign Affairs mentioned that Quebec could provide help—if requested—in five areas: agriculture, communications, education, energy, and transportation.

On August 20, 1987, Amnesty International—Canadian French Division—published a thirty-two-page document on capital punishment in Vietnam (especially p. 16) and on the thousands of people incarcerated in "re-education camps," without trial, whose only crime has been to serve in the army and in the administration of the former regime. In front of several hundred journalists from the five continents, Amnesty International revealed that out of the thirty-eight members present at the summit, thirty-one have violated human rights in their countries. According to the Montreal *Gazette* of August 29, 1987, Vietnam is one of the nine states arresting people without trial and one of the thirteen countries known for practicing savage torture and capital punishment. In Quebec, Amnesty International erected a wooden cell in the yard of the Anglican Holy Trinity Church—near the château Frontenac—in which victims of nations violating human rights were invited to relay one another, twenty-four hours a day, whatever the weather. On September 3, 1987, a Vietnamese woman locked up herself in the cell from 8:00 to 9:00 P.M.

On September 2, 1987, the day the summit opened, hundreds of people from Somalia, Burundi, Cambodia, and Vietnam gathered to denounce the human rights violations in their respective countries and together to expose Hanoi's hypocrisy of prohibiting French and yet being present at the francophone summit. The delegation from Canada and Quebec have refused Mr. Nguyên-Huu-Tho's request for an interview.

The aim of the Vietnamese delegation was to solicit aid from Quebec on the five subjects already mentioned and to paint a picture of a "new opening," "transparence"—"Soviet Glasnost" fashion—to invite foreigners to consider the "new investment law with assured benefits" and invest their money in Vietnam. Despite the promise that French would be taught again in Vietnam and that prisoners in re-education camps would be released, it seems that not much response has been given to the Vietnamese delegation—publically, at least.

The sine qua non condition for Canada to send aid to Vietnam is the withdrawal of Vietnamese troops from Cambodia; a promise made in Paris by Mr. Nguyên-Huu-Tho to the effect that no matter what, Vietnam will pull its forces out of Cambodia in 1990.[6] As far as the United States is concerned, President Reagan authorized private humanitarian aid and the end of the trade embargo if and when the 150,000 *bô-dôis* get out of Cambodia.[7] However, their withdrawal does not change the fact that the civilians who support the regime and who will remain there are North Vietnamese. Minh Hiên insists upon the figure of two hundred thousand bô-dôis[8] being in Cambodia. It is also said that a U.S. delegation has established quarters in Ho Chi Minh City to study the files of some twenty-eight thousand Vietnamese seeking refuge.[9]

During a lecture he gave in Melbourne, Australia,[10] Mr. Nguyên Ngoc Huy[11] said that if the communists are sure of the withdrawal of their soldiers from Cambodia, it is because since 1979 they have been implementing their plan of Vietnamization of Laos and Cambodia. In the latter, there are already eight hundred thousand Vietnamese settlers, and their number is growing daily. They have been ordered to take Cambodian names, to learn the Cambodia language—Khmer—and to become Cambodian citizens. In a few years, they will be 2 to 3 million. The Vietnamese Communist party will then be able to recruit two hundred thousand soldiers and policemen, which will be used officially as national forces of Cambodia but will remain under the direct control of Hanoi. The communist Vietnamese will then be able to withdraw their troops and keep very tight control over Cambodia.

Can it also be done in Afghanistan? And elsewhere? Then the so called "national forces" will be able to perpetrate even more inhuman crimes, and nobody will say anything about it, except maybe that "it is a matter between nationals."

NOTES

1. The international edition of *Le Monde*, no. 1933, November 14–20, 1985.
2. Fighting has been reported on Hill 538 on the Khmero-Thai border (TVFQ 99, November 5, 1986).
3. J. C. Pomonti, *Le Monde International*, May 14–20, 1987.
4. "Plongée dans l'enfer du génocide." ("Deep into the hell of the genocide" could be the translation.)
5. Radio Canada (CKTM-Indep), August 18, 1987.
6. Also on CBC, June 30, 1988.
7. *l'Express*, October 2, 1987.
8. CFTM-TVA TV Montreal mentions the same figure on June 2, 1988.
9. *Lang-Van*, October 1987.
10. September 17, 1987.
11. Already mentioned, author of *A New Strategy to Defend the Free World against Communist Expansion*, Thanh-Phuong Tu-Quán, USA.

THE INTERNATIONAL CONTEXT

The deterioration of a government begins almost always with the disintegration of its principles.

—Montesquieu

Species dying out, problems due to the desertification of the Sahara, droughts, the decline of the elm tree (in Europe), women allowed in office (and in the clergy), insecurity in the Near and the Middle East, colonization and independence, the secret monopoly of silver (to mint money), the first bill of exchange (the first check), and the end of the world are more or less today's news, but these events, for example, took place from 8000 B.C. until A.D. 1057, except that at that time democrats were imperialists and conservatives pacifists, all arguing about the way war should be conducted—it has not changed much since—and faced with diseases from Egypt and China and great famines plaguing the West.[1]

Free enterprise may well have started when the first man split a stone into pieces and when the first woman used one of the splinters to clean the skin of a wild beast. Later on, it was when men and women began to sow wheat, harvest it, and plan for the future, therefore, "capitalized." War was invented at the same time, when the nomadic tribes of the time discovered that it was easier for them to steal the harvests of the sedentary people than to sweat producing them.

Dictatorship and bureaucracy already existed thousands of years ago in Asia, and despotism was given its name in ancient Greece. Communism was also around: an elite aristocracy—today we would call it an elite or Nomenklatura—was to lead "the Republic" of Plato, in the fourth century B.C. He was then advocating the community of goods and of women, and children were to be taken away from their families to be brought up by the state.[2]

In 1516 Thomas More described in *Utopia* a socialist society he had imagined, suppressing private property, not governed by an elite this time, but resting with the people. In 1623 Campanella's concept of communism reposed on Christianity, and its goal was to bring back mankind to its original divine state, probably forgetting that if human beings had fallen low then, it was not with the already cumulated mistakes that they would rise again. Campanella was to suppress the family also.

Then all schools of thoughts get representation during the seventeenth and the eighteenth centuries; Christian with Winstansley; end of private property with Abbot Mably: return to nature with Morelly; opposition to religion, considered long before Lenin himself to be the opium of the masses, with the parish priest Meslier. It is with the French Revolution that the modern form of communism as we know it today appeared, the way it is practiced in socialist states.

Identity searching and territorial definition took place early in the history of nations. The aristocracy that had served the kings and queens, emperors and empresses, grabbing whatever they could, was rewarded with estates and titles, money and privileges to enjoy itself. The eighteenth century was to change all that, or so it seemed, and shift the center of power to the economy. For the first time, it dominated politics and triggered wars and revolutions; it was the beginning of political economy.

The eighteenth century was also a period during which the ideas of progress, enlightment (even enlightened despotism), humanism (the human being becoming the center of society), pursuit of happiness (in the Epicurean sense), scientific thinking, universal love (Schiller, for example), and nationalism (Kacinczy) were on the agenda of the time. What was to become a worldwide form of economy was changing the division of time and work itself, but for the moment children of twelve and women were laboring in coal mines under atrocious conditions. Beside this revolution of ideas, four other revolutions were in the making.

Early in the eighteenth century, a Scot, John Law, proposed a financial revolution: the changing of coins for banknotes, the creating of a state-owned bank that was to lend money to business people, manage large enterprises, and make profits, the "intelligent" exploitation of colonies through monopolies whose revenues were to go to the state, the recovering of taxes that were to bring in more money to the state than the farm system of that time did—like sharecropping for instance—and the reimbursement of debt with the profit from these measures. Law was ahead of his time then, but the road was now open to finance as we know it today, and the crashes of 1929, and 1987, since in December 1719 the collapse of this new financial system left the people in total shock—some having been ruined, while others became a lot richer—and the material situation in shambles.

The Industrial Revolution began in Great Britain around 1760 with craftsmen who believed that every human being is master of his own destiny. It started out in the countryside with practical inventions, results of cumulated discoveries over the centuries, and made businessmen out of these inventors and not the other way around: people who would have created inventions to make money out of them and therefore have the means to oppress the masses, as propaganda would have it.

In 1776 the War for Independence in America—not to be confused with a revolution—established freedom and democracy as a way of life, while the French Revolution—attempting to do the same?—ended up in blood, unscrewed aristocracy from its pedestal, established a centralized government in Paris that beheaded the king and those resisting its dictatorship, and gave Napoleon the opportunity to democratize war and impose his dictatorship over Europe.

The eighteenth century is also a socialist revolution with Saint-Simon (1760–1825). Born after the Financial Revolution, with the Industrial Revolution, he grew up with the French one, all representing a need to reorganize a world already going wild. The aristocracy knew very well what was going on, and that the name of the game was to give the feudal system a new orientation, while remaining in power and enjoying the privileges, and avoiding the people's legitimate anger: in short, to create more goods so that everybody could be satisfied. The thing turned out to be bloody, ruthless, which made Danton tell Robespierre that the revolution would devour him the way it was killing himself, which it did.

To understand modern socialism and communism better we need to go back to their roots: the Saint-Simonian doctrine. The economic, political, and social doctrine of Saint-Simon[3] was developed to "replace" the monarchy obviously in jeopardy as a way of life. For him, society having gone through a theological and military age (feudalism), then through a metaphysical and democratic one, it would reach a scientific and industrial era in which administration would replace the political governments. A central body—a *Nomenklatura*, or elite, as we call it today—is to lead a scientific organization (a new aristocracy?), governing more and more by knowing what others do not. It will favor those supporting the system based not on agriculture as in the past, but on industry. This means looking for resources, and the systematic exploitation of the planet so dear to colonialists. Budgets will be allocated to the representatives of the industry replacing more and more the clergy in the exercise of the spiritual power. Today we would say that dialectic materialism in the East and consumerism in the West are replacing religion in order to go, as suggested by Saint-Simon, from a celestial morale toward an earthly one. Associations (Unions) will be linked together toward a grand common goal in order to improve the fate of the workers. This doctrine includes the elimination of the non-industrious, non-productive (idle) people. In the East, it is the Gulag, the New Economic Zones, and/or the genocide solution. In the West, unemployment, welfare, and down the road, the jobless, homeless, and under-the-poverty-level percentage. Government will be reduced and will disappear completely, to be replaced by an administration. It means that we will probably not vote anymore. This era is supposed to be the exploitation of nature by man, and not the exploitation of man by man. If it is true, ecologists should have some difficulty with human rights activists. A central, state owned bank would become the sole inheritor and manager of the financial system. This was, by the way, already advocated by John Law some decades earlier. All this was supposed to bring perfect equality and the end of private property. The five-year plans are not an invention of the Soviet system, nor of Marx, but are Saint-Simonian. The Constitutional changes, more and more advocated in our Western countries, the legitimization of insurrection, the clearing sweep of the past—the "Tabula Rasa" formula we have been hearing about for two decades or so now—are also part of the same doctrine. All this, to give people a sense of history in order to attain universality. What is important in all this is that it has been implemented in communist countries alright, but it was invented by a Westerner, and our daily reality reveals that it is being advocated here in the West.

The historical perspective that comes to mind first goes back to ancient China, where the emperor's administration then was already keeping people pretty much under control. Plato described a similar society in *The Republic*, during the fourth century B.C., and monarchy has already set the pattern for this type of structure: emperor/empress/king/queen—"Nomenklatura"/privileged; aristocracy-scientific/industrial/technocratic elite; artisans-workers; peasants-farmers; serfs–forced laborers. All this looks pretty much like a replay of the successive past experiences of mankind, under the roof of the same doctrine.

The nineteenth century accentuated the trends of the eighteenth century: war and peace, sharing the colonial world, leading to the systematic exploitation of the planet for supplying resources for the Industrial Age, revolutions and independences to get out of monarchy, free trade and tariffs, industrial development, and a socialism in its various forms: socialism through association (universal harmony); Christian socialism (sovereignty to the people);[4] social democracy (equality, a religion for mankind, and the emancipation of women); mutual socialism (end of property, decentralization, developing unions); state socialism (organization of work, suppression of private industry, and collectivization),[5] all being more or less facets of the Saint-Simonian doctrine.

In 1848 entered Karl Marx, influenced by Saint-Simon, among others. Whatever positive things are said about what he advocated and the hope he may have given to the workers then, reality shows that if Marxism, and by extension Marxism-Leninism, is what the world has seen for the past seventy years—from the Soviet Union to Vietnam and other countries like them—no matter how good the intentions may have been, they are not supporting his claim that they will form a better society. Marx based his analysis of capitalism on its contradictions presumed to be its downfall. Yet at the very same time a very close follower of Saint-Simon Marx cannot have ignored or not known—Saint-Amand Bazard (1791–1832)—had said that the domination of capitalism was already yielding ground.[6] As a matter of fact, capitalism being identified with knowledge and technology more and more people were being acquainted with, the various facets of the human nature could not keep a monolithic view of it. What was thus far the basis for the class struggle was the frustration of the workers who did not have the knowledge that industrial leaders had and could have been an identical problem for the Saint-Simonian doctrine of governing by knowing what others do not. Today the spreading of this knowledge—willingly or not—and the taking over of companies by former employees is becoming grass-roots capitalism.

Lenin introduced violence to impose the "dictatorship of the proletariat," that is, the taking over by the workers of the means of production, power to the producers also being, and by the way, part of the Saint-Simonian doctrine.[7] So much so that Trotsky himself wrote to Lenin that a proletariat able to impose its dictatorship on society would certainly not accept to be dominated by it. To make sure he would not share this idea with others, Lenin had him killed in Mexico. Since then we have seen who has exercised what on whom and how; why is to be seen later. Marx is also said to have envisioned a classless society; Lenin created the first totalitarian state with several classes: the ruling class (Nomenklatura), the intelligentsia (new aristocracy), the working class (artisans), the farmers (the peasants; Marx did not like them very much, but it was Lenin who called them the "last capitalist class"[8]), and the forced laborers in the Gulag (the serfs): pretty much a monarchy.

Behind Marxism, which was and still is said to be the cure for all the ills of society and for which people have given support all around the world, the horrors and the repressive nature of communism have made some people say, "If Marxism-Leninism is that good, how come it has to be imposed through violence, murder and starvation?" This difference between the two expressions of socialism (persuasion in the West and the use of force in the East) may explain why at times the Western side is upset with the way the East is perpetrating genocides. It discredits its name and scares people away, but most of all, it makes public opinion aware that under the same regime, what happens there may happen here someday. But the doctrine is never questioned as far as the end is concerned. Conversely, the East considers Western socialism to be a substitute for real communism, hiding itself behind "helping people" by organizing the entire planet, as if to save a bunch of snails, someone were to create a system with its bureaucracy, its elite, and its privileged, in order to control the entire so-called endangered species. Eastern communism is more direct about it.

People may not always know what an illegitimate use of power is, because the tolerance margin may vary according to history and the country in which it takes place. If evolution and even revolutions with, of, by, and for the people are supposed to be all about, it should make us wonder what this illegitimate use of power may do to us when it is used, sometimes with great subtlety, in order to prevent the public from picturing a clear definition of it and forming its own opinion.

During World War I, European empires and the last one of the Near East began to crack. Two of them, the Austro-Hungarian and the Ottoman empires sank into a storm that killed about 9 million people, mostly farmers, mown down like wheat in fields. Between 1917 and 1922, the Soviet Revolution put an end to czardom and most communist parties were established around the world: Germany: 1918–19; France: 1920; Spain: 1921; the United States: 1919; Great Britain: 1920; Italy: 1921; Japan: 1922 (illegal then, re-established officially in 1945); Yugoslavia: 1919; China: 1921; et cetera. Later, some of their members infiltrated Western countries and their governments, thanks to their collaborators, as with the Philby, Hiss, and Revers affairs, for example.

By and large, World War II is the story of two trains. "Beware," warns the signpost, "a train may hide another one." Soviet totalitarianism in particular and communism in general hid behind Nazism and a conflict that killed about 49 million people. When some Soviet official said during the Reagan-Gorbachev meeting in the United States that the USSR saved the world from Nazism,[9] it is appropriate to remember that from 1922 until 1941 Germany—which became Nazi in 1933—and the Soviet Union were allies and collaborated (even their secret services) for nineteen years, of which two during World War II, against Western democracies. If 20 million Soviets died during the conflict (this does not include those who had been eliminated by the political police), it is mostly due to the fact that, despite the clauses in the Treaty of Versailles that forbade it, Germany was allowed to rebuild and train its army and air forces on Soviet soil, thank you.

Hitler killed between 10 and 11 million people, including 6 million Jews, representing 40 to 41 percent of the entire Jewish population in the world at that time. Stalin eliminated between 30 and 65 million people, according to Western and Soviet experts.[10] Therefore, Hitler can be credited with an average of about 830,000 to 917,000 dead per year and over a period of twelve years, whereas Stalin would score an average of 1.25 million up to 2.8 million a year over a period of twenty-four years.

World War II is also the story of the nuclear bomb. As horrible as it is, its use brought the war with Japan to an end. However, some people repeatedly conjure up the ghosts of Hiroshima and Nagasaki as if today's nuclear arsenal of the United States was the one wielded against the two cities back then. More "moral, conventional" bombardments, followed by house-to-house fighting between the United States troops and Japanese men, women, and children ready to die rather than to surrender would have set the death toll much, much higher. Both the Nazis and the Soviets worked on their bomb during the war,[11] but they were too late for mankind to know if they would have used it to impose the Aryan or the communist race on the world. This being said, and now that people know what it does, the threat of it can achieve the same goal anyway.

After World War II, colonial empires tried to cling to their former possessions, but by 1960 most former colonies were able to choose between one side or the other of what Yuri Andropov called "the historic confrontation between Socialism and Capitalism." The West being the symbol of colonialism then, it is not surprising that many newly freed nations sought the support of the USSR to fill in the political vacuum. Yet it was the signing of the Atlantic Charter by Churchill and Roosevelt on August 14, 1941, that gave nations the right to choose their form of government and the right to dispose of themselves as they saw fit. It inspired the United Nations Charter signed by fifty states, including the Soviet Union. Decolonization was not invented by the communists, as it has often been propagated at the grassroots level, but by some Westerners, and many nations that expected to get out of bondage to discover freedom have ended up in the communist claws. Beginning with World War I, and confirmed with World War II, decolonization marked the end of European pre-eminence in world affairs.

What began as a "mere wandering" some 2 million years or so ago became a real "migration" between 30,000 and 15,000 B.C. By 8000–6000 B.C. it was already war indeed, colonization or being colonized.

Two major movements took place in early history. The first one, with the tribes coming from the bends of the Amur River (today the southeastern part of the Soviet Union) crossed the Bering Strait and successively populated what are today the Americas: from Ellesmere in the north to Patagonia in the south.[12] The second one,[13] which took place somewhere between 2000 and 3000 B.C., was also a continuous movement of tribes coming from the Altai region—the triangle of Mongolia, China, and the USSR—and Turkestan (today south of the Soviet Union) invaded part of the Middle and the Near East and Europe. They brought along the tripartition of government we have kept for centuries: priests/kings, warriors, farmers. Revolutions may have invented the separation of powers, but they have divided only what was there before. These people were integrated to or imposed themselves on existing populations in Europe, submerged during the fifth century A.D. by hordes coming from the same regions. A little more than one thousand years later, these Indo-Europeans were to meet people of the first wave in the Americas during the European colonial era.

European colonialism did, in fact, what other nations, kingdoms, and empires of yesterday had done, in Europe itself as well as in other parts of the world, for thousands of years before. The treatment people had to endure was the same: murder remains murder, theft, theft, and slavery, slavery. All of them, though, brought something new, which opened up the societies they conquered to inventions and new ways of life, not necessarily welcomed then. What was different, though, was the time spent, the means of communications, and demography. From a political-economic point of view, and this was a major change, Europe was playing with rules that it had invented, then unknown to other nations and which completely changed the balance between rulers and ruled. Europe was not a ground for invasion anymore, but a group of nations at odds with one another and bouncing the colonial migration effect to the four corners of the world by new means. Now if one wants to know what colonialism is all about—for better and for worse—just turn the table on those who have and/or are still practicing it: by now almost everybody.

The Marxist-Leninist approach to history cuts this perspective into convenient parts when it comes to propagate its views of the world today and "forgets" about reality, in order to draw the public's attention to that era alone and therefore justify its ideology, bringing nations back into the communist basket and justifying its very "raison d'être," which strangely enough in that case takes a "historic" perspective when it comes to telling people about the struggle between socialism and capitalism, in the name of decolonization and for the unification of the world.

Today the means of communication, the demographic explosion, and the will to eliminate people who want to cling to freedom are such that communist colonialism has perpetrated genocides of an unprecedented magnitude. By and large, it has killed "270 people per hour for the past 70 years":[14] 270 × 24 × 265¼ × 70 = 165,677, 400.00 people, roughly 2.8 times World War I and World War II put together.

In early history, the motivations for colonization were food and gold. Later on food, gold, and spices, in the name of religion and civilization. Today it is still food, gold, and spices, but also raw material and people in the name of an ideology and of a civilization without God. Tomorrow should mankind settle in space, it will be probably considered an "exploratory migration." That is, if no one else is out there; otherwise it will continue to be war, colonize or be colonized, from space this time. And God knows, and censorship as well, how often we have been visited during our entire history. Maybe the UFOs and flying saucers of the kind are only a pretext to "bring people together" into the science and technology space age.

Vietnam, which is our example here, began with the promise of liberation from a form of colonialism. It has ended with the invasion of the country, its plundering, the establishing of a police state, re-education camps—some say outright concentration camps without barbed wires—the suppression of freedom and liberties, the manipulation of the masses reduced to mere statistics, disinformation, the trading of human lives as if people were only beasts of burden, the impoverishment of the remaining population, corruption as a way of life and survival, the stealing of international aid, and, worst of all, a genocide through artificial famine.

This policy is becoming normal procedure for establishing a communist regime in a targeted country. According to the plan, Thailand should be next—combat has been reported on Hill 538 on the Khmero-Thai border[15]—which does not preclude the fact that another nation will not be subject to the same fate, should the opportunity arise, like the Philippines, for example. Vietnam is indeed in a position to back up a revolution in the Philippines, which would mean the loss of the Subic and the Clark Bases for the United States. Now it is common knowledge that whoever controls the Philippines controls Micronesia and that whoever controls Micronesia controls the South Pacific.

When one looks at a map, one can see the huge landmass of the Soviet Union (partly Asian, partly European, resembling a gigantic sea elephant whose tail is in Western Europe and head in the Chukchi Peninsula, "barking" at a stubborn, really American-looking Alaska) driving the wedge of Mongolia—militarily and economically integrated with the USSR—into China's nape, itself resembling a round-bellied bird staring at Japan, the Philippines, and all the other good-looking islands of the region.

Today in 1988, Afghanistan is becoming scorched land, from which the Soviet Union, stretching its neck toward the Indian Ocean, will be able to invade Pakistan and Iran in due time—the Soviet Union still has an accord with Iran stipulating that any invasion of Iranian soil by a third party would give the USSR the right to come into that country[16] and cut the oil jugular vein of the West: the Persian Gulf, first target of the USSR, as stated by Leonid Brezhnev.[17]

For the time being, the Soviets are stealing electricity from

Afghanistan,[18] natural gas, herds of sheep and cattle, tapestries, tin, chromium, copper, zinc, lead, manganese, and even salt (looks like "déjà vu"), in the name of brotherly assistance to pay a so-called debt to the USSR.[19] It probably means that the puppet regime of Kabul should feel indebted to the Soviets for having been put into place by them. They are also interested in the lapis lazuli,[20] This fine intense blue stone, Afghanistan alone exports in the world. Yellow rain is also used (or has been), wells are poisoned, land and people burnt like cockroaches, old men tied to the ground and run over by tanks, men nailed alive to trees with bayonets; children killed or maimed by booby-trapped toys, women raped and/or killed. Survivors fled to Pakistan or to Iran, where the men were forced to fight against Iraq—exactly the way things were done with South Vietnamese against Cambodia. Now the Soviets are also talking about the withdrawal of their troops from Afghanistan within a year;[21] living behind a puppet regime in Kabul, exactly the way North Vietnam is doing in Cambodia for example? In that country indeed, the Vietnamese troops can go home: by now, nearly one million North Vietnamese "civilians" have disguised themselves as "Cambodians," and are supporting the regime put in place by Hanoi. As far as the Soviets are concerned, and according to experts, if they withdraw from Afghanistan it could be to regroup in the northern Balk-Jouzian region, and create a north-south situation, as in Korea and Vietnam, whose experience has cost us so much. In both cases, the communist regimes are doing enough to improve their trade and diplomatic relation, with the West, and cash in its aid vital to their respective "glasnost" at home, but not enough to be called a real change. In Afghanistan, the Soviets are next door to Iran with whom an old treaty allows them to interfere any time they want. They are also close to a weakened Pakistan—particularly since the death, if not murder, of President Zia—at odds with a non-aligned India asserting itself economically (the only country with China in that part of the world to have progressed, thanks to its internal market,[22] versus Japan, for example, which relies heavily on its external trading), but allowing the Soviets to have four naval bases on its shores.[23] India, on the other hand, has also ethnic, linguistic, religious and social differences, and external tensions with Pakistan and China.

Peking, which has been reading maps for quite some time now, since it was probably the first to have mapped this region—long before Christ—understood very well what the membership of Vietnam in the COMECON meant (June 29, 1978), the signing of the Friendship Treaty between Moscow and Hanoi on November 3 of the same year, and the establishing of Vietnam's puppet Heng Samrin in Cambodia soon afterward.

This surrounding of China will allow the USSR to isolate Japan and South Korea—though these two have been traditionally at odds with one another—with their industrial potential, and to cross swords with the new Peking-Tokyo Axis (which is in the making) and to approach the Anglo-Saxon Axis (London, Washington, Canberra, Wellington), that is, if there is no trouble between the United States and New Zealand.

In a way, it is the meeting of the "Great Axes" that wants to write history in the Pacific of the twenty-first century. As if those who left Asia for Europe thousands of years ago met, some five hundred years ago, their predecessors, established themselves in the United States, and are now face to face in the Pacific with those who stayed in Asia. Everyone wants to have a front seat to watch and participate in the show titled "The Alpha and the Omega of Human Civilization." By the way, nobody knows if there will be a replay of it.

The Moscow-Hanoi Axis strategy of nibbling one country after another in the region is aimed at establishing a "balcony fortress" on the South Pacific shores to control the entire area without triggering a major conflict with the West. This technique began with a big chunk in Eastern Europe (World War II)—Finland being a "mild" example up north—and in Southeast Asia. Next, Africa and Latin America.

In general, and as far as the supply of raw material is concerned, South Africa seems to be more important to Europe and to Japan than it is to North America. However, and from a strategic point of view, it is of vital importance to all. The fall of that country into communist hands would put an end, for twenty-four hours, to an unfair, undemocratic, racist apartheid, but it would be replaced by something even worse right afterward. The far right maintaining it gives all the reasons to the far left to fight it, and the two are perpetrating in South Africa what they have in other parts of the world since 1917. A leftist minority resorting to violence wants to make this country a communist land. This time, however, and in this country in particular, deception will not be sufficient and socialism will have to be imposed through a bloody war between the communists and the whites, then be followed by an even bloodier one among blacks struggling for tribal survival and the communists killing to gain power, by purges and ultimately by genocide. This is the usual pattern known for decades throughout the world.

However, the thing barely mentioned by the media in general is that anti-apartheid laws have changed and are changing the country, and people saying that they want to give peace a chance should consider this part of reality as well, even if we do not see much of it on our TV screens and in our newspapers.

The African National Congress—the leading group among those resorting to violence and certainly given visibility by the media—was created in 1912 to oppose the white rule by peaceful means. In 1919 Lenin conceived the Third Communist International (Komintern). In August 1920 the Second Congress of this Komintern declared that all wanting to join would have to help the Soviet republic and by any means—including illegal—fight against their own government and establish underground organizations. The Communist party of South Africa was founded in 1921 and was affiliated with the Third Communist International (Komintern) in 1923, at which time the African National Congress was likely to have come under the influence of the Communist party of South Africa.

Considering the fact that this ANC is posing as a nationalist movement—an ideology considered at other times despicable by the communists and some Westerners when it opposes their own aim of uniting this world their way—one cannot avoid drawing a parallel with Ho Chi Minh in Vietnam who, while posing as a nationalist, was himself an agent of this same Communist International (Komintern) as early as 1923–1925:[24] the time at which the ANC seems to have come under the influence of the Communist party of South Africa. Today nineteen communists out of thirty members constitute the executive committee of the African National Congress (ANC), and the only white—Joe Slovo—is suspected to be a KGB colonel. The leadership of the

United Democratic Front ("democratic" always sounds good to Western ears) is made of 90 percent of former ANC members,[25] and some of its adherents have participated in atrocious assassinations.[26]

Either apartheid will have to be dismantled or a South Africa led by an ANC and/or affiliates will resemble countries like Ethiopia, Tanzania, Angola, Mozambique, Zambia, and others like them in the rest of Africa, where one-party dictatorships are in many ways similar to the regime in Vietnam. The transition, however, has to be as smooth as possible; otherwise what will happen with this country is what happened with others expelling colonialism but leaving the door open to outright repression and disaster.

The ANC draws its support from the Xhosas: 6.2 million people, if one is to assume that they all stand behind it. Against it and with the same kind of consideration are the Zulus (6.5 million), the anti-ANC blacks of the Zion Christian churches (5 million), those of the Reformed Independent churches (4.5 million), and other minority groups. These people represent two-thirds of the South African black community against which an ANC would lose in an election. No wonder, then, that it wants to keep using violence to impose its minority on the majority of South Africans.

The view of this majority, who certainly want an end to apartheid and are working toward it by peaceful means, is not reflected by any media; neither is the fact that indeed 75 percent of the black people reject sanctions against South Africa, whose neighbors are trading with, nor is reflected the view of the three hundred thousand American workers thus far who have lost their jobs in direct connection with the sanctions adopted by the U.S. Congress against South Africa, costing a tremendous amount of money in lost trade.

As a matter of fact, one of the things that have not been reported at all by the media is that when antiapartheid laws have begun to provoke irrevocable changes for the better—among which the right and the practice for black workers to be unionized, ask for better wages and conditions, and therefore request more money from the companies employing them—some Western governments, banks, and economic sectors have also begun to fear for their profit margins, while others, it is true, have not. They have withdrawn under the pretext of apartheid—that is the part we were told by the media—but they also increased their trade with the Soviet Union, and that is the part we were not told about by the same media. The profit margins are certainly more substantial there, and the communist system, which has an even worse human rights record than that of South Africa, seems to be more convenient for these people than the end of apartheid: true enough, too, free people would not be so easy to manipulate, whereas those under dictatorships or totalitarianism are not allowed to say much. Perhaps they are waiting for South Africa to become a communist country so that they may come back and get the resources even cheaper? What blacks? What Indians? What Asians? What whites? What genocides are you talking about?

Thus far terrorism used to prevent the coming together of various South African communities dedicated to nonviolent changes is directly connected with the African National Congress for a great part (supplied by the USSR) and has been on the increase since 1976. This includes the burning with tires and gasoline, known as necklacing, of moderate black people who, like many others in South Africa and elsewhere in the world, do want an end to apartheid, but by peaceful means, not genocide, result of a policy such as the one implemented in Vietnam, Laos, Cambodia, other places in Africa itself, and in the world.

By the way, it is not customary to name parks and squares after Marx, Lenin, Stalin, and others like them in the West—at least not yet—but contemporary revolutionaries must be very much "in" these days, since on January 29, 1988, the city of Montreal decided to rename one of its parks after Nelson and Winnie Mandela, who advocate the assassination method of necklacing in South Africa. What about Amerindians who, witnessing this incitement to imported, publicized revolutionary terrorism, were to decide to use this same necklacing on moderate and decent Montrealers in the name of a "struggle against the white people who massacred their ancestors and deprived them of their land"? Would parks be renamed after them? Would concerts be organized for them in order to finance the tires and the gasoline they would need? Nelson Mandela has been offered freedom under the condition that he would not resort to the use of violence. He refused, and he is not considered a political prisoner by Amnesty International. To remain in jail, though, is also good business, since the name and anything related with it is being commercialized.[27]

Not much reflected either by the media is the fact that some members of the clergy in South Africa create a climate of confrontation leading to violence, divert foreign financial aid for political ends, and advise donators not to send their money to needy groups, but to churches and organizations approved by the ANC.[28] As a matter of fact, the African National Congress has a special Religious Affairs Section, based in Lusaka, Zambia, in charge of infiltrating religious groups of absolutely all denominations.[29]

Paris Match published on July 22, 1988, an article on black African writer and journalist Gaoussou Kamissoko (Ivory Coast), who says that it takes courage not to howl with the pack against South Africa, over which hovers the threat of a new Vietnam able to set ablaze the entire continent. On the other hand, should South Africa solve its apartheid problems, it could become a center of development for the rest of Africa, and many African leaders who at the U.N. are the champions of human rights should first clean up their own house, since freedom and the respect of people are still an exception in that country. Violence is certainly not the way to solve any problem, and if 1.5 million black Africans were happy with their fate, they would not have left their communist Mozambique and Angola to work in mines and fields under apartheid. In both cases there should be more room for more real freedom.

Although there are some variances between the *International Conservative Insight*,[30] *l'Etat du Monde* (*The State of the World*),[31] politically different, and *l'Atlas Stratégique* (*The Strategy Atlas*,[32] it is clear that all agree about the fact that in terms of minerals, South Africa and the Soviet Union are two of the major producers in the world. Should South Africa fall into communist clutches, it would mean that Moscow would have the upper hand on some of the rarest minerals and would have the largest production and reserve on gold of this planet—gold which could replace the dollar—diamonds, and other minerals the West needs not only for its economy, but also for its survival.

Today, the United States, and it would not come as a surprise to anyone to discover that other Western nations are doing the same thing, has increased by thirteen times their import of chromium (needed for missiles, ships, and submarines, for example), ferro-silicone (required for armored plates, ships, military vehicles, and tanks) by five times, antimony (used for ammunitions, computers, and radar) by ninety-eight times, and industrial diamonds, platinum, rhodium, from a Soviet Union that is basically an enemy, since it has sworn the destruction of the West. It sounds like: "Of course we intend to protect our freedom and our democracy, and we may even have to flex some muscles to show that we mean it, but first sell us what we need to beef up our military." Why not? After all, and for entirely opposite reasons, that is exactly what the Soviets have done with the West since Lenin.

All this to bring nations together? Could it be that all so-called revolutions to "free" people, all wars heading toward "better tomorrows," all treaties—particularly Teheran and Yalta among all the others—have taken place to that end but are tragic farces about real freedom and democracy? If such is the case, what can we expect? By paying too much attention to only the Far Right and/or the Far Left, the media forget to talk and to write about the vast majority of people who represent decency, balance, and good common sense.

In Ethiopia, 2 to 7 million people—according to various sources—may die of starvation, due to collectivization, arms spending, and lavish festivities. The Soviet Union has increased its military and economic aid to Angola—where the communists have executed black people from the resistance movement through circular saws,[33] and Mozambique. Zimbabwe, Zambia, and Tanzania, where 10 million people have been displaced by force,[34] are leaning toward the Soviet Union.

In Latin America, said to be the soft belly of the United States, Soviet-supported Cuba (geopolitical aircraft carrier or strategic missile planted on the flank of the United States) is projecting communism in neighboring countries, while throwing out some of its malcontents to the United States. Nicaragua, its like, intends to build up a force of six hundred thousand men justifying this with its so-called fear of a U.S. landing on its shores and will therefore receive Migs from the Soviet Union. This means that almost a quarter of today's population will be under arms. It is also said that Sandinistas disguise themselves as freedom fighters to kill people[35] and therefore make public opinion believe that the contras are responsible for this dirty job, which maybe explains why it was so easy for some journalist to take a picture of a "contra" killing a man, as if the real ones had wanted to advertise something of the kind. However, very few pictures, if any, have been made of the Miskitoe Indians massacred by the Sandinistas, the way other people have been eliminated in Vietnam, Laos, Cambodia, and elsewhere—the same technique. Haiti, with its frustrated elections, the specter of the "Tontons Macoutes," the military dictatorship, and its fifteen to twenty-five thousand nationals being used as slaves in neighboring Dominican Republic,[36] is a real time bomb that can be activated by Cuba next door. Since drugs are a deadly weapon against America, one wonders if Panama is a friendly country or a foe.

Should Latin America catch fire—and it is beginning to—North America might suffocate with entire populations fleeing tragedy. Refugees—though no fault of their own—are another way of transferring populations to the West by force, and by the same token to infiltrate agents known to be the backbone of political and social unrest and the most striving drug and prostitution rings financing the disintegration of the West.

The signing of the INF Treaty may have been a nice Christmas gift, but somehow the batteries were not included; now that the Pershing missiles are not going to protect Europe anymore, the only batteries available around are the SS-24 and the SS-25; The SS-20s scrapped by the INF treaty were too old and would have been replaced anyway by the SS-24 and SS-25. From a conventional and a nuclear point of view, Europe is no match for the USSR, and in order to avoid destruction, it will have to accept "pacification" as suggested by Saint-Simon.[37] Mutual Assured Destruction will have worked against the West unless Europeans give themselves a defense that American tax payers have heavily financed thus far, give a new meaning to NATO or create a new system to protect themselves. Now if the world is to be united, as some are suggesting, Europeans may want to simply wait and see—since the deal became obvious between the United States and the USSR with World War II—but it will open a window of vulnerability to Soviet expansionism in the West.

While some Western media are reporting words of "peace," "new thinking," "cooperation," and "arms agreement" before and during the summit meeting between President Reagan and Premier Gorbachev—exactly the way words of "reconciliation," "tolerance," "magnanimity," et cetera, were spread before the invasion of South Vietnam by the North—two documents written by Tiouchkevitch, and Krivine, Popov, and Savouchkine in 1986 and in 1987 for Party and military consumption, reveal that the sayings of Lenin are far from dead,[38] that as Yuri Andropov wrote, the world is the arena for the confrontation of socialism and capitalism, that World War III is likely to take place, that it is necessary to act by surprise while lulling the West with words of peace, that should a conflict break out the odds are in favor of socialism, and that small but disciplined communist groups can penetrate parties of the left and manipulate them.[39]

The oil of the Persian Gulf is the first target of the Soviet Union. Minerals of South Africa are the second. Most certainly Canada and Australia would not mind replacing that country as mineral suppliers—and maybe the actual footwork concerning the free-trade agreement attempt between Canada and the United States, if not rejected by the Congress, could be a preparation to that end—but, in the case of platinum, for example, Canada does not come close to either South Africa or the USSR, let alone these two countries together. In terms of diamonds, another example, the same applies to Australia.[40] As far as antimony is concerned, the South African and the Soviet productions are about the same, but Canada and Australia combined do not equal either one. In manganese Australia produces about half of what South Africa produces and one-sixth of what the USSR produces. In gold, the United States, Canada, and Australia combined produce about the same quantity as the USSR, itself producing 2.3 times less than South Africa. Together the Soviet Union and South Africa would produce 3.3 times more gold than the United States, Canada, and Australia combined, et cetera.[41] What is important to know is that the Soviet Union depends very much on gold for financing its military expansion. Are we being forced to get together?

From a strategic point of view, the USSR, like Russia before, tries to get control of the straits, choke points in the world for Western navies. One of the most important things to remember, though, is that the Soviet Union does not need to protect vital communication lines, but to cut those of the West. When one looks at a map, one realizes that the seas and the oceans represent 71 percent of our planet and the importance of the supply routes around the world. From where their bases are located, the Soviets can cut any vital line for Japan, Europe, and the United States with a minimum of effort. The control of South Africa would, in one blow, cut all the lines and isolate the West and Japan from their most vital resources. One understands also that the Falklands were more than just a matter of honor: they are also another important choke point. Speaking of straits and choke points, Turkey, surrounded by Syria, Iran, the USSR, Greece, and Cyprus, controls the entrance and exit of the Black Sea and the Aegean Sea to the Mediterranean Sea. Isolated and a forward Western base in that part of the world, it could be a prime target in times of war. So would Panama, whose situation today does not augur well for the future. If one looks at the globe upside down, and from the South Pole, one can see that the Falklands (Patagonia), South Africa, Australia, and New Zealand are the main check points of an Antarctica holding vast wealths and promising resources similar to those of South Africa.

When reading books on the subject of the Soviet military[42] it becomes obvious that the USSR (and all communist countries, for that matter) is allocating its best resources to it in terms of financing, technology, skilled labor, and industry, when it knows all too well that nobody will attack it: had it been the case, it would have been done a long time ago, and if the world is supposed to get together, why then attack it indeed? On the one hand, some Westerners want to unite this world their way; on the other, the communists are trying to dominate this planet in their own manner. But in order to achieve that and since the system does not work too well, they need the technology of the West itself. Therefore, we have glasnost and perestroika. Westerners who do not despair of getting the Soviet market are ready to believe in the movements posing as changes, when in fact what is taking place is only a replay of Lenin's NEP to prevent a total collapse due to the system and the ideology, to grab whatever can be gotten from the West before tightening up the rope again to head socialism toward domination.

In order to achieve that, some Westerners are selling the best computers we have to improve research and development for the Soviet weapons that ultimately will equip all communist nations[43] and pass on to them many of our scientific secrets: from lasers to sensors and from electronics to radars and communication systems.[44] In the end, Western taxpayers have to pay billions of dollars to counter this arming of our enemy,[45] unless, indeed, it is really intended to arm the Soviet Union for another purpose.

From an economic point of view and exactly seventy years after the Soviet Revolution, the West sort of wished the USSR a "Happy Birthday" with the crash of October 19, 1987. Not everybody was hurt by this economic setback, though,[46] but it may be the pretext to force Western nations to cut down further their defense budget,[47] therefore not keeping up with the Soviet Union, and let down nations that would have been our allies.

Speaking of defense, we are told in the West that the U.S. Strategic Defense Initiative is "not feasible," "unrealistic," that its space program cannot go ahead because of the impossibility of developing a small rubber joint for its *Challengers*. Yet in a TV speech Premier Gorbachev clearly said that the USSR has its own Defense Initiative program.[48] Once again, and since it is part of the Soviet military program, the Party allocates the best of its resources to it, and in some fields it is twenty years ahead of the United States.[49]

The Soviet Union is also exploring all new and modern weapons such as lasers, X rays, particle beams, et cetera, and some of them are even near deployment.[50]

How come, then, our technology cannot do for us what it does so well for the Soviets? How come the U.S. Strategic Defense Initiative is "not feasible" when that of the Soviets is going full speed ahead?

To close this chapter and go back to Southeast Asia, one can say, without oversimplifying the case, that the history of Russia/USSR, Japan, China, and the West is almost repeating itself in that part of the world.

A few years before Marx wrote the *Communist Manifesto*, Alexis C. de Tocqueville foresaw—along with a handful of others—the emergence of two nations: America and Russia. Japan was opened to the West in 1854 by the American commander Matthew Perry. Between 1840 and 1860, Russia started its Industrial Revolution, one century after Europe. In 1867 the population of Japan had gone from 30 million, half a century earlier, up to 50 million. Short of resources, Japanese began to migrate massively toward Australia and the United States.

Within half a century, Meiji Japan, which had started its own Industrial Revolution a little later than Russia, was to impose its supremacy in Southeast Asia, China taking the brunt of this expansion. Russia was already in Afghanistan (1884–85) and managed, with the help of France and Germany, to grab some places Japan had in China (1898). As a matter of retaliation, Japan launched an undeclared war against Russia in 1904, and won in 1905. Japan, a tiny island, able to be so powerful, and yet apparently difficult to understand in its culture, was to be feared more than anyone else.

During World War I, Japan, then allied with the West, made significant gains in Asia. The Austro-Hungarian and the Ottoman empires, which had been in rivalry with Russia, were not a problem to that country anymore: they disappeared in the storm. The socialist revolution in Russia, supported by socialists elsewhere, allowed itself to be brutal, violent, and bloody because it was fighting capitalism. Yet capitalists and communists have been working pretty well together since. The myth of the besieged Russia—the one in permanent need of buffer zones—was also born at that time, and yet again the number of foreigners engaged in the Red Army then exceeded, and by far, that of the Entente, that is, the Westerners serving in Russia.[51]

Japanese expansionism in Asia and in Siberia worried the United States, who did not want the market of China to be monopolized by Japan. In 1921–22—the Meiji era ended in 1912—Washington forced Japan to abandon its gain in China, withdraw its troops from Siberia, and limit its navy. In 1922 an influential capitalist supporting the USSR[52] told Lenin that capitalists and communists should work together in order to keep the world at peace. Business they did and they do, but peace?

This may have prompted Lenin's answer that Western capitalists and their governments (are we still voting?) would one day sell the rope to hang themselves—and us, one might add. All that in order to lay a hand on the Soviet and the Chinese market. How true!

Japan, opened up to the world, needed to get out of its tiny island; industrialists needed a market and therefore to have a universal system to make the most out of the economy, and the USSR wanted to get rid of both of them, to impose its own view and system on the planet.

In 1923 Japan exports all over the world. In 1924 Washington cuts down Japanese immigration to the United States. Japan leads a policy of expansionism and was the only industrial nation not affected by the crash of 1929. In 1933 Hitler takes over power in Germany, and Japan leaves the League of Nations. In 1934, Japan denounces the Washington Treaty limiting its navy.

During World War II, F. D. Roosevelt tried to asphyxiate the Japanese economy, with the result of strengthening the war party in Tokyo. The U.S. ambassador to Tokyo then said that sanctions against Japan could very well end up in war.[53] Thus Pearl Harbor, December 7, 1941, without any declaration of war.

At this time, Japan is practically master of Southeast Asia and threatens even Australia. However, Midway, in June 1942, stops this pressure and 1943 is the turning point of the war: the pendulum swings back against Germany, Japan, and Italy. It stops—momentarily—in Berlin in May 1945 and on August 6 of the same year, over Hiroshima; three days later, over Nagasaki, Moscow having "forgotten" to tell Washington that the emperor of Japan wanted to talk peace with the Americans, who knew it anyway, since they had broken the Japanese "Purple Code" of communication.[54] The USSR, formerly allied with Nazi Germany, itself allied with Japan and Italy, used the pretext of war to be given people and territories even the czars never had before, in Europe and in Asia, as buffer zones, probably, to "protect" the "besieged" Soviet Union.

History after World War II is a sort of repetition of what happened so far: the United States, which wanted to dismantle the Japanese army and economy, the way it had planned to do with Germany, "reopened" Japan with a new constitution. After the expansion of communism in Asia (China, 1949; Korea, 1950, signs of things to come in the region), things turned the other way round: it was "containment" and the enemies of yesterday became allies. Japan was on the move again.

This time, it did not colonize Siberia, but in the seventies invested heavily in that region. It also began to export all over the world again. It did not place China under a Japanese protectorate, as in the past, but signed a peace-and-friendship treaty with that country on August 12, 1978. Since then, Japan has not colonized any nation in Southeast Asia, as it did in the past, but has invested a lot of money in the countries of that region, and elsewhere.

By the end of the seventies, the United States, China, and Japan worried about Soviet expansion in Southeast Asia: Vietnam, Laos, Cambodia—though by proxy—with an eye on Thailand, directly in Afghanistan, with ambitions in Iran, the Persian Gulf—energy source of the West in general and of Japan in particular—and the Indian Ocean. Since then, Japan has become the second economic power in the world, third in exportation. By the next century it could be even richer than the United States.[55]

This time though, there is a difference: Japan is not a military power as such, but some worry that if it becomes the leader of a world economy, and the USSR the major military power on this planet, we will be in for great, great troubles.[56] And what if, for example, both could acquire economic clout (through glasnost and perestroika) and military power? As for the West, it has been driven out of Southeast Asia, or almost, and the only place it seems to be able to stay a while longer is the Pacific Ocean itself, rich in natural resources . . . and political sharks.

Some people say that to be anticommunist is to push Vietnam further into the arms of the Soviet Union. For one thing, Vietnam chose the embrace of the Big Bear in order not to repeat the long experience with the Chinese Mandarin and to stay away from a West it had kicked out of the country. As for anticommunism itself, people like or dislike things for what they do, and as far as communism is concerned, they prefer to stay away from its ideology and practices. Yet, ordinary citizens who are shocked with the results of such a policy are usually told that "there are good things with Marxism-Leninism." Such as? Morphine and dynamite were also supposed to help people, too.

For another thing, the checks and balances in this region affect the West and the rest of the world. Japan needs resources as close to home as possible, especially if South Africa falls into the hands of Moscow's proxies. China, often ranking first to sixth in the world, could offer just that, and it needs a development Japan could provide. Should this Asian Axis become powerful with its connections around the world, the political cards could be shuffled once again, as never before. It would not be surprising to see people in power in the United States support the Soviet Union the way they did during World War II; against an Asia with a very different background, and a tremendous potential to become another power? Against an oil-rich Middle East, systematically and traditionally considered to be "an enemy" of the Western culture? "Or God knows who else?"

Finally, behind the Soviet, consequently, the Vietnamese "glasnost" and "perestroika"—or the "détente" in Central America that Nicaragua is promising—lies a motivation: every time communist leaders have needed a break to prepare their next move against free democracies, they have talked peace. Some Westerners marvel on about "restructuring," "new thinking," the way Europeans did with Hitler on the eve of World War II. Yet both ideologies have sworn the destruction of the free world.

NOTES

1. From the records of history books, chronologies, and works on civilization, listed at the end of this book.
2. This is pretty much the case in socialist states today.
3. Emile Durkheim, *Le Socialisme—sa définition, ses débuts, la doctrine Saint-Simonienne (Socialism—Definition, Its Beginning, the Saint-Simonian Doctrine)* (Paris: Félix Alcon. 1928).
4. Reported by "Cité FM Montréal," January 9, 1988: Mr. Jacques Parizeau, the new leader of the Parti Québécois was told by a woman that sovereignty is an outdated form of social democracy, itself standing for: equality, a religion for mankind (which one by the way, and in the event it is a mixture of all existing ones, written by whom?), and the emancipation of women. Will state socialism be next?
5. According to Pierre Bornecque in *La France et sa littérature—guide complet dans le cadre de la civilisation mondiale (France and Its Literature—a Complete Guide in the Context of World Civilization)* (Editions de Lyon), p. 462.
6. Emile Durkheim, *Le Socialisme—sa définition, see débuts, la doctrine Saint-Simonienne (Socialism—definition, Its Beginning, the Saint-Simonian Doctrine)* (Félix Alcan), p. 317.

7. Ibid., p. 193.

8. "De Marx et du Marxisme" ("Of Marx and Marxism"), *l'Express*, Raymond Aron, May 13, 1983.

9. AIM Report, December-B 1987.

10. Robert Conquest, Joseph Dyakin (sent to the Gulag for saying it), and A. Antonov-Oyseyenko, in *National Review*, May 31, 1985; and Solzhenitsyn in *l'Erreur de l'Occident (The Mistake of the West)* (Grasset).

11. Harrison E. Salisbury, *The Unknown War* (New York: Bantam, 1978), pp. 7 and 125–219.

12. Ivar Lissner, *Dieu était déja la (God Was Already There)* (Robert Laffont).

13. There are other migrations, of course, particularly from north to south, but these two are probably the most important.

14. *News Center* 22, November 6, 1987.

15. TVFQ 99, November 5, 1986.

16. Ali Pahlavi in *Paris-Match*, December 11, 1987.

17. Quoted by R. Nixon in his book *The Real War* and *International Conservative Insight*, January/February, 1987.

18. *Paris-Match*, June 5, 1987.

19. Ibid.

20. Ibid.

21. "Nightline," December 9, 1987.

22. According to *L'Etat du Monde 1987—1988*, Maspero.

23. Gérard Chaliand and Jean-Pierre Rageau, *Atlas stratégique (Strategic Atlas)* (Fayard).

24. See p. 3.

25. *Actualité Sud-Africaines*, March 1988.

26. *La Presse*, February 22, 1988.

27. ABC, July 26, 1988.

28. *Actualités Sud Africaines*, February 1988.

29. *Actualités Sud Africaines*, April 1988.

30. *International Conservative Insight*, January/February 1987.

31. Maspero.

32. Gérard Chaliand and Jean-Pierre Rageau. (Fayard, 1983).

33. *International Conservative Insight*, January/February 1987.

34. Ibid.

35. From "God and Politics," PBS, December 9, 1987. Americans had to bombard North Vietnam in order to hit the communist bases. It will be interesting to see if the Sandinistas are going to do the same in Honduras and how public opinion will be led to react on that.

36. From TV Hebdo, November 11, 1987 (fifteen thousand); OXFAM in *La Presse*, November 28, 1987 (twenty thousand to twenty-five thousand).

37. Emile Durkheim, *Le Socialisme—sa définition, ses débuts, la doctrine Saint-Simonienne (Socialism—Definition, Its Beginning, the Saint-Simonian Doctrine)* (Félix Alcan), pp. 246–47.

38. For external consumption Marx is put up front; for internal consumption it is Lenin who advocated the use of violence.

39. From *l'Express*, October 16, 1987.

40. Figures from *l'Etat du Monde (The State of the World)* (Boreal, 1987–88). In this issue though, diamonds do not seem to be mentioned; is South Africa out of stocks?

41. Ibid.

42. Such as *Devant la Guerre (Facing War* could be the translation) by Cornelius Castoriadis (Fayard, 1981).

43. *Le scandale français (The French Scandal), l'Affaire Richard (The Richard File)*, and *Hélice au pays des Soviets (hélice* means "propeller", in French, but sounds a little bit like "Alice"; the general meaning would be: "Hélice/Alice in Soviet Wonderland") (*l'Express*, October 23, 1987).

44. John Barron, *KGB Today* (Pleasantville, N.Y.: Reader's Digest Press, 1983), p. 223–24.

45. *International Conservative Insight*, July/August 1987.

46. A multimillionaire is said ("Cité FM Montreal," November 20, 1987) to have pulled out his money before the crash and to have reinvested it afterward. As the journalist said: "Some people know things we do not."

47. For the United States in 1960 9.5 percent, 1970 8.3 percent; 1980 5.0 percent; 1987 6.4 percent. For the Soviet Union about 17 percent of its GNP (from 12 percent in the early seventies). (*National Review*, March 4, 1988).

48. "ABC News Brief," November 30, 1987.

49. William A. B. Campbell and Richard K. Mechlin, "Western Security and Strategic Defense Initiative," *Studies in Foreign Policy*, Canadian Conservative Centre, pp. 48–50.

50. Ibid.

51. Christian Jellen, *l'Aveuglement: les Socialistes et la naissance du mythe Soviétique (The Blinding: The Socialists and the Creation of the Soviet Myth* could be the translation) (Flammarion), pp. 120–28.

52. Joseph Finder, *Red Carpet* (New York: Holt Rinehart Winston); p 8 and 11. The father of the man referred to in the book was a member of the Socialist party in New York (p. 12), both preeminent figures in economic aid to the Soviet Union. Described also as the son of a co-founder of the Communist party in the USA. (*National Review*, March 4, 1988).

53. Denise Artaud and André Kaspi, *Histoire des Etats-Unis (History of the United States)* (Paris, 1969, 1980), p. 275.

54. Harrison E. Salisbury, *The Unknown War* (New York: Bantam, 1978), pp. 215–19.

55. "Japan: Behind the Mask," TV Ontario, December 7, 1987, which happens to be the anniversary of Pearl Harbor, by the way.

56. From *l'Express*, November 20, 1987.

WHAT A WORLD

Whoever holds Central Europe holds the Heartland. Whoever holds the Heartland commands the World Island. Whoever holds the World Island commands the entire planet and the Oceans.

—Mackinder

Our world is supposed to be united. Referring to the United Nations as a possibility,[1] it is worth remembering that this organization was created to maintain peace and to develop a New International Economic Order; most books on this will tell you that. In 1922 an influential capitalist told Lenin something to that effect. On May 2, 1987, Georges Marchais, head of the French Communist party, exposed on TV[2] the policy of his party, based on a "New World Economic Order." The French Communist party being not the one that decides world policy, one wonders who can be behind this?

Is all this a similarity of language for two different things or two expressions, apparently different, for a same policy?

The world is not divided between East and West, Left and Right, North and South, Communism and Capitalism. Of course, when it is convenient for some we hear people talk about the struggle of one against the other, while at the very same time, but on another channel, we hear that "things are more complex than that." By and large, we have seen that since the eighteenth century various political parties have come out of the monarchy: socialism in its various forms, communism also in its various forms, capitalism, free enterprise, and private property, which was to protect citizens against aristocratic usurpation, et cetera. It appears that socialism considers communist violence as a major difference to its vision of the world and society, yet often both share some basic concepts on economy, politics, and social issues. In political terms, some of the people can be called the doves and others the hawks of the Left, the way there are doves and hawks on the right.

The pillars of freedom, real democracy, and free enterprise

are said to be "backward" people, *réactionnaires*, since according to the Saint-Simonian doctrine held as a pillar of any form of socialism, society having gone through various stages—a theological and military age (Plato's elite in his communist "Republic" was a military one, by the way, and of scary significance today) then through a metaphysical (Campanella) and a democratic one—we should be in the middle of a scientific and industrial era in which free elected governments would be replaced by a centralized administration or bureaucracy.

What opposes the supporters of freedom and real democracy with the Left in general is that the former are saying that people know what is best for themselves—given freedom and correct and complete information—whereas the others claim that an elite alone knows better what is good for the people: by knowing what others do not, or are made to believe that they do not, in order not to use their own judgement. The first group holds that freedom and economic development are directly connected. They are also warning the leftist doves that the leftist hawks are certainly not going to let them run loose if they can get the upper hand on this planet. Yet the doves and the hawks of the Left have been working together more than once, World War II being a good example of that.

In his book *The Decisive Battles of the Western World* J. F. C. Fuller wrote something to the effect that when Hitler attacked the Soviet Union in 1941, the Allies should have let the two dictators annihilate each other and then, afterward, bring a lasting peace to this planet, and that to help Stalin would only allow communism to expand in the world.[3] How true.

One: the Atlantic Charter, signed in August 1941, defined the principles of future peace, renouncing any territorial expansion—that is probably why we gave Eastern Europe to Stalin—the right for the people to choose their form of government—idem—free access for all nations to natural resources, freedom of the seas, and the condemning of the use of force. It was approved by the Allies, including the Soviet Union, and inspired the United Nations Charter. It also triggered decolonization and what went on with it.

Two: Signed two months after J.F.C. Fuller's crucial observation, this shows that it was already planned to be the guiding policy for the rest of the war and after.

Three: A golden opportunity to bring the world a lasting peace, offered on a silver plate by the very nature of the two dictators themselves, was lost. This was confirmed with Teheran/Yalta/Potsdam and became the source of dissension among the Allies since then, including some people from the Left itself.

Four: It gave Soviet totalitarianism a marvelous opportunity to put itself on the "right"—and winning—side of history and to continue its conquest of the world, undisturbed in that even today.

Korea made us doubt that we were on the winning side of history, and shattered the great dream of a prosperous and peaceful world. By reaction, we tried to contain something that was already planned otherwise. Vietnam was a big nail in the coffin of freedom, but most of all, it made us feel—more than we understood it perhaps—that human rights and development were not enough to keep communism at bay: it had been invited. This is probably one of the major reasons why genocides perpetrated by the communists, like in Vietnam, for example, and in other places, may have been loathed by people from the right and the left side of the political spectrum in the West, but have not been brought to light the way they should have been.

Why all this? To make sure that our world is going to get together?

Who and what is going to be the driving force behind the political unification of the world? Freedom, democracy, and free enterprise? Communism, since Premier Gorbachev said that it is what this world is going toward[4]? Like the Soviet Union, Vietnam, Laos, Cambodia, Afghanistan, Ethiopia, Angola, and other countries like them? A so-called social democracy (names also used in communist countries, by the way) which pretends to be a middle of the road solution between capitalism and communism, left and right, et cetera?

How can that be? Where there is communism there is no real democracy. Look around. Besides, a member of the French Communist party said on TV that social democracy is only a substitute for real communism.[5] As for socialism as we know it today in the West, it would surrender to the Soviet Union right away or in the best of cases, try to put on a coat of "liberalism" (in the original sense of the word) to achieve the same result.

Already in the West, in Sweden, often portrayed as an example of social democracy to be duplicated—"a fascinating country" even said a journalist—many Swedes are finding their "paradise" suffocating, repressing: ten thousand new laws in ten years, Big Brother knowing everything about anyone thanks to interconnected computers, twenty-two thousand children (whose parents are supposed to be unacceptable by bureaucratic standards) taken away from their families by social workers, 6 percent under state tutelage, with no possibility of contesting such an action in court. A judge of the court of appeal said that the way children and their parents are treated is inconceivable. At times children are requested to describe the whereabouts of their parents and reveal their own political orientation. Children of foreigners are to be, literally and in every sense of the word, "Swedished": a British woman whose son was speaking English at home saw him taken away, probably thanks to one of the "benevolent" neighbors who have denounced some thirty thousand Swedes, often on false charges. The only official medicine is the one recognized by the state, and everything else is strictly forbidden.[6] People's organs belong to society, et cetera.[7] No wonder Sweden has the highest suicide rate in the West and Swedes are migrating to more hospitable countries.

Yet it was predicted that since the authority of the state, the administration, comes not from sheer power, but from knowing what others do not, it was not supposed to be arbitrary, or coercive, according to the principle of the socialist policy.[8] Pretty much déja vu.

" . . . Socialism has opened up to Communism; it has undertaken the task of playing the two characters together. In that sense, it has really inherited from it; that is, without deriving from it, it has absorbed it while remaining distinct."[9] Is it the old "sedentary" way to assimilate the "nomads," the latter trying to dominate the former in order to levy tribute? However, to absorb means to be, become "what you eat," what you integrate. History shows that this is how early civilization has been destroyed.

When President Mitterand said before his re-election that the Soviet Union is neither foe nor opponent,[10] it is certainly an attempt to facilitate the getting together. However, one should not brush aside that, from an etymological point of view, the word *adversary*—which he used in fact—and the word *adversity* are synonymous, given the context, of trouble, hardship, poverty, et cetera. And that, along with the privileged of the system, is what Premier Gorbachev has to deal with. So do we from our standpoint.

If the world is to be politically united—a principle found in the Saint-Simonian doctrine[11]—either the West will have to become like the communist countries or the communist countries will have to become like the West. And surrender their formidable power backed up by the military might they have built thus far? Throw Marxism-Leninism—foundation of their very own existence—into the bushes? And what about those who have perpetrated genocides at the rate of "270 people per hour for the past 70 years"? Are they going to disappear, just like that? Are they going to be on unemployment insurance or under "legal tutelage"?

The Saint-Simonian doctrine also reveals that " . . . there are only two ways to keep the mass of the have-nots bound to society: by force" (as in the East in general) "or by interest" (persuasion, as in the West, also in general). "They have to be tied down so that they will not be able to rebel, materially, or to make sure that they will not have the desire to do so; or, to impose upon them a social order by constraint, or, to make them like it."[12]

It was Gustave Flaubert who once wrote "the problem for the electors is that a government powerful enough to give them what they want is also powerful enough to take away from them what they possess."[13]

The very question remains: how good will a united world be for the people if, in the name of socialism at all costs, it has perpetrated and/or has tolerated genocides around the globe, knowing that by the year 2000 it is said that two-thirds, or up to three-quarters of the earth's population will be made of have-nots and that those in charge of this system will want to stay in power?

We can expect more repression everywhere. One can bet also that if we are politically united, information in the world will be different and genocides are going to take a subtler form. We will get even more information about the yellow-and-black-striped snail, more dramatics about "could-be-real-life-situations-but-are-not," and little, if anything about our own reality as human beings.

The problem with failures of magnitude is that their originators usually take society along with them, like Nero or, closer to us, Hitler. World War III would be a classic case and AIDS the ultimate of its kind, a result of the sexual revolution of the sixties, advocated, by the way, by one of the followers of Saint-Simon—Enfantin—who recommanded the emancipation of the flesh. Those in possession of the virus (transfusions) and of the antivirus (when discovered) will literally hold life, death, and money (real power) in their hands.

NOTES

1. Gwynne Dyer in his series "War."
2. Antenne 2, France,"l'Heure de Vérité" ("The Hour of Truth"), rebroadcast in Canada by TVFQ 99.
3. Published by William Aspenwall Bradley in English, Berger-Levrault in French, p. 293.
4. From AIM report of December-B 1987.
5. *Antenne* 2, France, January 27, 1987. As a matter of fact, he used the German word "ersatz," which means a substitute for the real thing, the way roasted acorn was used during World War II, as a replacement for real coffee.
6. Given the attacks of official medicine against acupuncture in Quebec, one could say that some people would certainly welcome such a system.
7. From an article in *l'Actualite*, February 1984, based on the testimony of a French correspondent working with "le Point."
8. Emile Durkheim, *Le Socialism—sa définition, ses débuts, la doctrine Saint-Simonienne (Socialism—Definition, Its Beginning, the Saint-Simonian Doctrine)* (Félix Alcan), p. 282, a Central body (p. 197) is to lead a scientific elite (pp. 195–97, 205–206) governing people by knowing what others do not (p. 223), while culture and politics will be the realm of a particular class of scientists who will silence debate (p. 226).
9. Ibid., p. 244.
10. *l'Express*, December 25, 1987.
11. Emile Durkheim, *Le Socialisme—sa définition, ses débuts, la doctrine Saint-Simonienne (Socialism—Definition, Beginning, the Saint-Simonian Doctrine)* (Félix Alcan), pp. 187, 247, 251, 254, 309.
12. Ibid., p. 241.
13. In *Le Candidat (The Candidate)*, a practically unknown play.

CONCLUSION

The great error of human beings is to believe that God is not necessary for their happiness.

—Saint Augustine

There is a direct relationship between freedom and economic development. Free enterprise started long before the invention of any regime, and every time oppression has manifested itself, in whatever manner or form, it has been a dark age, but also a test, for those used to, or in search of, a God-given freedom.

People and nations, often with different backgrounds but with freedom in common, are examples of how mankind can evolve. All the Vietnamese communities that have found refuge in still free countries around the world are also proof of that. Their success—often starting from scratch—is in total contradiction with the artifical man-made famine and misery of communist Vietnam, which had, however, all possible means in its hands, had it wanted to build a prosperous society. This goes for all nations under the communist yoke.

Communism is said to have come about because of the failures and ineptitude of bad regimes, of "imperfect" governments, according to communist criteria. This is partly true. But most of the time, nations that wanted to get out of bondage and experience freedom and real democracy have been crushed by a regime more eager to impose socialism at all costs and fast, and has revealed itself to be worse than what was there before—be it in Vietnam, Laos, Cambodia, Ethiopia, Angola, Afghanistan, or anywhere else.

In Vietnam it started with the struggle against a form of colonialism: a legitimate right, but which soon turned out to be unacceptable when it was for the sake of freedom. When it was recovered by communism, that is socialism by force, it became the "indomitable will of the people" and was lauded in the West by those supporting the internationalization of such a regime. Of course, the means used to that end were "drastic," but their results were kept in a low profile. Mind you, the purges of tens and hundreds of thousands of people became the "inevitable losses," "mere statistics," not to be emphasized in view of the grand design.

It was followed by a military takeover violating all the treaties and agreements signed just for that purpose, it seems, and carefully crafted a long time ago. Then the police network took care of all the freedom lovers who were sent to the "re-education camps" in order to learn that freedom is "passé." The future is collectivization, the sharing of so-called limited resources, managed by those who "know best." People tried to flee the country, leaving their ancestors behind. They were sold like cattle. A quarter of them died on their way out. Many were children.

Then people were impoverished by successive campaigns; money was invalidated. To make sure that people were going to accept this way of doing things, they were brainwashed by propaganda telling them that since the leaders came from the people, it was a popular movement. Farmers were deprived of their lands, which were collectivized. Entire populations without knowledge of agriculture were sent to the New Economic Zones, which often were outright concentration camps without barbed wire.

Medicine was stolen. Food was stolen. Goods were stolen. International aid was stolen. And then people were artificially starved to death by the hundreds of thousands. Later the authorities will "recognize the mistakes of the regime." In fact, it is no accident: communism is being imposed in order to prevent people from recovering their freedom and maintain them in a socialist context. Those who pretend to manage the world cannot let ordinary citizens do that by themselves, mind you.

The conclusion of this tragedy comes in part from the communists themselves[1]: a demographic increase for the same production of rice—18 million tons for the past three years—millions of workers out of work or underemployed, shortage of first necessity goods for most of the population, severe hygiene and health conditions, tens of thousands of houses without sanitary facilities, water, or electricity, bad management of companies and of the land, resources wasted, environment destroyed, degradation of the economy, and people distrustful of the regime. And, at the Sixth Congress of the Vietnamese Communist party in December 1986, the leaders recognized the mistakes and the failures of the regime since 1975.

Why? Since Western tourists are given the impression[2] that despite mistakes, Vietnam is already familiar with free enterprise, the presence of the police is not even felt, and given more socialism things will be just great. It does not matter if the situation is absolutely catastrophic as long as Westerners, particularly at the grassroots level, can be made to believe that socialism can work. Ideological support does not come from those who know it first hand anymore, but is sought from Westerners with vested interests or those who, knowing only one thing, believe it is the entire perspective and, even worse, an end in itself.

On June 4, 1988,[3] for 7 million North Vietnamese people food is in short supply and Vietnam needs sixty-five thousand tons of rice and milk powder from the West. Three million of them—40 percent children—are in critical condition.

However, no journalists are allowed in, no figures have been released, and according to some foreign experts, the Vietnamese Agriculture Department says that the only things the country needs are fertilizers and pesticides. ABC News "Nightline" of June 8, 1988 stated that thirteen years after the communist takeover the tragedy goes on, with famine, economic hardship, ten years in re-education camps, and political and religious persecution, which will end up pushing more and more Boat People out to sea. Vietnam tries to smuggle its nationals to Thailand. Do not forget that this country is one of the next targets.

Therefore it appears that, on the one hand, Westerners at the grassroots level are the target and the tools of propaganda, public pressure and generous aid, while on the other hand, politicians are saying that should they get more time, they could make socialism work. For an insider like Minh Hiên all this means rationing of the food, the request for foreign aid, the extortion of money and goods from Vietnamese families now living in the West, postponing of the debt with the International Monetary Fund, and sending more and more South Vietnamese into Economic Zones that are absolutely not New anymore. Journalists are not issued visas to check out what is going on—and could they, under tight control?—and the contradictions with the various games played inside the Vietnamese administration itself and at the international level concerning the real needs and/or failures of this regime that has everyone and everything in its hand, have not been able to correct the situation it initiated and produce its own fertilizers and pesticides. Hanoi is the source of the problems and should indeed solve them. It did not need the West to create them; it should not need it to get out of the mess it has created. Socialism is old now and does not need to be held by the hand in taking full responsibility for its actions.

Once mistakes have been made—on purpose, since they have been repeated carefully over and over again for seventy years—the West is asked to give, blindly, with the belief that aid may help to open up, even if only a tiny bit, countries that are unwilling to manage normal times and keep everything and everyone under tight control. The way the West has behaved politically and economically for seventy years has encouraged nations such as Vietnam not only to reject the responsibility for what they have done, but also to continue. After all, are we not supposed to be all united? Why then bother being efficient and yet caring?

By the way, what makes the West so sure that these things happen only "out there"? Wars have always been the opportunity—if not the motive—to impose changes. Take World War III. A Middle East nation, for example, does something foolish. The United States responds to that, then the USSR embarks on the bandwagon, and here we have it. Then words of "reconciliation," "peace," "tolerance," "new thinking," and "getting together" will let the people understand that the only choice lies between a "promise" and further war. Follows, shall we say, impoverishment with a crash whose seismic repercussions will leave people poorer than December 1719, September 1929, and October 1987 put together, just to make sure that they will have to depend upon the state for their survival. Next, probably, will be overtaxation and massive land foreclosures to deprive the farmers of their land and to force them into collectivization. It took seven years in Vietnam; how long will it take here? Then our constitutions could be "amended" in such a way that we would face the worst form of tyranny. Private weapons—particularly in the United States—will be confiscated, and a police network will make sure that everybody is under control. Finally, artificial famine: food, medicine, and first-necessity goods will be taken away by those who want to "manage" this world and redistribute limited resources equally, something that has never taken place in any communist country anywhere in the world. It will not take long before any nation ends up like Vietnam, in starvation. This time, though, there will be no West to give a hand, but as the saying goes: "You do not know until it happens to you."

The twentieth century witnesses the outgrowing of all the excesses born in the past, from despotism through administration, thousands of years ago, to totalitarianism through a social doctrine, with a brief interlude of freedom between the end of monarchy and the implementation of the social order. It seems that all the past mistakes have been gathered under the same roof and are supposed to prepare a brave "new world of communism" for our children. The struggle is not between socialism and capitalism anymore, as it is often suggested, but rather with communism that scared people away because of its violence and socialism that wants to recover them through persuasion.

Most mass communications are making sure that we are being kept abreast of all the "ills" plaguing our world, from the disappearance of species—which began thousands and thousands of years ago and is the natural evolution of our planet growing old—to the "imperfection" of nations considered to be unable to govern themselves and therefore "justifying" the intervention of a world system, the need to "bring us together," creating problems or "discovering new ones" and then involving the state more and more in "solving" them is the new game in town.

Capitalism is said to have overdone it, but socialism and communism were also supposed to produce so much that no one would be in need anymore. Communism claims to be the thing for the future when its nineteenth-century theories are outdated. The most important thing, indeed, is that freedom, real democracy and efficiency, are the goals and the means to a better life—except for a few who want to consolidate socialism and therefore need to control people through society and social changes. Western socialism, perceived for a long time to be a "third possible option," was known—though hiding it today—for its ties with capitalism and communism to be a real compromise between the two: it will have to lean always to one side or the other. Being the two at the same time would mean to become a "productive, centralized, and controlled society," an impossibility in itself, since where there is no freedom there is no production. It has tried to bring the Financial Revolution, the Industrial Revolution, communism, and even the old monarchy under the same roof, and people are supposed to look at the bright side of things; it will turn out to be the best way to make the world blind, unable to learn from its differences, with production—or the lack of it, as is the case with most nations under such regimes—being the means and the end of an evolution limited to that. Mankind was not sent on earth to do just that.

The domino theory has proven to be correct and will again. General MacArthur was right when he said that if a war has to be fought, it has to be won; the communists, at least, are convinced of that. Maybe the solution in South Vietnam, as well as in other countries—Afghanistan being a good example—would have been to help people help themselves against North Vietnam, China, and the Soviet Union. Freedom and real democracy have been denied to them, because the ultimate goal is to bring this world together with those who have sworn the destruction of the West.

Yesterday a red flag with a swatiska on it was flying over Europe and part of Africa. Today another red flag with a hammer and a sickle, or a star—depending upon the country over which it flies—is covering 39 percent of this planet and shadowing another 24 percent,[4] some of it under right-wing dictatorship, most of it under leftist totalitarianism; what a choice, what a world, in which only 37 percent of the population can still claim to be free. The emergence of international socialism and of communism with worldwide ambitions has given rise to fascism and nazism. However, we must bear in mind that Mussolini (fascism was born before nazism) was a socialist at the age of seventeen, thirty-three years before Hitler took power in Germany. His dictatorship was centralized around and for the state, something socialists of all kinds could claim as their own. As for Hitler himself, he said that he had brought socialism to Germany.[5] They are said to be the reason for more communism today, itself in turn reactivating far right wing groups: a never ending down spiral, and both the recto and the verso of a coin always tossed on the side of suffering, misery, and loss of freedom for real democracy.

If communism has not worked over there, why should it here? It appears that socialism, which began with the idea of sharing with all, is to establish itself and at all costs, without bothering much about the right of people to decide what is best for themselves or not, or even paying attention to their ability to do so. Vietnam, which is an up-to-date example, proves that it does not work.

It may look nice to take care of the poor and the downtrodden, but this also reveals itself to be a very controlled way to protect those who organize it: people are given just enough so that they will not want to rebel, are dependent upon it for their survival, and lose their ability to become self-sufficient. It leaves the system at ease to protect itself and those who implement it, yet perpetuates the two-hundred-year-old myth that socialism is here to protect the poor.

Communism uses force to make sure that nothing will escape its control, because it considers that goods and resources are in limited supply, and that it is self-appointed to manage them. Western socialism thinks that we can produce so much that nobody will be in need and that everybody will remain quiet. Then how can one set the portions, the limits or lack of them, to material happiness, since to produce is to consume in proportion and, without central planning, the key to disaster of communism itself? Distribution does not work too well, even when free countries are involved; we know that. Organized production? At what price? At the cost of suicide, as in Japan or Sweden? Alcoholism? As in the USSR (although there is a natural penchant for it there), but more and more in other parts of the world as well? Drugs? Prostitution and its diseases? An opportunity for the state to be more "involved" and absorb everything into its perspective.

The world suffers? It sure does, as in the past. But who can say that since the advent of socialism, and particularly communism, it has suffered less? Human beings were created to be free before they invented anything else: free to choose between their will, and guidance from the One Who created the universe. We do not drive cars, and we do not take medicine unless we have read, at least, the directions for use. Do we not? Especially that now we know that drinking, taking medicine, and driving do not go well together. The same applies to people and the planet earth. Some people tried to confine God to Heaven, while they would take care of this world. They separate the soul from the body, the way they separate the germ, the starch, and the bran of a wheat grain—and sell everything separately—when each part needs the other to be a complete and balanced entity. Having discovered such things, the human mind has begun to worship itself as the means and the end for exploiting and justifying everything. This "ersatz" situation leads no higher than the motivations of these minds.

When men and women began to rely solely on their knowledge and on their own strength to organize this world, they accumulated mistakes upon mistakes, as if, having taken the wrong medicine, they had to work on the side effects, then on the side effects of the side effects, and so on and so forth, and believed that having discovered errors leading to errors was the acme of knowledge and civilization. Today the planet is really sick, the result of cumulative mistakes, like apprentice sorcerers trying to imitate and to impose what they believe is the quest for the primeval state of happiness, but ending up with a big mess.

Material decency and comfort are all right and needed. But now that universal abundance has been promised without really knowing how to achieve that in its entirety—replacing God implies a promise but not necessarily the real knowledge and wisdom to do it—those more and more numerous on earth to be deprived of even the essential (by the year 2000 two-thirds to three quarters of the world's population will be made of have-nots) will be infuriated. Any system will have to prove itself to be extremely efficient, or people will have to be repressed, controlled, and probably eliminated, which means more genocides disguised, of course, under "natural causes." Now even if the world were to lay a hand on the horn of plenty, how can one define material happiness and set a limit or lack of it? Again, will this sort of happiness be sufficient to make people really feel that they have fulfilled their life and purpose on earth? Probably not: Some people are certainly going to look for more stimulating pleasures, as with drugs for example, and will not be satisfied with the system itself. Others will be searching for something that makes them real human beings, and will not be satisfied with the system either, since it evaluates happiness only in terms of materialism. Otherwise, like animals, we will end up feeding ourselves on the weakest and maintain the "ecological balance" between "limited resources" and the demographic explosion of the human jungle: pretty much the message genocides are sending around the world today. War being another form of it, World War III would be the ultimate: on a wide screen and with special sound effects, of course.

Yet freedom allows even bad and tragic experiments to take place. Evil himself was given the choice between his knowledge and his pride, the recognition of human beings acting then in accordance with the will of God. And "the work of providence takes time; only evil is in a hurry," says an Asian, an Arab, and a Western proverb. Mankind indeed walks at the speed of its slowest, so that the inner experience may become reality, and reality itself becomes an inner experience in that perspective. How long are these experiments going to last? As long as we try to prove that we can continue only on our own, over and over again, a period of 2 million years and so that we cannot say, "Had we had more time, we could have made it our way." The situation in the world today shows that we did not do too well.

If the world of tomorrow is to be invented without economic, political, cultural, or even "religious" oppression, it will not be by believing that we can save the world—we cannot even save ourselves—and by projecting all of mankind's past and current mistakes into the future as a system. André Malraux, who can be said to have had a foot on each side of the political fence, once said something to the effect that the twenty-first century will have to be spiritual or not be at all.

Almost a century and a half ago Alexis C. de Tocqueville wrote: "Human beings put the greatness of the concept of unity in the means, God in the end; hence, this concept of greatness leads to a thousand smallnesses. To force human beings to walk at the same pace, towards the same goal is a human idea. To introduce an infinite variety into the acts, but to combine them so that they all lead by thousands of different ways towards the accomplishement of a grand design, is a divine concept.

"The human concept of unity is almost always sterile, that of God immensely fertile. Human beings believe that they give expression of their greatness by simplifying the means: it is the object of God that is simple, His means vary infinitely."[6]

God Begins, Continues, Ends, and May Start all over again with the individual, and it is when people fulfil their destiny as individuals who experience their inner development under His Guidance, that harmony, the outer aspect of people going through this process, can become a thriving reality.

NOTES

1. Gérard Hevvouet, "*Le Vietnam à l'heure des décisions (Vietnam at the Time of Decisions)*, p. 209. Mr. Hervoet is from the Political Science Department of Laval University, and director of the review *Etudes Internationales (International Studies)*. He was invited by the International Institute of Hanoi to go to Vietnam in July 1987, in *Institut Canadien pour la paix et la sécurité internationales (Canadian Institute for International Peace and Security)*, Winter 1988.
2. *Le Bulletin national du Mouvement socialiste (The National Bulletin of the Socialist Movement)* 7, no. 2, (April/May 1988); *Temps Nouveaux (New Times)*, March 1988; and *Le monde à bicyclette (The World on Bike)*, Spring 1988.
3. *La Presse*, Montreal.
4. *International Conservative Insight*, May/June, 1987.
5. Seen saying it in a French war archive documentary 39–45.
6. "De la Démocratie en Amérique" ("Democracy in America"), Garnier-Flammarion; p. 407 (II). Paris, 1981.

BIBLIOGRAPHY

VIETNAMESE AUTHORS

Doàn-van-Toai. *Le goulag vietnamien (The Vietnamese Gulag)*. Paris: Robert Laffont, 1979.

Hà-thúc-Sinh. *Daï hoc Máu (Bloody University: 1685 Days in Reeducation Camps.)* San Jose, Cal.: Nhâu-Vàn, 1985.

Hoàng-vàn-Chì. *From Colonialism to Communism*. London: Pullman Press, Inc., 1964.

Kim-Nhât. *Committe "R": The Story of the Clandestine Provisory Government*. Saigon.

———. *The Passing Shadow: The Story of the Communist Underground*. Saigon.

Lê-huy-Linh-Vũ. *Ba ngày cuôi cũng o' Bô Tu' lênh Tüong Giai (The Last Three Days at the Headquarters of General Giai)*. Saigon, 1973.

Lê-Quang-Gérard. *La guerre américaine d'Indochine (The American War in Indochina)*. Paris: Editions Universitaires, 1973.

Lê-tâń-Trang. *Nhân loai Dā thay gì tû hoá Nguc Vietnam? (What Does Mankind Know about the Vietnamese Hell?)*. Published in Vietnamese by Liên Minh dân chú, Santa Ana, California, 1982). Not yet translated into English.

Mai-thu-Vân. *Vietnam: un peuple, des voix (Vietnam: A People and Voices)*. Paris: Pierre Horay, 1983.

Nguyen-Ngoc-Huy. *A New Strategy to Defend the Free World against Communist Expansion*. San Jose, California: Alliance for Democracy in Vietnam, 1985.

Nguyen-Van-Canh. *Vietnam under Communism, 1975–1982*. Stanford, Cal.: Hoover Institution Press, 1983.

Nhâ-Ca. *Un linceul pour Huê (A Shroud for Huê)*. Saigon.

Pham-quang-Giai. *Trai Cai Cao (Reeducation Camps)*. Houston: Liviko Printing, 1986.

Pham-quôc-Bao. *Cùm Dó (The Red Carcan)*. Westminster, Cal. The Vietnamese, 1985. Not yet translated into English.

Phan-Nhat-Nam. *L'été sanglant (Bloody Summer)*. Saigon, 1972. (This author is still in a re-education camp.)

Ta-Ty. *Day Dia Nguc (Down to Hell)*. San José, Cal. Thang Mo, 1986.

Toan-Anh and Cúu-Long-Gian. *Cao nguyên Miên Thüong (The High Plateaux), Glendale, Cal.: Dia-Nam, 1981.*

Trân-huynh-Châu. *Nhũng nam cái tao o' Bào Viêt (The Reeducation Years in North Vietnam)*. Published in Vietnamese by TTNS (Culver City, Cal. 1981). Not yet translated into English.

Trân-trong-Kim. *Vietnam sú Hüoc (The Abridged History of Vietnam)*. Saigon: Centre du Matériel Educatif, 1981.

Trân-trung-Quân. *Trong lòng dich (Behind the Lines)*. Published in Vietnamese by Vàn-Húū (Houston, 1984). Not yet published in English.

Trân-Vān-Thái. *Trai Dâm Dùn (The Camp of the Dùn Lagoon)*. Saigon: Sóńg Móï, 1979. Reprinted under the same title in the United States, since the death of the author.

Trûóng-Nhu-Táng. *A Viet Cong Memoire*. New York: Harcourt Brace Jovanovitch, 1985. Also published in French by Flammarion.

Truong-Xuan-Hy. *Mourir pour la colline 30 (To Die for Hill 30)*. Saigon.

Vān-Tiên-Dūng. *Dai thāng mà Xuân (The Great Spring Victory)*. Translated into several languages, 1976.

Vū-Thuy-Hoāng. *Rôǹg Vâng vuöt biēñ (Sea Crossing)*. Springsfield, VA.: Vietnam Books Inc., 1983.

Xuân-Vū. *Düōng di Không dên (Dead End: The Ho Chi Minh Trail)*. Saigon, 1973.

WESTERN AUTHORS

Amnesty International. Reports of 1980, 1981, 1982, 1983, and 1984. EFAI.

Ansart, Pierre. *Sociologie de Saint-Simon (Sociology of Saint-Simon)*. Paris: Presses Universitaires de France, 1970.

Arendt, Hannah. *The Origins of Totalitarianism*. New York: Harvest, 1973.

Artaud, Denise, and André Kaspi. *Histoire des Etats-Unis (History of the United States)*. Paris: Armand Colin, 1980.

Aron, Raymond. *Paix et querre entre les nations (Peace and War between Nations)*. Paris: Calmann-Lévy, 1984.

Banerian, James. *Losers Are Pirates*. U.S.: James Banerian, 1984.

Barron, John. *KGB Today: The Hidden Hand*. Pleasantville, N.Y.: Reader's Digest Press, 1983.

Binyon, Michael, *Life in Russia*. London: Hamish Hamilton, 1983.

Bornecque, Pierre. *La France et sa littérature: guide complet dans le cadre de la civilisation mondiale (France and Its Literature: A Complete Guide in the Context of World Civilization)*. Les Editions de Lyon, 1953.

Bronowski, Jacob. "The Ascent of Man." BBC, 1973.

Campbell, William A.B., and Richard K. Melchin. *Western Security and the Strategic Defense Initiative: Studies in Foreign Policy*. Vancouver: Canadian Conservative Centre, 1986.

Chalian, Gérard, and Jean-Pierre Rageau. *Atlas Stratégique/Géopolitique des rapports de forces dans le monde (Strategic Atlas/Geopolitical Rapport of Forces in the World)*. Paris: Fayard, 1983.

Charter 78. *The Prison System in Vietnam*. Montreal: Human Rights Movement, 1978.

Colby, William. *Honorable Men: My Life in the CIA*. New York: Simon and Schuster, 1978.

Darcourt, Pierre. *Vietnam, qu'as-tu fais de tes fils? (Vietnam, What Have You Done with Your Sons?)*. Paris: Albatros, 1975.

Delvert, Jean. *Le Cambodge (Cambodia)*. Paris: Presses Universitaires de France, 1983.

d'Encausse, Hélène Carrère. *Après la détente (After Détente)*. Paris: Hachette/Pluriel, 1982.

Doré, Amphay. *Le partage du Mékong (The Partition of the Mekong)*. Paris: Editions Encre, 1980.

Durkheim, Emile. *Le Socialisme: sa définition, ses débuts, la doctrine Saint-Simonienne (Socialism: Definition, Its Beginnings, the Saint-Simonian Doctrine)*. Paris.

Paris: Librairie Félix Alcan, 1928.
Finder, Joseph. *Red Carpet*. New York: Holt Rinehart Winston, 1983.
Fontaine, André. *L'histoire de la Guerre Froide (The History of the Cold War)*. Paris: Fayard, 1983.
Irvine, Reed. *Media Mischief and Misdeeds*. Chicago: Regnery Gateway, 1984.
Isaac, Rael Jean, and Erich Isaac. *The Coercive Utopians*. Chicago: Regnery Gateway, 1983.
Jacquin, Henri. *La Guerre Secrète en Indochine (The Secret War in Indochina)*. Paris: Olivier Orban, 1979.
Jelen, Christian. *L'aveuglement: les Socialistes et la naissance du mythe Soviétique (The Blinding: The Socialists and the Birth of the Soviet Myth)*. Paris: Flammarion, 1984.
Kirk, Russell. *The Portable Conservative Reader*. New York: Viking Portable Library, Penguin Books, 1982.
Kirkpatrick, Jeane J. *Dictatorships and Double Standards*. New York: Simon and Schuster, 1982.
Lamour, Catherine, and Michel R. Lamberti. *Les Grandes Manoeuvres de l'Opium (The Great Maneuvers of the Opium)*. Paris: Editions du Seuil, 1972.
Lartéguy, Jean. *Voyage au bout de la guerre (Journey to the End of War)*. Paris: Presses de la Cité, 1971.
———. *L'adieu à Saigon (Farewell to Saigon)*. Paris: Presses de la Cité, 1975.
Lissner, Ivar. *Dieu était déjà là (God Was Already There)*. Paris: Robert Laffont, 1965.
Manac'h, Etienne M. *Mémoires d'Extrême Asie; la face cachée du monde (Memoirs of the Far East: The Hidden Side of the World)*. Paris: Fayard, 1977.
Gèze, François, Yves Lacoste, and Annie Lennkh. *L'Etat du Monde 1982 (The State of the World 1982)*. Paris: la Découverte/Maspero.
———. *L'Etat du Monde 1983 (The State of the World 1983*. Paris: la Découverte/Maspéro.
Paquot, Thierry, and Alfredo G.A., Valladão. *L'Etat du Monde 1987–1988 (The State of the World 1987–1988)*. Paris: la Découverte/Boreal.
London, Herbert I. *Why Are They Lying to Our Children*. New York: Stein and Day, 1984.
Nixon, Richard. *The Memoirs of Richard Nixon*. New York: Warner Books, 1978. In French: *Les Mémoires de Richard Nixon. Paris: Editions Internationales, Stanké, 1978.*
———. *No More Vietnams*. Arbor House, 1985. In French: *Plus Jamais de Vietnams*. Paris: Albin Michel, 1985.
———. *The Real War*. New York: Warner Books, 1978. In French: *La Vraie Guerre*. Paris: Albin Michel, 1980. In Canada: Montreal: Québec/Amérique, 1980.
Rangel, Carlos. *L'Occident et le Tiers Monde (The West and the Third World)*. Paris: Robert Laffont, Libertés 2,000: 1982.
Rémy, François. *40,000 enfants par jour: vivre la cause de l'UNICEF (40,000 Children per Day: To Live the Cause of UNICEF)*. Paris: Robert Laffont, 1983.
Salan, Raoul. *Mémoires*. Paris: Les Presses de la Cité, 1971.
———. *L'Indochine Rouge (Red Indochina)*. Paris: Presses de la Cité, 1975.
Salisbury, Harrison E. *The Unknown War*. New York: Bantam, 1978.
Servan-Schreiber, Jean-Jacques. *Le Défi Mondial (World Challenge)*. Paris: Fayard, 1980.

Shultz, Richard E. and Roy Godson. *Dezinformatsia*. McLean, VA. Pergamon-Brassey, 1984.
Sleeper, Raymond S. *A Lexicon of Marxist-Leninist Semantics*. Alexandria, VA. Raymond S. Sleeper, 1983.
Solzhenitsyn, Alexander. *L'Archipel du Goulag (The Gulag Archipelago)*. Paris: Hachette, 1974.
———. *L'Erreur de l'Occident (The Mistake of the West)*. Paris: Grasset, 1980.
Suant, Jacques. *Vietnam 45–72*. Paris: Arthaud, 1973.
Viatteau, Alexandra Kwiatowska. *Katyn*. Bruxelles: Editions Complexes, 1982.

DICTIONARIES

Boudet, Jacques. *Chronologie Universelle (Universal Chronology)*. Paris: Bordas, 1983.
Mourre, Michel. *Dictionnaire d'Histoire Universelle (Dictionary of Universal History)*. Paris: Bordas, 1981.